Unhindered

Healing from Spiritual Harm and Discovering True Relationship After Religion

KATHRYN J. L. ROBERTS

Published by hope*books
2217 Matthews Township Pkwy
Suite D302
Matthews, NC 28105
www.hopebooks.com

hope*books is a division of hope*media

Printed in the United States of America

First paperback edition.
Paperback ISBN: 979-8-89185-167-2
Hardcover ISBN: 979-8-89185-168-9
Ebook ISBN: 979-8-89185-169-6
Library of Congress Number: 2025931418

Book cover art by Timothy Fisher, www.waveswindcreative.com

Scripture quotations marked (AMP) are taken from the Amplified Bible, Copyright © 2015 by The Lockman Foundation. Used by permission.

Scripture quotations marked HCSB are taken from the Holman Christian Standard Bible®, Copyright © 1999, 2000, 2002, 2003 by Holman Bible Publishers. Used by permission. Holman Christian Standard Bible®, Holman CSB®, and HCSB® are federally registered trademarks of Holman Bible Publishers.

Scripture quotations marked MSB have been taken from The Holy Bible, Majority Standard Bible, MSB

Are you tired? Worn out?
Burned out on religion?

Come to me.
Get away with me and you'll recover your life.
I'll show you how to take a real rest.

Walk with me and work with me—watch how I do it.
Learn the unforced rhythms of grace.
I won't lay anything heavy or ill-fitting on you.

Keep company with me and you'll learn to live freely and lightly.

—Jesus

Matthew 11:28-30, MSG

This Book is Dedicated To

My first Love—the One who, through His cascading grace, changed my mind about everything I thought I knew. He set me free, and my heart ablaze to run with Him to a higher place, partnering with Him from those days forward to help set the rest of the captives completely and wonderfully free.

My true love—Forrest. You are my beloved, and I am yours, and that fact is purely a miracle in every way. Your belief in this book since the moment you heard of the tugging at my heart still means the world to me. I love you in all the ways, always.

My Liam love—you are the reason why I could finally grasp His love for me and all of us—because it still somehow surpasses my boundless, indescribable, unconditional, and never-ending love for you, my precious son. You are indescribably wondrous to me, and I love you more than words can ever express. Nothing could ever separate you from my love or His. You do not have to be shackled by the lies and false beliefs I once was. This book is for your freedom, for your wholeness—that you may experience Him sooner than I got to and enjoy life abundantly beyond all you could ask or imagine, to degrees surpassing even that which I've come to know.

My dear reader—You picking up this book gives wind to the sails I loosed by faith long ago, trusting that the wind would come. When I agreed in my heart to the calling God placed on me, to dedicate years of my life to birthing these pages you now hold, I couldn't see your face, and I may not have known your name—but I believed that if you needed to hear something that I needed to share, God would divinely orchestrate in the way He does, and we would come to this moment of meeting each other between these pages. The belief that you would come here and let me walk alongside you for part of your journey to greater measures of healing and freedom kept me writing when it was the hardest thing to do.

Thank you, with all of my being, for being here.
I'm so deeply glad that you are.

Note to Reader

Out of sensitivity to the wounds you may carry, whether from personal or collective injustice or loss, I want to preface that the wounds I primarily reference in this book stem from religious abuse within Christianity. My most formative traumatic experiences occurred between ages 7 and 15 in a small, evangelical fundamentalist church, which was heavily involved in the Institute in Basic Life Principles (IBLP)—later exposed as a cult.[1]

Understanding that I grew up in a cult environment has given me a new language to process the harm and continue to heal from that experience, as well as the other negatively influential religious messages surrounding my early childhood through young adulthood. Despite all of this, following a crisis in my late 20s, I came to personally experience God in ways that challenged everything I thought I knew about Him. The rich and life-giving faith I now have is authentically my own and rooted in what I have now experienced to be the truth of who God really is.

I share this both as a trigger warning for the themes of religious abuse and associated harm ahead and to encourage you to read at your own pace, honoring your personal journey. My hope is that the words of encouragement in this book will outweigh the heavy ones, offering hope, clarity and even some humor as you seek healing and truth.

When I reference "the church" in this book, it's not just about my experiences in various churches and ministries but any group that leaves members confused, afraid, or harmed, opposing and angering God's true heart for us. Regardless of the severity of "church wounds," it all matters—deeply. I wrote this book as a reckoning so

---

1 *Shiny Happy People*, Season 1, Prime Video, 2 June 2023.

we may heal, reclaim what was lost, and come to know God's true goodness, our true selves, and our valuable place in community with each other.

Table of Contents

"God cares about the religious-y things that we have believed about Him and ourselves that are false. The dead things that promised a good future but brought nothing but disillusionment and pain. He wants to help us shed those old beliefs so new ones can grow that will bring us true life."

Maggie Paulus [2]

---

2 Paulus, Maggie. Facebook, date unknown.

DIARY OF A FUNDAMENTALIST CHRISTIAN KID

February 11th, 2001

Dear Diary,

I just don't really feel like I know God that well. Like I understand Him or obey or love Him as much as I should. I always hesitate to set money aside for offering, and I only do it out of obedience, not because I want to. And when I read my Bible, I pretty much do it for the same reasons. Although I do enjoy it sometimes but like, I'm afraid He will get mad if I don't do it. I know that if you don't do things out of love for God, you might as well not do it at all, but I just can't stop having quiet time or tithing because then I would feel like an atheist. I just long to be close to God, but it seems like an on/off period of being close to Him. I hope that will change because I know that no matter what, God still loves me. Me, a worthless sinner of who I am very ashamed of. God, help me to not sin but to please you and love you with my whole heart. Amen.

12-year-old me

February 13th, 2001

Dear Diary,

I still feel as though I am separated from God. I long to be close but it just seems like I never have time to pray; which, if I don't talk to God, I can't grow with Him. As soon as the rain stops, I want to go to the woods all by myself and talk to God. That must be my problem. How can I read His word and praise Him and learn anything if I don't talk to Him? I need to get away in a quiet spot every day to pray. That's what I should do.

12-year-old me

March 1st, 2001

Dear Diary,

I can't wait until we get to heaven! It will be so wonderful! No more tears! No more hatred! No more sin! Everything sparkling and clean, fresh and new! Streets of gold, seas of glass! Mansions! And God. Oh, my wonderful Savior! How I can hardly wait to see You, face to face! I want to jump into your arms and hug you for hours! I will feel safe, secure, forgiven and free! What a wonderful feeling that will be! While I'm still down here, help me to flee temptation, do what I know is right, and please You in everything I think, say, and do. I love you Lord! Amen.

12-year-old me

———

If my 20+-year-old journal entries struck a familiar chord with you (whether with your previous or present self), I want to say how deeply sorry I am for what you've experienced. Religious trauma is served up on a spectrum, on which anywhere and any amount of it is grievous.

Growing up slowly simmering in a steaming pot of the legalist lifestyle that was fundamentalism—unbeknownst at the time to those terms or how to describe what I only knew as my "normal"—felt like living in a state of constant hypervigilance over what I must have done wrong yesterday and searching endlessly for what I might do wrong today. That all took place subconsciously, mind you. I still don't even know exactly where its influence began. Like drinking from a contaminated water source, who knows where along the way it became corrupted? That's just what the water tasted like—we didn't realize it was the source of our soul-sickness.

From being involved in small, medium, to near mega-churches—all claiming to be non-denominational Christian churches but all twisted at the roots with heavy involvement in organizations from Bill Gothard's Institute in Basic Life Principles to the Southern Baptist Convention—none of them were "non" anything. All were deeply ingrained in doctrines that, no matter how different in name, had this in common: they twisted Scripture and used it to coerce, control, and intimidate others—which is, in short, the definition of abuse.

While I don't know your specific church/religious background, I know many have been able to relate, even without being able to trace the messages back to a specific organization or leader. Maybe you were indoctrinated to similar ideas in your family of origin or in religiously rooted cultural movements that you were affected by as well. (Purity culture, anyone?)

Whether or not you've personally identified toxic Christianity or religious abuse experiences, the effects of its messages are often what stays with us more than the experiences themselves. For example, if you've ever thought that God is quick to anger and unpredictable in love (the literal opposite of the verse "slow to anger and abounding in love"), been through rounds of "He loves me/He loves me not" or the even more terrifying, sinister game, "I'm saved/what if I'm not saved?"—you may have experienced religious harm to some degree. If that's you, friend, I want to pause here and give you the biggest book-hug through these pages. I pray that words of healing and freedom find you here and wrap around your war-torn heart like my arms would if we were having these conversations face-to-face.

I know too well the stress of that way of thinking and believing, which felt more like existing on a tightrope of trying not to screw things up. I know the terror of guessing, wondering, fearing, and feeling like a failure in the eyes of a God you don't even know if you know, no matter how much you may long to. I'm sorry for the hurt, confusion, and alarm you've been caused by poor theology and well-meaning but misguided folks. "Hurt people hurt people," and it's safe to say similarly, "confused people confuse people" and "fearful people instill fear in others."

Let's get this cleared up straight away: *none of the above is true to God's heart, a part of His nature, desires, or ways of relating to His children.*

Zero. Zilch. Nada.

In the coming pages and unfolding chapters ahead, I hope you become fully convinced not only of the truth of who He's *not* but secure in the truth of who and how He *really* is.

How deeply He loves. How creatively He speaks. How soft and safe a landing place is His grace. There is endlessly *more*—far more good and beautiful than we've known or dared to imagine that is true of Him. And in turn, that means there is endlessly more of you—and me, too—that is good and true that many of us have never known from the brand of faith that's been told or sold to us inside (or outside) the walls of some churches.

In most of my church experiences of youth, if the church culture (because it wasn't always direct from the pastor, rather some influences of other leadership, parents, and even peers) wasn't "hell-bent" on making me terrified of eternity, they'd at least do a thorough job of calling out supposed failures, keeping them at the forefront. I was given one-way tickets on guilt trips aplenty, convincing me I was a wretched sinner with a wicked heart that couldn't be trusted and that I might as well get used to my inherent sinful nature and never stop being on alert for ways in which I might stumble, or—heaven forbid—cause my "brother" to.

I wish I could have gotten to know the real God that I *now* know better at the time. Ironically, it was around the time I took a break from church that I really began to encounter Him. That should tell us something about the damaging messages being preached in many churches today that are actually hindering us from knowing the true Him.

But being in the legalistic churches I found myself in during my most formative years kept me quite busy, really. In short, the frenzied and impossible task of constantly trying to be perfectly "good" to gain and then maintain everyone's approval consumed me.

I remember the latent anxiety in the pit of my stomach going to church most of my childhood. The pre-guilt feeling about what I would likely feel "convicted about" after the sermon, the sickening feeling of having to "confess" my "sins" even if just to God quietly, the cold shoulder the mean girls would turn to me, the rumors that circulated about me and the boy I liked, being shunned by some church members, confronted by others rather than loved by them. Between the fear-mongering, rule-following, and back-watching, trying to "be a good person"—much less a "good Christian"—felt like an impossible, rigged, but required full-time job.

I continued year after year to try and jump through enough hoops and remember all the cumbersome choreography constantly being thrown at me by "authority figures." I was immersed in teachings of everything from the Bill Gothard cult to purity culture that swept the American evangelical church scene in the 90's–early 2000's, which had me feeling awful about even thinking a boy was cute and like a total failure if I didn't "save my first kiss for marriage."

Good times, am I right? You can imagine (and if you've trudged through similar trenches yourself or alongside a loved one, it's not hard to) how the above religious experiences created a lot of chaos for me around everything to do with God and well—me, too. It's what spurred me toward writing this book, which I've felt called to for years leading up to this breakthrough moment.

That's the sweet thing about how the Lord gently leads. He might give us an idea, an inspiration, a nudge in a direction, but He might wait for the whole picture to unfold slowly in its own time. I knew I was supposed to write a book over a decade ago, like a slow-burning calling you just know is inevitable. But it wasn't until a few years following that I began to see what it needed to be about. I can't even tell you when I knew it would be titled "Unhindered," but God revealed that to me at some point along the way through a deep inner knowing that it's as though it's always been called this.

Years of this book waiting in the wings of my heart to be written "for such a time as this" (a reminder to my calling to this work that God has gently nudged me with from Esther 4:14), and here it is at last, in your hands. There's been a constant ache and longing in my heart for you that, through reading these words, you may experience a fresh wind filling your tired sails. That you'll watch with wonder as your wounds close in at the seams with refreshing truth like new skin.

May you lock heart-eyes with the One who's been holding you in His gaze all this time, waiting for you to look up and meet His bright eyes, glistening with tears of love for and joy over you. May you hear His gentle whisper, "*I have made you and I will carry you; I will sustain you and I will rescue you*" (Isaiah 46:4, NIV). For this, my dear ones, is the Love I've come to know and love, and knowing Him has freed me from what I *thought* I knew—about Him, myself, and everyone around me.

LOVE'S LETTER

(A long overdue reply from the God I now know to my 12-year-old self.)

Dear little Kathryn,

My precious girl. You are amazing, and I love your heart! Oh, how I wish you could fully understand, see, and feel how very much I adore you. You are My treasure! Just as you are. Today and every day. That has never changed, not for a moment. When you read My words, when you talk to Me, and when you don't—has nothing to do with the fact that you are My beloved daughter, and I take great delight in you, the good fruit of My creation. Perfectly and wonderfully made.

Hear Me, please: you don't have to be afraid of Me, or anyone. Don't be ashamed, either. It makes Me sad to hear you say those things—because you have nothing to be ashamed of. Anything grievous you've ever done or could do, I have resolved on your behalf, and your shame is no more. You are made new. You are free! Oh, how I hope you'll believe Me and live your one beautiful life in that truth.

Kathryn, I can't wait to hug you too! I love to hear how excited you are for that day we are together face-to-face. That feeling you described? Of wanting to feel safe and secure, *forgiven and free? Love, you don't have to wait till then. You can feel that **now**! That's what I gave My life for—so that you could have all of that and more in Me now, "on earth as it is in heaven." I came so that you could know Me and have life in abundance—because I am Life, and all it encompasses.*

*If you could hear Me yet, if you were awake to Me as you will be one day soon, you'd know in the depths of your soul how deeply held, safe, and secure you already are. I know it may not always feel like it in this still-broken world, but trust Me—**believe** Me—I have called you by name, and you are irrevocably Mine. The more you believe and remember that, I promise you, the more you'll feel it's true, too.*

Know that nothing can ever separate us. Not bad days or good days. Not days you feel closer or further from Me. Those are feelings, like how the clouds pass by. What's true, regardless of the feeling, is that the sky is blue and will be there each day you wake up and each night when you go to sleep. Remember how close we are like that—an unchangeable fact.

I love how often you think about Me and how deeply you long to do the right thing. I wish you could rest and relax into the truths that you're not aware of yet or have been misinformed about. I'm sorry those you look up to have twisted things into making Me seem scary, distant, or hard to please. It grieves Me because I went to the furthest lengths—laying down My life for you—to prove My Love for you so that you wouldn't have to strive, earn, or prove anything ever again!

*So here's what's true and what you **can** rest in right now.*

You can always come to Me and lay any heaviness down. Any burdens you have, I want to carry. I want your load to be easy and your burdens to be light. I want you to link arms with Me and learn from Me. My pace and My ways are sweet, easy, steady, and light. You can rely on Me. You can trust Me. I want what's best for you, and I am already taking care of guiding you into the good plans I have for your life, one step and one day at a time.

*And little love, did you know that you are **constantly** on My mind? Yes. I've engraved your name in the palm of my hand. I never sleep and I watch over you every moment of every day. You are precious and honored in My sight, and Kathryn, I **love** you. Deeply. Unshakably. Whether you ever tithe another penny or not. Which, by the way, you don't have to do. I see your heart in it of wanting to give, be selfless, and honor what you've been taught I desire of you, but for the record, the verses about tithing are often taken out of context, and I want you to be free of the financial burden of your church, especially as a 12-year-old. Lay it down, sweet one. That's not for you to worry about, and I'm sorry the grown-ups made you feel like you had to "do" things rather than just "be" with Me—being who I've created you to be.*

I wish you could see the tears I've cried on your behalf as you've remained in the dark to My true nature and My ever-turned-toward you good, good heart. I'm angry over the confusion caused to you, the harm done in My name that's hindered your faith and held you at a distance from Me in your mind. Because that couldn't be further from the truth.

The enemy is crafty and has infiltrated even My church with lies and a religious spirit that's convinced some that I'm far-off and distant, hard to please, and handing out favor in exchange for following rules. They've forgotten I fulfilled the law already and that you are not under the law but under grace now. I took care of that to make a way for us to all be together in perfect unity and harmony.

Oh, how I can't wait for you to discover these things! I can't wait to fan the flame I've started inside your heart that will expand like wildfire as we consume the lies and reach others with the truth. I have such adventures waiting in store for us together. I promise I am fighting on your behalf and will see to it that every twisted verse is made clear, every lie is smote with truth, and every law used against you is shattered by My love.

The time is coming, sooner than you think, when the eyes of your heart and the sensitivity of your spirit will be opened more and more to My heart and ways. I'll be whispering to you more and more as you grow, so keep looking up and keep listening—you're on the brink of discovering My wildly creative voice.

You haven't recognized Me in these small ways yet, but since you were young, I've winked at you through the glittering stars, glowed with joy over you through the moon, kissed your face through the warmth of the sun, played with your hair through the dancing wind, tapping you on the shoulder through every raindrop that's ever touched you.

I'll whisper to your heart and answer your prayers before

you even ask. I'll put things in front of you that may seem like a coincidence, but don't be too quick to write it off or explain it away as some do. Look again, look closer, and listen to the promptings of My Spirit alive in you. It's Me! I'll order your steps and lace things together through your days that will put you in the right place at the right time to remind you of Me. Before too long, a rainbow will come across the countertop in a mundane moment, but you'll look up and think of Me. The clock will strike 8:28, and you'll remember the verse I'll teach you soon, the promise about how I'm working everything together for your good. It's going to be the sweetest relationship and the most alive life together—soon, little love.

Have faith, take heart! I have overcome all that has hindered you, and that victory is slowly unfolding in your priceless life, day by day.

I'm here. I'm not going anywhere, ever, no matter what anyone says, no matter the doubts. I made up My mind about you from the beginning of time, and I'm never going to change it.

> *Love you wildly,*
>
> > *Your Adoring Heavenly Father*

Part 1:
ENTANGLED
Where we got trapped

Chapter 1

Everything That Hinders

"Everybody, I believe, is injured in some way. We're all wearing casts. When somebody is wearing a cast, we navigate around it as gently as we can. If they can't run so fast, we don't tell them to hurry up. We move at their pace."

J.S. Park [3]

Wounded

If there's one thing I've been consistent in throughout my life, it's been my inconsistent relationship with running. You could say I'm more of a walker or wanderer. I love hiking, yoga, and horseback riding. But for some reason, across the seasons of life that I've attempted to "be a runner," it was short-lived. Sometimes that was due to time constraints in my vibrant, self-employed work schedule, sometimes due to injuries, or the weather turning dangerously toasty—living in the sweet Southern state of Arkansas, where temps surpassing 100°F are not uncommon in our summers. The other constant obstacle that tends to keep the desire to sweat at bay is the fact that I'll have to wash my long hair, which is a whole thing. I try not to have to summit the "Everest" of long-hair-care more than absolutely necessary.

---

3   Park, J. S. *The Voices We Carry: Finding Your One True Voice in a World of Clamor and Noise*, Northfield Publishing, 2020.

Thus, I've never made it far enough in my running journey—which itself has been more like a brief jog—to qualify in joining the culture of those who are consistent in their relationship with running. You know the type (or perhaps you are the type, and if so, well done to you, my speedy and far more endurant friend)—where it becomes part of their identity made known through car bumper stickers adorned with impressive mileage distances that read like a secret code of accomplishments.

But when I think back to the most successful bouts of my on-again, off-again running seasons—two true accomplishments come to mind.

The first was back when I was about 17 years old. I hadn't been in a running "season" at the time, but nonetheless, I stepped up to the pavement to carry the torch for a group of middle-aged moms who'd signed up for the Little Rock Marathon relay. Unfortunately, a couple of weeks before the race, their fourth member was out with an injury and couldn't participate. My mom and her friends did what made the most sense, of course: recruit a semi-athletic-build, late-teens gal who hadn't trained or been running at all the months prior leading up to the race. Brilliant! I did what I thought any good daughter or decent citizen would do and accepted the challenge so that they didn't have to drop out of the race or, worse, have one of them pull a double shift of the relay. They were so grateful that they even saddled me with the longest leg of the four-part relay: the 7-mile stretch that included going up Little Rock's iconic, historic, steep and winding Kavanaugh Hill.

I will never forget that 7-mile run. Sure, diving in with less than two weeks to prepare my body to undergo the journey was a definite challenge, but what caught me off guard was the mental challenge of running a race. I have always been competitive (don't ask my big sister about why she stopped playing Monopoly with me), but as this felt like a more collaborative group run of which I had no intention of "winning," I was still surprised how hard it was for me to slow down when I needed to, to stop and walk when necessary. I wanted to run and run well. I didn't realize at the time that *slowing down and walking when needed is a part of running well.*

But as I rounded the final stretch of pavement where I could see the end in sight, the "finish line" for my leg of the relay, I really pushed myself. I wanted to cross the finish line running even if I collapsed on the other side of it. My body was aching, my lungs out of breath, my vision becoming blurred, and I felt pain in my knees and feet with every movement. But I made it. It was one of the hardest things I've ever done, but I did it. And promptly following the whole marathon, told my mom that should they find themselves down a woman in the future, I'd happily provide referrals for a replacement. As surprisingly rewarding as it felt in my heart, my body had other feelings about it and did not want to go through that again.

The second running feat I recall as a "win" was a few years ago. During the beginning of the pandemic, the yoga studio I've gone to for years was suddenly only able to offer virtual classes. With the weather turning nice for spring, I turned to the outdoors for exercise and began walking, then running, on a 2-mile trail not far from where I lived.

I continued this into the spring of the following year, which is the longest I've stuck with a running routine. That spring, my dad and a couple of my brothers ran the Little Rock half marathon, and as I've always done for other friends who'd run it in the past, I went to the finish line to cheer for them. Something about the energy there lifted my spirits. The air was saturated with full-blown support and celebration for total strangers, and people came together to cheer each other on in a positively inspiring way. I was brought to tears watching a young boy who couldn't have been more than 14 collapse after he made it across the finish line, and people rallied around him to make sure he recovered.

Watching how much these runners poured every bit of themselves into reaching their goal took me back to that feeling of the 7-mile run from over a decade ago. I decided I'd spent enough time at the finish line cheering for others through the years following—I set my eyes on the goal of running a half marathon myself. While that goal has yet to be reached, it was in the literal running towards it that I consider a victory.

I began training that spring and continued through part of the summer, adding length to my runs incrementally. Week after week, I showed up consistently and stuck with it—which was a first for me. I made it all the way up to a 6-mile route that was the furthest I'd run without having to stop to walk—until a foot injury that still pains me today caused me to stop shortly afterward. I don't know if or when it will be healed to the point of being able to pick back up and press toward that half marathon goal once again, but no matter what, what I learned about "running the race with endurance" will always stick with me.

Somewhere around the same time as my running "career" concluded, I was reading the well-known verse in Hebrews 12:1, which reads: "Therefore, since we are surrounded by such a great cloud of witnesses, let us throw off everything that hinders and the sin that so easily entangles. And let us run with perseverance the race marked out for us" (NIV).

Though I've read it many times throughout my life in various translations such as the one above (where the title of this book came from), this time, I was reading The Passion Translation Bible. For some reason, the words and even footnotes jumped off the page and into my heart like a lightbulb moment (as often happens with this translation that I am, in fact, quite passionate about). Rather than "so we must throw off everything that hinders" (NIV) or "lay aside every weight" (HCSB), it reads: "So we must let go of every wound that has pierced us."

As I read it, I was viscerally aware of every invisible wound that had pierced me throughout my life. Imagery of a sharp object making contact with my chest, like an arrow to the heart, flashed across my mind. I believe God often speaks through imagery, and sure enough, as I looked to the footnotes at the bottom of the page, the imagery I had just pictured is exactly what the original intent of the verse points to:

> "Or, *'get rid of every arrow tip in us.'* The implication is carrying an arrow tip inside, a wound that weighs us down and keeps us from running our race with freedom."

Gasp* I thought back to my running adventures, picturing trying to run my 7-mile and 6-mile stretches with gaping wounds in my chest. I pictured heavy arrowheads still lodged in my flesh and bone and me trying to continue running on rather than addressing the obvious problem lodged inside me, causing pain with every hindered breath. "How illogical!" I thought. "Who would do that?"

"You. Them. Everyone, really," I imagined God answering.

Gasp again* Now that imagery and those words lodged in my heart have gripped me ever since, and I've felt a growing urgency and burden to not only identify and remove the arrowheads I didn't realize I was carrying but to help shine light to all who have eyes to see and ears to hear the absurdity of trying to continue running before addressing first things first: to remove what's been weighing you down and causing you harm, to tend to your wounds and begin healing before taking another blind and painful step.

Our Western culture as a whole commends those who keep limping along, wounded and breathless in their lives. What we actually *need* to commend is pausing, turning toward, naming in truth, and tenderly removing the arrowheads so that then we heal and grow stronger—continuing on, truly unhindered.

Believer or unbeliever, none of us have escaped the unhelpful influences that have told us messages such as to "suck it up," or "just pray through it," or "trust God more." That type of dismissive language denies the reality that all of us have wounds inside of us, whether inflicted by others or ourselves, that are hindering our optimal functioning and realizing our total freedom. What we need first is permission to pause and intentionally tend to those places.

Quite similar to when, rather than listen to my body, I drove my unprepared and untrained self that was *technically* unfit to run 7 miles to run that long leg of the relay with no preparation. In that case, it was my pride and ignorance inflicting my own wounds and turning a blind eye, forcing myself to continue running when the wise thing to do would have been perhaps to decline the opportunity to begin with or, at a minimum, walk it to be gentle to my suffering self.

On the contrary, after my 6-mile run, when I became aware that my right foot was unwell, as much as I hate slowing down and sitting things out, I listened this time. I stayed off of it and have continued to let it heal, finding alternative and lower-impact activities to work toward my health and fitness goals in the meantime.

I'm on a quest now to listen to my heart injuries and to take everyone that I can with me along for the adventure as we discover that God's heart for us is not like the task-mastery ways we've been conditioned to treat ourselves and expect of others at times. His heart longs for us to listen to ours, to know and name our wounds so that we can partner with Him in our healing. We can learn to lay down the burdensome weights of the arrowheads we learn to bravely face and work with Him (and often a good therapist and/or friend) to delicately remove them. He has ways of laying His hands over our wounded places and stitching them up with His love for newness to fill like sweet meadow grass taking over a barren landscape.

While I'm no stranger to invisible (mental/emotional/spiritual/relational) wounding of many kinds and many contexts throughout my life, it is "arrowheads" of religious origin that have perhaps sunk in the most deeply and wreaked the most havoc. Like a spray of shotgun pellets hitting every organ rather than being isolated to one area of damage, when proverbial shots are fired from places of perceived higher authority, such as ministries and churches, the whole framework of our being is impacted.

As I've navigated my way back to the origins of many of the hindrances that held me back for the majority of my life, religious trauma seems to be the biggest common denominator that shaped me to the core, which is why it's the focus of this book. I want to get to the root of what harmed so many of us, setting us up for failure, fear, and fear of failure in many or all other areas of life—quite the opposite to the "freedom" it was marketed under.

From faulty black-and-white thinking that had me harshly judging others and myself, to being afraid of disappointing everyone from God to my parents, to just being plain afraid of interacting with the opposite sex, to other's opinions of me, to having low self-esteem and high self-loathing, to having no self-trust and lacking discernment in relationships, having low to no boundaries (or not even knowing what a healthy boundary was until my mid-twenties), to fear of vulnerability and transparency, to preparing for the worst, expecting the least, to experiencing yet being unable to identify various injustices because "love covers" and "forgiveness = forgetting"—everything warped about the theology I'd been hit by harmed my world view, inner world, relationships, education, and more.

It came into play when I entered the professional world, keeping me bound to working under toxic leadership for too long because I was trying to "consider it pure joy" that I was "facing trials of many kinds." It came into play as the root cause of much relationship dysfunction of every type, including dating and my first marriage. Since I was trying to "turn the other cheek," "suffer as Christ suffered," and "forgive 70x 7," I allowed much relational harm that perhaps I could have prevented by standing up for what's right sooner—had I not been so disoriented and confused about what was actually right. It's been something I've worked overtime on to ensure my own child isn't affected by the wounds I'm still healing from as I entered motherhood in the last decade.

I'm sure you have your own examples of what I'm speaking to. For your harmful and wounding experiences, I grieve with you. It makes sense that if the belief systems we built on are full of life-draining toxins, the air rising up from that compromised ground would pollute and cause harm to everything we've built from there.

Doubting

After the arrowhead epiphany, I kept reading as the verse moves from "every wound that has pierced us" straight to "and," and the two translations I had before me both used the same word in the next part:

"... and the sin that so easily entangles...." (NIV)

"...and the sin we so easily fall into..." (TPT)

That word "sin" is not a pretty one and still rubs me the wrong way when I hear it, which is why I've dedicated space in another chapter to unpacking its misuse and abuse. I realized, though, as I continued more thoughtfully and intentionally this time, that I had never really studied what it's inferring in this particular passage.

I'd always assumed it was referring to collective, common "sins" that are "easy" and as common as a cold. I'd filled in the blank with things like pride, selfishness, dishonesty, and other slippery things that trip all of us up at some point. My curious eyes fell to the footnotes once again, which led to another "aha!" moment of enlightenment on what he was getting at:

> "Or 'the sin that so cleverly entangles us.' The Aramaic can be translated 'the sin that is ready [and waiting] for us.' If this is speaking of one sin, the context would point to the sin of unbelief and doubting God's promises."

"Doubting God's promises is a *sin*?" I thought to myself. (Which also piqued my curiosity even more on the topic of what is and isn't sin.) "I thought that doubt was just a weakness, a struggle we all have to overcome?" I pondered more. It's as though God answered in my spirit, "Yes, but choosing to live *in* doubt is what becomes unbelief, which leaves you vulnerable to harm. It causes you loss. It causes you to miss out on all that I have for you. Like in James 1:8, 'the man who doubts is unstable in all he does.'"

It hit me: how can we run life's "race" well if we're moving forward from a place of chronic doubt and the unaddressed pain often causing it? How can we run wholeheartedly towards a goal of any kind when we're *choosing* to live unconvinced and doubtful about the goal, the path, and the purpose of it all anyway?

As I'll elaborate on more later, if we understand "sin" as "harm" (because that's essentially what it is and what it causes), and if we understand the intent here is that there is something harmful ready and waiting to trip us up—that it is choosing to live from a place of not really taking Him at His word and doubting the good promises He gives to us—we can see that of course, we'd do well to avoid choosing harm.

Since doubt typically arises as a form of self-preservation (think of it as a way to keep from getting hurt or disappointed), it may not sound harmful, rather smart, even. For a time, doubt does its job of trying to keep us safe. I think what it's saying is that when doubt is given the right of way to take root and grow into unbelief, it harms us and others in countless ways, perhaps the most tragic of all: keeping us from experiencing the fullness of abundant life intended for us.

Through noble self-preservation efforts and very valid trust issues that created an unhealthy and tragic "fear" of God (rather than the "awe" that is intended by the term when used in the context of "fearing" the Lord), we become entangled in our doubts about God's promises to the point that we don't even recognize what we're missing out on. If left unaddressed, we bench ourselves from the fullness of life and relationships with God and others, sidelined from the very life we were designed to live.

For example:

If we don't really believe in the existence of or transforming power of God's grace (unmerited favor), which is promised and freely extended to us every moment of every day, we won't know how to receive it when it's extended to us, and we sure won't know what it means to truly give grace to others.

If we don't believe that all things are possible with God, we'll live within the bounds and limits of the natural world and our humanness, discounting or explaining away the miraculous and not being able to be astounded by the supernatural ways He shows up in our daily lives.

If we don't believe that we are loved beyond measure, we live believing that we are partially or conditionally loved; any smaller degree falls vastly short of the grandeur of how deeply and irrevocably loved we truly are.

Please hear me when I say this: *you are not to blame for the way in which you've been hindered by doubt that petrified into unbelief.* Doubt goes up like a default wall of protection when we've been hurt. It makes *sense.* But when you become aware of the ways doubt is causing further harm now than the temporary protection it offered upon activation, then it's up to you to decide if you stay behind it or step out in faith in front of it. Like the man who cried out, "I believe; help my unbelief!" (Mark 9:24, HCSB), stepping out can begin with simply asking for help with the hindrance. God absolutely hears us and helps us.

I believe that at the root of doubt lies the sneaky, twisted spirit of religion (different from a chosen "religion," such as Christianity, Catholicism, Judaism, etc.). It has ensnared so many of us in its life-sucking legalism without our even knowing, rendering us unable to operate in true faith—hindering us from running our race well. Many of us were brought up in churches that struck more fear in us than love, which goes expressly against the truth of God's heart and is explicitly stated in the verse, "...perfect love drives out fear, because fear involves punishment" (1 John 4:18, HCSB). This part of the verse has to do with throwing off the harm that's been dished out to us that we consumed, often without our knowing. But once we know, we can choose to throw it off. We can let Perfect Love help drive out the fear that's stunted us by causing our doubt and building our walls of unbelief. We can learn to partner with—and become like—Perfect Love, driving away the doubts that dare to hinder us from our divine destinies.

Able

What is the goal of all of this untangling, unhindering, healing, and believing, anyway? I love how the last part of the verse vision-casts for us of what we'll be able to do once we start taking care of first things first in their proper order:

> "*Then* we will be *able* to run life's marathon race with passion and determination, for the path has already been marked out before us."
>
> Hebrews 12:1b, TPT (emphasis, mine)

When we're throwing off "everything that hinders"—those sharp, painfully heavy arrowheads that we carry—when we take them out and lay them down at His feet, our wounds feel even more vulnerable once cleaned out. At first, they're just gaping open. But hiding behind the weapon that dealt the damage isn't true vulnerability. At best, it's avoidance. At worst, it's holding on to what's causing the harm, thus enabling and perpetuating the harm. But we can trust Him—we can allow Him to begin stitching up our open wounds. We can let Him tenderly love us into wholeness. We can learn gentleness and tenderness with ourselves and others from this place. We can heal—and often, through our own healing, we get to participate in the healing of those around us.

When we're awake to the doubt-traps that have entangled us—the falsities, the "truth" we were taught that's full of so many holes that our boats have been sinking, and we've been drowning for years. When we're no longer scooping buckets of water out of the boat but diving into the ocean itself and swimming to solid ground...

Then, we are able.

Able to face reality and call things by their real names.

Able to heal from the hard things we name.

Able to help heal others by sharing what helped us.

Able to support others as they do their tending.

Able to feel empathetic, love deeply, trust again, speak from experience, lead by example, and in short, run the race with passion and determination.

He's already marked out the path for us during His time here on earth as one of us, experiencing His own wounding—in body, soul, and spirit. He met His wounds with vulnerability—crying when he needed to cry, being angry when he witnessed injustice, pouring His aching heart out before God, experiencing the sting of betrayal, false accusation, and actual impalement by nails. And He modeled complete healing when, after dying, He rose again on the third day. He didn't deny all of the pain and suffering had happened—on the contrary, He made a point to prove it did, that He was the same Him, fully healed and fully alive again, as He pointed to the scars that now covered where nails once pierced Him.

Arrowheads. Nails. Removed. New flesh. Abounding. Scars remain to bear witness to the truth of His story, which means that in every way, He has lived and relates to us. He's cut the trail for each of us, and we're invited to accept this invitation, rise to the challenge, answer the call and follow in His footsteps to the victory that is healing so that we can continue running our race with all the passion and determination we can carry, that will in turn have a way of lifting and carrying us instead.

That is the vision for living unhindered. I hope you will have felt chains fall off of your heart and felt cage doors swing wide open in areas you may not have even realized you've been held back from running your race with all the freedom and grace available to you.

But as with most transformational journeys, it often has to get worse before it gets better. We'll explore more about where many of us had our doubts, fears and other hindrances forged and have had our healing hindered—whether deliberately or out of ignorance—largely due to the influences, direct or indirect, of the church.

Broken Sanctuaries

"Sanctuary: 1: a consecrated place... 2: a place of refuge and protection"

Merriam-Webster Dictionary [4]

Genesis

If I could write my own beginning or "Genesis" regarding my journey with the church, it would read something like this: In the beginning, the church was created to be a sanctuary. But sadly, in many cases, it instead became a den of thieves and a lair for wolves in sheep's clothing who beckoned in the innocent and impressionable, wounded-but-hopeful believers (or want-to-believe-ers.) And so, it lived up to the opposite of the meaning of 'sanctuary' and instead became a place of harm. And God said that it was *not* good.

Although my memories of the first church my family attended in my early childhood are vague, I still recall enough of the fear-based messages from those Sunday school classes and the broader Christian community to have vivid memories of the following: I distinctly remember being a frightened 5-year-old, pacing in my parent's backyard, anxiously repeating the "sinner's prayer." I was

---

4 "Sanctuary Definition & Meaning." *Merriam-Webster*, Merriam-Webster, www.merriam-webster.com/dictionary/sanctuary?utm_campaign=sd&utm_medium=serp&utm_source=jsonld. Accessed 15 Oct. 2024.

overwhelmed with fear and uncertainty, not knowing if I had done it correctly—if the prayer had "worked" since I didn't feel any different. I worried that if I didn't pray it perfectly or truly mean it, I would go to hell someday. Looking back, it grieves me deeply that this was the conclusion I reached with the limited and distorted understanding I had. The idea that a child must "join the club" of Christianity or risk being excluded from God's family instills fear and isolation that led me, and I'm sure other children, to "invite Jesus into my heart" just to feel safe, to be "good," to seek approval, and to find belonging. It's a terrifying place for a child to be.

Now, I realize that there are many wonderful (or, at the very least, not harmful) churches and Christian communities in existence. I am thankful that on this side of the journey, I've been able to experience a healthy church family. It is the closest imagery of the body of Christ I've corporately experienced to date. So while I mean no disrespect to any one church or religion in particular, I *do* mean to call out any building, group, or person that claims to believe in Jesus the Son of God as the Savior of the world but who has instead preached directly or indirectly any fear-based messaging in attempt to coax, coerce, or manipulate others into compliance with their prescribed methods of "achieving" salvation (as if it's something we could achieve—that's why Jesus took care of what we couldn't) and remaining in "God's" (read: their) good graces. It is sadly my experience that this description encompasses many portions of Western Christian churches today, specifically those that would fall under or overlap with fundamentalist, conservative, and even evangelical schools of thought.

My personal experiences were in churches and ministries with fundamentalist ideals—that is, legalistic, actively prioritizing strict rules, conservative ideals, emphasizing male leadership and superiority, patriarchy, complementarianism, and encouraging what I now know to be called a "religious authoritarian parenting"[5] style (thank you D. L. and Krispen Mayfield for that verbiage I was lacking until recently.) These groups are often characterized as having extreme focus on the outward appearance of their organization, families, and concerned primarily about behavior modification and compliance with those in their congregation over the inward heart and wellness of an individual or family.

If we were to venture all the way back to my most impactful "church burn" experience, you might get a picture of what I'm referring to. I know that you may have your own church war story as well, and for that, I am so deeply sorry. Please accept this book as a healing balm from me to you and your loved ones who've trudged parallel, or perhaps, the same trenches as I did.

I remember it like it was yesterday—though now, decades later, it feels like watching my own story unfold from a fly-on-the-wall perspective.

Everything changed when we visited a small rural church near Greenbrier, AR. A homeschooling family friend had invited us to visit. Our dads worked together and thought we might enjoy it since the church was full of like-minded families. One of the most defining shared traits was the influence of the Quiverfull movement, which had shaped many families there, including mine.

While the movement began before the 1990s, Rick and Jan Hess's book, A Full Quiver[6] (published in the early 90s), became a leading influence at the time. In essence, the movement centers around the belief that children are a blessing from the Lord, encouraging married couples to forgo birth control and allow God to determine the size of their family.

---

5   Mayfield, Krispin, and D. L. Mayfield. "Chapter 1: What Is Religious Authoritarian Parenting?" *Strongwilled*, Substack, 8 Apr. 2024, https://strongwilled.substack.com/p/chapter-1-what-is-religious-authoritarian. Accessed 15 Oct. 2024.

6   Hess, Rick, and Jan Hess. *A Full Quiver: Family Planning and the Lordship of Christ.* Wolgemuth & Hyatt, 1990.

As you can imagine, most families at this church had more than a few children. Many embraced old-fashioned values, adored the Little House on the Prairie[7] TV series, and homeschooled their children. It wasn't uncommon to see 12- or 15-passenger vans parked outside to accommodate large families. In the years to come, my sibling count grew from four to seven, and soon after, we upgraded to a used vehicle we affectionately called Clifford—the big red van. Our family of ten fit snugly inside, with extra seats for friends who often tagged along.

I'll always remember my first evening church service there at age 7. We went into the building a bit late after the service had begun, as our larger family typically ran late. The church was also about a 45-minute drive from our home on the far west side of Little Rock, so the distance was something we were not used to accounting for either. But nevertheless, we slipped quietly into a back row near our friends who had invited us.

The worship was old school in that it was just a pianist and the music minister leading worship. They sang from hymnals and used an old-fashioned slide projector when they sang original music by one of the congregation members. The congregation was small, with less than 100 people, and about half of those were kids. My parents liked that the children sat through the whole service with their families. I, for one, not used to attending the "grown-up" service, was bored out of my mind. I passed some of the time propping my feet up on the back of the row of chairs in front of me, promptly being directed by my mother to stop doing that, and eventually, drawing doodles with the pocket-sized pencil on the offering envelope tucked in the back of the seat in front of me.

---

7   Hawkins, John, and William F. Claxton. *Little House on The Prairie*, NBC, 1974.

We didn't talk to many people after the service, as my mother was great at doing that on all of our behalf with her endearing, outgoing, never-met-a-stranger personality. My sisters and I stuck together and socialized a bit with the family friends who invited us. Other than that, there was nothing super memorable about that first experience at the new little church that would become our church home for nearly a decade. There was no way of knowing it would become such an emotionally and spiritually traumatizing environment to me and many others.

We began attending the little church "religiously" (pun intended) and with great dedication, considering the drive from Little Rock to Greenbrier each time. We were there Sunday mornings, often returning for Sunday evenings—or passing time in town or at another family's home until the next service—and again on Wednesday nights. We especially made the trip for potluck Sundays, when everyone brought a dish for a buffet-style lunch in the fellowship hall downstairs after the service.

At first, it felt charming and harmless. We started making new friends—some of whom became lifelong connections, the saving grace and most redemptive part of our too-long time there. We got "plugged in," so to speak, and for a while, nothing seemed out of the ordinary compared to the conservative and unconventional home life I was already used to. We were an odd bunch—we just didn't realize it—and we fit in better with the families there than at the larger church we had previously attended in Little Rock.

Most families, like ours, listened primarily to classical music and hymns. This was largely because those genres didn't have a "drum beat," which was somehow linked to a "secular" style of music. Though I can't recall who said it, the phrase "drum beats are of the devil" struck fear in me and stuck with me as I grew up.

Most of the girls at the church wore dresses, just like my sisters and me. The few who didn't were often met with disapproving looks. The boys shared an intense fascination with the military, and it wasn't unusual to see them wearing camouflage combat-style pants. Many children were interested in historical time periods—just like us. My older sister even served as president of our own "Old-Fashioned Club," which raised funds to donate Beanie Babies to the children's hospital. Later, we used donations to purchase a butter churn. And by golly, we taught ourselves how to churn butter.

A lot of our friends from church were into Civil War history, and before long, we sewed "Southern Belle" style dresses as part of a project with some of them. Sometimes, we'd dress up as French Revolution-era aristocrats and watch films like The Scarlet Pimpernel. Ironically, we weren't allowed to watch more age-appropriate films—like some Disney movies—because they contained "worldly influences" such as magic. Never mind the guillotine gore in the French Revolution films—we'd close our eyes or fast forward. Usually, at least.

As we got older, we were allowed to watch some R-rated films such as The Patriot and Black Hawk Down, yet still not allowed to read or watch what kids outside of our bubble were at that time—such as Harry Potter—because again, magic was more harmful than violence, and the war movies taught us about history and patriotism. (Or something along the lines of that justification since war films could be considered part of our homeschool curriculum.)

That's just a small picture of some of the ways in which we as a church community were already a bit strange, but thought we were living in a more wholesome, subtly superior, and more holy way, you could say. This high-horse mentality bred judgement toward those outside of our church at first, but it wasn't long before I realized how much it set up standards for comparison and judgement within our church community as well.

As I got a bit older, 11 or so, it felt easier to make friends with both the girls and boys. Though we didn't have a children's program or a youth group, all of the kids would hang out on the lawn after church, sometimes playing tag, sometimes dancing the Virginia Reel (yes, we were also into square dancing, if that doesn't surprise you by now.) Being a country girl made me a bit of a tomboy, too, and I felt quite comfortable socializing with the boys, sometimes more so than with the girls. Especially when I started recognizing a group of girls slightly older than me, who had a subtle and stinging way of excluding me from conversations when I'd walk by or try to join the conversation. I was met with a few shouldered-out circle-ups, where they'd cast discarding glances my way as they whispered or giggled just below what I could hear. It wasn't long before word got back to me that rumors were being started about me being a "flirt" for hanging out with the boys. Also, that my mom must have allowed my sister and me to start wearing makeup as pre-teens in order to attract and "seduce" the boys. (I only found out about that one in my adult years, and it still cuts.) I guess I shouldn't have been surprised that it was frowned upon to have struck up friendships with some of the members of the opposite sex, as that was the very reason the church was against having a youth group—to avoid any "temptation" or "stumbling" or other "gray areas" between boys and girls.

Like Sleeping Beauty's parents trying to control outcomes by burning all of the spinning wheels, the parents of that church took control to new levels with their choice to eliminate any sort of inclusive group for the adolescents to have some normal model of socializing together. We were all homeschooled, mind you, so we didn't get this co-ed time at school. They made sure it was minimized at church, too. Because that doesn't make for an awkward and ill-equipped teenager, right? You may find it as no surprise, then, that the majority of the families at the church had a no-dating rule for their teenagers (and 20-somethings). Old-fashioned chaperoned courtship relationships, however, were the encouraged path should one arrive at such a relational bridge to cross.

The segregation between boys and girls was furthered at the weeklong summer day camp that all of the kids looked forward to every year. It was hosted by the pastor and his son at their home on many wooded acres, and was one redeeming quality of our time there. I still have many good memories from our outdoor adventures. We'd all deck out in camo for those days, as we enjoyed the combat elements of the epic games of Capture the Flag, water balloon fights, and other competitive activities requiring stealth mode. They worked in Bible study time as well as some swimming time in the pastor's pool, which is where the segregation between males and females reared its head again. The boys would go far off into the woods away from the pool during the girls' swim hour, and likewise, we would give the boys space to have the pool to themselves during their designated swim time. However, both genders were still required to wear full-coverage swimwear. By that, I mean boys were required to wear sleeved T-shirts with their swim trunks, and girls were required to wear large T-shirts and knee-length shorts over their one-piece swimsuits. It seemed a bit extreme to me even then, but of course, I didn't question it at the time.

Another key focus, besides the extreme purity culture—such as those exhausting efforts toward modesty and segregation of sexes—was a major emphasis on authority.

This went beyond good parenting of teaching respect and obedience among children, but taken to unparalleled degrees of driving fear into the hearts of children of ever usurping any authority figure, whether accidentally or through outright rebellion. It didn't stop at a fear of stepping out from under our parents' authority, but virtually any adult, especially male, especially pastors, elders, or other leaders—church or government sanctioned. This messaging and fear were driven into us by a variety of means, from threats of punishment to stories of consequences others had suffered when not fully submitted to their "God-given" authority figures, to content consumed in sermons, by special speakers, at other church-condoned conferences and events—especially those put on by or affiliated with Bill Gothard's Institute in Basic Life Principles (IBLP).

IBLP was like a slow-growing cancer, sneaking in and infecting the worldview of so many families in our church and nationwide, which we later learned was a part of their "infiltration" strategy. As if we weren't being immersed enough in Bill's "Umbrella of Authority" model at church, a hefty dose was also included as the basis of IBLP's homeschool curriculum put out by their sister "ministry," ATI, which stood for Advanced Training Institute. Originally published under the organization's former name, Institute in Basic Youth Conflicts, and ironically named "Wisdom Booklets," many of the families, including mine, utilized this homeschool curriculum, further cementing the nail on the coffin of complete submersion and total indoctrination into the ideals of this man and "institute" that would later be revealed as a cult. He would later be removed as leader of the institute on numerous counts of sexual abuse allegations among the young women he'd give the "special opportunity" to come "serve" at one of his "training centers." *Shudder* Even speaking the language again is a dead giveaway to the "cult"-ture masquerading as a ministry.

It's not to say that they didn't also include some great Bible stories and some lovely verses or that some at the organization didn't have the right heart and were genuinely trying to help families. It is to say that it was so entangled with unbiblical and completely off-base personal and even political propaganda that they were calling "biblical truth." They influenced and misled the masses, of which we were a smaller part of the plague reaching far beyond the borders of our small congregation. To be continually exposed to the content this organization put out was to be slowly brainwashed into normalizing abuse, objectification of women, patriarchy, white Christian nationalism, and more.

I recently came back across a page of one of the old Wisdom Booklets and was in horror even these decades later to read afresh the atrocities I consumed under the guise as "truth":

"HOW DOES TURNING THE OTHER CHEEK HELP US OVERCOME THE ATTITUDES THAT CAUSE A SLAP?

Wrong attitudes are so potentially destructive to a person's life that God will use many means to correct them. His goal is that they will be eliminated during a person's youth. Toward that end, a young person should quietly accept the discipline that God brings in the form of sharp reactions from others."[8]

It goes on to detail a list of attitudes that are "unbecoming of a Christian" and "deserving of swift and harsh rebukes," asking the child to number these attitudes from mild to severe. The attitudes range from indiscreet to brash, from rude to impolite. With grief, I see now where many of my ideas about emotional suppression being holy and expressing emotions being disobedient or sinful were rooted and watered. I can also see where fear of punishment primed us to accept mistreatment, stunted our growth in developing agency to stand up for ourselves, and crowded out room to become curious about the responses prompting our "unbecoming" emotions. I'm sure now that most, if not all, of our responses were completely justified and our little God-given alarm systems were going off try-

---

8 "Power through Precision B." *Wisdom Booklet #28* , Institute in Basic Youth Conflicts, 1987, p. 1313.

ing to draw attention to the harm we were experiencing.

In another booklet, a page showed the sketch of a woman in the center, with bullet points detailing every aspect of her posture as being the "appropriate" way a woman should stand, such as "shoulders rolled back and down, relaxed rather than stiff" and "Back-straight and tall, having only a slight curve at the waistline" and more that make my skin want to crawl right off of my imperfect posture. This was after the page teaching on how to avoid what they referred to as "eye traps" and how to draw people's attention to your Christlike countenance rather than distracting them with your physical appearance. They wanted to control even how we stood, so as to be pleasing to God and our parents. The heading over the sketch of the woman read:

"STAND TALL - SIT GRACEFULLY
Sagging posture draws attention to itself, slouching in a chair communicates a lack of alertness, and often disrespect. Flaws in the posture draw the observer's attention away from the face and to the problem."[9]

Perhaps the most ridiculous one I came back across in recent months was this one, which was further evidence of where much of the messaging about women needing to spend every waking moment striving not to become a "stumbling block" for men came from:

"HOW ARE EYELIDS USED FOR SEDUCTIVE PURPOSES
The eyelids are also noted in Scripture as a weapon that is used by those with impure motives.[10]

---

9 "Medicine Resource H." *Booklet #15–Preliminary Edition*, Institute in Basic Life Principles, 1986, p. 624.

10 "Medicine Resource H." *Booklet #3–Preliminary Edition*, Institute in Basic Life Principles, 1986, p. 98.

The above examples from the textbooks embraced by many of the families at that church, including my own for a time, still make me wince. It's just a fraction of the abhorrent doctrine we were force-fed on a slow drip from Gothard's cult, seeping into our church and lives masked as "biblical truth." My family was among the many that would attend Gothard's in-person seminars when they came to Little Rock, which of course, came complete with a program for the kids they aptly called the "Children's Institute." It was like Awana meets Basic Training meets Miss Trunchbull from Matilda. But the local events weren't the only time we got an extra helping of Gothardism—our family was also sadly a part of the pack that would travel all the way to Knoxville, TN once a year for the Advanced Training Seminar. It seemed like a normal, supplemental activity that so many in our church were involved in that it became synonymous with "church activities," though it was not expressly a part of our church's doctrine.

Exodus

As time went by and we continued to attend that little church that was now mostly made up of families involved in Gothard's "institute" as a part of their home education, things, of course, continued to go from bad to worse.

My mother—admired for her beauty and youthfulness despite having carried many children—began facing exclusion from women's circles, much like I was experiencing with the "mean girls." Her fun-loving, outgoing personality—something we had always adored about her—seemed to step on the toes of some of the quieter, more traditional women there.

Our family also began facing criticism for our friendship with a brother and sister duo a few years older than my older sister and me. Initially, their father had come down to do carpentry work on our home build. As they'd learned construction skills from him, this eventually led to them being hired as a part-time summer job, staying with our family for a few days of work at a time due to the travel distance. We all got along like siblings, and this sparked gossip among some families who felt we were overstepping by welcoming them into our home, leading to hurtful rumors that we were trying to "steal" them. We started receiving judgemental looks just for chatting with them at church. But that was only the start of the scrutiny we faced.

The following spring break, two of the music minister and lead elder's sons heard about the construction work opportunity at our home, which was still under construction. They were hired as extra hands for the week that one of our other friends was coming to work, too. They camped out at the job site, just across from the mobile home where my family was living during construction. My older sister and I were also honing our carpentry skills, learning how to do everything from cut and install trim to laying hardwood flooring to painting, staining, and hanging doors around the house. (This is where I developed my "design-bug" that eventually led to my college education and career in Interior Design!)

During the day, we worked alongside the guys and bonded over family dinners, card games, and raft wars in the pond. We'd go fishing in the evenings, hiking in the mornings, and play practical jokes and pranks on each other as much as possible. It was like we suddenly had big brothers, which, as it turned out, was tons of fun! Our adventures working and playing together during that time are still some of the best memories I carry from my adolescence.

They continued to work for my family on and off throughout the summer, and we all grew attached to each other like siblings. Except in the case of the oldest son—as we'd realized by the end of the summer, we began to have feelings for each other. *Gasp*

I know, right? Two teenagers liking each other—without even so much as a youth group setting to have enticed them. Outlandish!

But once word got out, the drama began. My innocent teenage crush became a scandal that rocked our little church. I felt like I was wearing a "scarlet letter" for falling in love with a son from one of the most revered families in the church. Despite the fact that he reciprocated those feelings, the blame was more directed toward me, as if I had somehow "seduced" him. My parents were aware of our feelings and didn't have a problem with it, but his parents reacted as if we had committed a crime. The situation escalated to the point that it was causing division among the church members, some siding with each of our families, but due to his parents' prominent place of leadership in the church, the majority followed suit in support of their disapproval.

One Sunday evening, a church elders meeting was called to address our "forbidden" relationship that was causing much upheaval among the congregation. The entire day, I felt a knot in my stomach leading up to this unprecedented confrontation. That evening, I found myself crammed into a tiny room with my parents, his parents, the church elders, and the two of us, facing their judgement. We were shamed for having feelings for each other without consulting our parents first, accused of "usurping" their authority—as if our emotions were something we could have gotten pre-approval for before feeling them.

I left that meeting feeling utterly exposed and embarrassed. A room full of church leaders had interrogated us about his feelings for me and mine for him, making me feel like a rebellious daughter and a moral failure for simply liking him. Worse, they threatened that we might never be able to be together, at least not without his parents' blessing. A few days following that traumatic event, his parents briefly gave their approval for a courtship—only to withdraw it the next day without explanation. It felt like a cruel tease, and we were utterly distraught, caught between trying to do the "right" thing according to our indoctrination, and what made common sense to us—young and naive as we were.

In a final attempt to understand his parent's change of heart, my parents kindly arranged a meeting with us and his father at a nearby coffee shop, as his mother was unwilling to communicate with us directly at that point. Again, we expressed our desire to pursue a relationship, hoping for some clarity on why their blessing had been withdrawn. Instead of providing clarity, his father exploded. The meeting ended abruptly with him standing up in the crowded coffee shop and pointing at us with a shaking hand, shouting, "I curse this relationship!" before storming off in a rage.

I was paralyzed with shock, unable to believe the verbal assault we had just experienced from a man who was supposed to be a spiritual leader. My parents, my almost-boyfriend, and I walked out of that meeting feeling disoriented, further confused, and now rattled by the public outburst. It became clear that there was no way to navigate their ever-changing rules and emotionally fickle climate, so we decided to move forward with our relationship with only my parents' blessing.

The relationship was intense, to say the least, not only because of its rocky beginnings but also due to the belief that relationships should lead to marriage. Not long after, we exchanged promise rings as a symbol of our intention to marry when I turned 18. But our young love didn't even make it to my 16th birthday. While our relationship outlasted my time at that broken sanctuary, it ultimately met its demise after a rocky few years of trying to make things work. Through much turmoil and disbelief that we could collapse after all of our "us against the world" striving and many gut-wrenching tears—I had to face the fact that there were chronic dysfunctional issues between us that created much emotional distress and distrust that was beyond repair. Before the breakup, my dad sat beside me at the kitchen counter as I cried over the latest wound after one of our last tearful and tense phone calls. I felt trapped; part of me didn't want to let go, while another part felt bound by the promise we'd made—as if we were already betrothed. Listening intently to my pain, he placed his hand firmly on the counter, looked me in the eyes, and gently but firmly spoke, "*Do not marry this guy, Kathryn.*" My dad is quiet by nature so when he speaks, I pay close attention. He had tried to support me, giving me space to fly or fall on my own, and hoped for the best. But now I could hear it in his voice and see it in his eyes—he was deeply concerned for, me—his daughter. And that was the moment I knew: I needed to end it.

It took me years to grieve the loss of a love I thought would last forever. I still mourn that what should have been a normal "first love" became one of the most demoralizing and traumatic experiences of my life—shaped by key figures in that church. What could have been a simple coming-of-age story for both of us was instead marked by deep emotional and psychological pain, intensified by religious overtones and undertones. Many years into my healing journey, I realized how deeply the toxic religious environment we had both grown up in had influenced our thinking, relationships, and behavior—essentially dooming our relationship from the start. I burst into tears of fiery anger for those truly to blame for the dysfunction in our relationship, grieving for the both of us. For the first time in years, I reached out to him—overwhelmed with compassion for our younger selves and the trauma we endured at the hands of that church. It was a moment of forgiveness, reconciliation, and healing that I never expected—and am so deeply grateful for.

But just before my first relationship met its tragic end, I'd left the church—making it out by the age of 15. Sadly, though, I didn't realize I was blindly diving head-first into my second most impactful church burn experience. My older sister and I had been extended a welcome invitation to a friend's youth group at a medium-sized church just minutes down the road from where we lived. Other refugees from the same little church in Greenbrier had somehow ended up at this church. The mere fact that it had a youth group felt like finding an oasis in a long, hot desert of awkward and heartbreaking teenage years. After years of suffocating in every way, it felt as though I was coming up for air. Eventually, my parents and younger siblings followed suit, leaving the small rural church that had caused all of us so much hurt behind and joining my sister and me at the new nearby one.

What we didn't realize at the time was that toxicity lives on a spectrum, and if you have been in an extremely toxic environment, even a step down into slightly less contaminated air may feel like clean air to pollutant-acclimated lungs. I will spare you all of the details of what transpired at the next one, but picture it as the miniature version of some of what we experienced at the former church, with less of Gothard's influence. There was more freedom but still high control. Opposite-gender friends were fine, but there were lots of worst assumptions and extreme boundaries. A bit more grace was mixed in with lots of law-based and still legalistic teaching.

At one summer youth event, for example, in contrast to the previous church's extreme swimwear policy, we were allowed to wear tank tops, not even for swimming, but just as casual wear! Just as I was beginning to relax and think that things were getting better, it was, of course, still an eggshell walk. Apparently, I missed the memo about only *high*-cut tank tops, and during an otherwise fun game of ultimate frisbee. I was pulled aside by the youth pastor's wife, reprimanded and shamed for being so thoughtless as to wear a scoop-neck tank, becoming a stumbling block for my brothers.

Who knew all it would take is an unidentified number of inches short from an acceptable amount of collarbone coverage to take a fun summer game south and into provocative territory? Clearly, not me. The next time I was shamed for my wardrobe was when I'd made the effort to still come to church one Wednesday night after getting off work late. A bit embarrassed that I hadn't packed a change of clothes and smelled like the frying vat at Chili's, I made a makeshift top out of a jean jacket I had with me, buttoning it up top to bottom. But that wasn't sufficient, and the modesty police (this time, a girl in the grade above me) pulled me out of a game of ping pong after the service, chastising me for the midriff she saw revealed as I'd reached to hit the ping pong ball across the table. I held back hot tears, embarrassed again that I'd somehow offended others again, all while trying so hard to do the right thing—in this case, work a part-time job and still make it to church. In short, being at this church was like escaping the fire but crawling right into the frying pan. A bit removed, but still in danger, and it would take a bit of the pan warming up to feel the heat was hot enough to burn me, still.

I wish that were the last "church burn" experience of my life, but sadly, even as they dissipated in legalism and intensity, church harm in other forms continued to occur through two more churches I attended following the last one of my youth. I won't detail the rest here for the sake of moving on to the reason why I'm writing this book, which is to offer the truth and life I've since discovered on the other side of these traumatic religious experiences, but I hope that this paints a picture of the damaging environments my spirituality and sense of self was informed and malformed in. I hope if you can relate in any way, that you feel less alone in your religious war stories.

It wasn't just that these experiences senselessly fixated on random and often unspoken rules aimed at controlling things that would supposedly please our parents, the church—and therefore, God—what was even more tragic was the utter *lack* of actual equipping with truth that should have been taking place. It was unsafe where there should have been safety. There was ignorance where there should have been education. There was widespread ignoring, shaming, or suppressing what begged to be acknowledged, accepted, and nurtured. It seemed a common theme across my experience that if I wasn't being oppressed by my religion, I was being taught through it, to suppress.

It wasn't until years later that I acquired the verbiage to name a destructive common denominator across my church and Christian circle experiences that I'd venture to guess you've experienced firsthand one way or another as well. The correct term for ignoring or suppressing circumstances or needs to the detriment of the afflicted, is spiritual bypassing.

Spiritual Bypassing

The first time I heard the term "spiritual bypassing," it resonated in my spirit as a missing puzzle piece to name many of the woefully-lived church experiences and "wisdom" dished out to me then. It seemed to make sense of moments where present pain was met with an ill-fitting admonition that, much like a backhanded compliment, managed to leave me feeling more confused and disheartened than I already was. Perhaps you've experienced being met with spiritual "advice" that discredited your actual need below the surface that spiritual bypassing can't dare to face.

For example, one might share that they're experiencing financial difficulty, and rather than being rallied around and supported with tangible financial support or solutions, the answer may have been something like to "just trust God," or "pray more," or "lay that burden down at His feet." Spiritual bypassing neglects to acknowledge real human needs that often need tending to in the natural, not just to trust God in the process spiritually. People have done it to us, and we have even done it to ourselves.

In the *Journal of Spirituality and Mental Health*, researchers Picatto, Neto, and Fox provide valuable insight into the background, displays, and outcomes of spiritual bypassing,[11] helping us better understand its use and serious detrimental effects. John Wellwood, who coined the term, noted that spiritual bypassing occurs when people attempt to use their spiritual practices to "suppress their personal needs and identity." He elaborated further, observing:

> Spiritual bypassers may read books on spirituality, engage in spiritual practices, visit spiritual teachers and gurus, go to spiritual retreats, be part of spiritual communities, but they do not care for and directly nurture their psychological needs, all the while believing that their spiritual work may deliver them one day from their psychological suffering.[12]

The primary symptoms of spiritual bypassing are described in the article as:

> ...repression and emotional alienation, exaggerated detachment, overemphasis on the positive, blind compassion or excessive tolerance, minimization or denial of the shadow side of one's personality, overconfidence about self-awakening, the notion that everything is an illusion including suffering, and disregarding the personal or mundane.[13]

---

11 Picciotto, Giovanna, Jesse Fox, and Félix Neto. "A Phenomenology of Spiritual Bypass: Causes, Consequences, and Implications." *Journal of Spirituality in Mental Health*, vol. 20, no. 4, 2017, pp. 333–354. https://doi.org/10.1080/19349637.2017.1417756.

12 Welwood, J. (2000). Toward a psychology of awakening: Buddhism, psychotherapy, and the path of personal and spiritual transformation. Boston, MA: Shambhala.

13 Masters, R. A. (2010). Spiritual bypassing: When spirituality disconnects us from what really matters. Berkeley, CA: North Atlantic Books.

The researchers also warn of the potential negative byproducts of engaging in or being the target of spiritual bypassing:

> …the need to excessively control others and oneself, shame, anxiety, dichotomous thinking, emotional confusion, exaggerated tolerance of inappropriate behavior, codependence, compulsive kindness, obsession or addiction, spiritual narcissism, blind allegiance to charismatic teachers, and disregard for personal responsibility.

I have sadly both experienced and witnessed these dysfunctional outcomes of spiritual bypassing.

It is sobering enough to take a moment of silence to process and grieve. It is unlikely many, if any of us, have escaped a brush or gouge with this toxic approach to "handling" very real issues in need of acknowledging, bearing witness to, and journeying through toward holistic healing. Before we go any further into this chapter, I want to thank you for staying with me through these weighty experiences I've shared, and I want to honor your negative religious experiences—be they suffocatingly toxic or paralyzingly traumatic. None of them were okay, and all of them testify to the fact that religion itself was never the goal or the plan. That was a man-made idea. Like in Galatians 2:21, if we were meant to obtain our own righteousness by doing enough "right" as dictated by spiritual leaders—then Christ died for nothing.

I now believe from deep in my bones, through the core of my heart, and soaring up through my spirit that a relationship with the Living God was always the goal. It is the only thing that will truly deliver the kind of vibrant, fruitful life that a man-made religion never can. Many of us were never introduced to that freestanding, sufficient idea. Rather, from what I experienced, my relationship with God seemed ever-tethered to the terrifying and confusing hellfire and brimstone sermons or supposedly well-meaning but nevertheless fear-mongering evangelism.

I want you to know that if you, too, have had or still have "trust issues" with church in general, a particular church personal to you, "church people" (or a person who has caused you harm, maybe even used out-of-context verses to justify their behavior)—your hesitation to trust is more than valid, it is wise. I hope that you hear God's heart for you behind my words: you are justified in feeling however it is you feel about it all. About what happened or what should've happened and didn't. It does not mean you lack faith, lack belief, have a hard heart, or are unforgiving (but spiritual bypassers love to over-spiritualize our emotions and miscalculate the origins of the negative ones as "lack of faith"). What it does mean is that your nervous system, which is wired to keep you safe, is working! Your heart, which is wired for what is right and true, is angered over what is wrong and false. That is also very, very good. And you aren't the only one who's angry about it. Because guess what else? If you've been harmed, ever—at all—but in this case, by the church?

God is livid about what happened to you. In Matthew 18:6 (TPT), Jesus expresses how much so with these strong words in our defense: "But if anyone abuses one of these little ones who believes in me, it would be better for him to have a heavy boulder tied around his neck and be hurled into the deepest sea than to face the punishment he deserves!"

Lies, exaggerations, suppression, and other manifestations of spiritual bypassing and religious abuse that distorted truth and withheld support that was actually needed? He's angry about it. What's worse is that these things were done under the confusing connotation that He was "all about" whatever it was. That He backed what these people were saying or doing that were detrimental to the well-being of your wholeness. He is on a mission to right the wrongs, bringing justice where there's been injustice, sifting the truth from the lies, straightening out what's been twisted, rebuilding what was demolished, and repaying more than what's been lost or stolen from you at the hands of misled and misleading churches and religious folk.

Jeremiah 6:14 (AMP) is a great example of spiritual bypassing happening in the Bible:

> "They have treated superficially the [bloody] broken wounds of My people, Saying 'Peace, peace,' when there is no peace."

If you read the surrounding verses for context, you see that God is angry about the way the leaders are falsely proclaiming peace where there is none while failing to appropriately address the wounds of His people. They are ignoring the truth and turning a blind eye to real needs. They were superficially slapping a bandage on still-gaping wounds, which actually required something more like surgery or, at a minimum, stitches (metaphorically speaking). That passage resonates deeply with what it seems the church has long done: superficially treated deep, bloody wounds with a pat on the back and a "keep a stiff upper lip."

It's time that we tend to them. It's time that we see them and name them so that we can treat wounds according to how they best heal, depending on the injury. When "thoughts and prayers" were handed out when instead what you needed was a real, flesh-and-blood hug intervention. When "just keep trusting the Lord" was incomplete, if not just bad advice, given in a misdiagnosed and minimized situation when you actually needed help physically removing yourself from. What you'd actually need in that situation might sound more like, "That's not right or okay, and God wants you to be whole. Keep trusting the Lord as you take steps away from this destructive situation and into a healthy and safe one. I'm here with you. You can count on me for tangible support. What would help you most right now?"

It is not enough to offer you a bit of scripture for your spirit, no matter how true the promises are, if I do not also offer you a drink of proverbial, practical water with which to quench the thirst of your weary body that's been spiritually bypassed more times than you can count. This is where the church at large lacks a bridge connecting us. Going from faith alone to walking in it in a life-changing way holistically changes our lives for the better: spirit, mind, and body.

Chapter 3

Embodied

"..where soul and spirit, bone and marrow meet."
Hebrews 4:12, TPT

Humanity & Spirituality

Emotional and mental well-being and awareness were not being taught in any circle I was a part of—religiously affiliated or otherwise. Hyperfixation on half of our make-up—our spirituality—was supposed to enable us to transcend earthly "woes" but seemed only to lead to despair, guilt, and striving. This is largely because what was being sold as relating to our spirituality was actually more strongly related to a legalistic religious institute—which, ironically, was actually spiritually dead. Thus, the prescriptions handed out by leaders and experts in this camp were, in effect, spiritual bypassing, just as we learned in the previous chapter—I just didn't have the words for it at the time.

Faulty or incomplete doctrine that focused heavily on spiritual realities led me to believe something akin to this devastating concept: that my body, being a temporary vessel born under the curse of sin in a broken world, was a lesser, if not ignored, aspect of my being. That it was normal to feel ashamed about and distrust my body. To make matters worse, the soul my body housed was surely born under a curse as well, giving weight to the verses I was proverbially smacked over the head with time and again about not "following my heart."

When "trusting God more," "praying with fervor," "confessing my 'sins,'" and "trying harder" didn't seem to fix my anxiousness or bring me more peace (if anything, the legalistic climate was the *source* of my anxiousness and the thief of my peace), it would send me on the defeating loop again, thinking I must just not have been a very "good" Christian or didn't "have enough faith."

On the other hand, from what I'd observed of the psychology and therapy world that focused on an ideology void of God and completely around science and our physicality, it seemed to create fragility, entrapment, and despair for some people. It was as though subconscious dependency on their humanity created a rather grim outlook for those completely wrapped up in and fixated on their past history, present repercussions, and current limitations. Only focusing on issues from a purely earth-bound perspective without also holding the other inescapable aspect of our being, the transcendent part of ourselves that holds space for additional possibility and promise—our spirituality—seemed to be a dead end as well.

It took me well into adulthood to sort through and wrestle into view why neither of these isolated approaches to healing and thriving worked apart from each other: *they were meant to go hand in hand.* To divide into two opposing belief systems attempts to segregate parts of our whole, isolating what is meant to be integrated and holistically embraced.

We can't sever our soul (which encompasses our mind, emotions, will, and other personality aspects) from our bodies (which, of course, refers to our physicality, including our nervous systems) and expect our spirits (the part of us that can transcend from this reality to another, filling and propelling our souls and bodies) to not experience unrest. Neither can we nourish just our minds and bodies and expect to have a robust spirit, either. Any combination that does not seek to know in a more honest way—and tends to in tandem with each other—leads to either the damaging ignorance of spiritual bypassing or stops short of the vastness of spiritual realities and keeps us stuck within the limits of our humanity, only—rather than opening the door to all that is accessible to us as spiritual beings.

In light of this truth, Scripture makes more and more sense—how "the Spirit gives life" (2 Corinthians 3:6, NLT) and "in him we live and move and have our being" (Acts 17:28, NIV). Of how awe of God and turning away from what is wrong will bring healing for your body and strength for your bones (Proverbs 3:7-8, NLT) or of how a cheerful heart (soul) is good medicine but a crushed spirit (spirit) dries up the bones (physical) (Proverbs 17:22, NIV). Suddenly, you see it everywhere!

We are integrated, multi-faceted beings, and there is so much scripture that supports it that I don't know how it was ever ignored. The way emotional pain can be strong enough to spur physical pain in our bodies (soul affects the body), emotional joy can cause health to our bodies. Spiritual aliveness causes health to our soul and thus bodies, and so on.

It's all connected. We are all connected. Because we are all made in God's image, and He Himself is "three in one."

A holistic view of self is finally being studied and taught now more than ever, which is so incredibly important if we're to partner with God in His mission of the "restoration of all things" (Acts 3:21 TPT), moving toward wholeness is His heart for you—for each of us. As my former spiritual director, K. J. Ramsey, told me once in a weighty session, "Instead of asking yourself what's right or wrong, ask yourself, 'What moves me closer to greater wholeness?' Because that is what God wants for you."

A recent article titled "Combating the Disease of Despair" by Jessica Athens of Trinity Church Wall Street notes:

"The loss of spirituality and religious practice has enormous implications for how the brain functions. The human brain is, in fact, 'hard-wired' for spirituality, which can then be nurtured through shared spiritual practice."[14]

I am so encouraged to finally see a shift in the tide that is on the brink of acknowledging and concurrently supporting human beings as spiritual beings, and our spirits, while they are at home with us in these blessed, earthly bodies. We've been entrusted with befriending, knowing intimately, nourishing, and maturing our whole selves—every aspect of our beings: body, soul, and spirit.

Imageio Dei (Image of God)

Perhaps the church hasn't been great at a holistic approach to living wholly because they haven't yet paused to connect the dots that point to why we are the way that we are.

And *the way that we are is made in God's image,* as Genesis 1:27 (TPT) so beautifully reminds us:

"So God created man and woman and shaped them with his image inside them. In his own beautiful image, he created his masterpiece."

Before we were these beautiful, complex, multifaceted beings, first there was God, who is a multi-person Being: a triune God,

---

14 Athens, Jessica. "Combatting the Diseases of Despair." *Trinity Church*, 22 May 2023, trinity-churchnyc.org/stories-news/combatting-diseases-despair.

made of up three persons completing one divine Being: God the Father, God the Son, and God the Holy Spirit.

The Trinity can be confusing, but one way I approach it—without getting lost in technicalities beyond full human comprehension—is by recognizing my own likeness in this multifaceted reflection of the One in whose image I am made. While we are not three people, there is a "triune"ness to personhood, in that we are made up of body, soul, and spirit respectively. Likening the parts of the "self" to His own has helped me to simplify and relate to a complicated concept such as the Trinity and better understand how I, too, am wholly one person while operating out of three complementary parts of self.

For example, Jesus would be the best reference for "body" because He had one! As Hebrews 2:14b puts it, "Jesus became human to fully identify with us" (TPT). For understanding our "soul," I think of God the Father because of the inner and invisible nature of that aspect from which we think, feel, will and act. 1 Timothy 1:17b references God as *immortal and invisible*—both attributes of our own souls, too. The Holy Spirit I liken unto our spirit since spirit can transcend realms or be in two places at once, such as Him being in Heaven but also with and in us, as it's His Spirit that animates and energizes, fuels, and fills up our own!

I also think a quick trip back to the original Greek Lexicon for these words, as defined in Strong's Concordance,[15] is a great way to clear up confusion about the many parts to our whole and how they dwell together.

Body: in Greek, the word "sōma" is defined, quite literally and generally, as a physical body: human or animal, stars or plants, or

---

15 Strong, James. Strong's Exhaustive Concordance of the Bible. Blue Letter Bible, 2024, www.blueletterbible.org. Accessed 15 Oct. 2024. Multiple words reviewed - please see individual entries.

a collective such as body of water or a body made up of other parts (such as the church being referred to as a "church body").

Soul: the Greek word "psuché," translated most often into "soul," is also translated many times to the word "life" and a few times to "mind" and "heart." Its two definitions include "breath," detailed as "breath of life, the vital force which animates the body, that in which there is life, a living being, a living soul," and "the soul," which is described as "the seat of the feelings, desires, affections, aversions (our heart, soul etc.)" and "the soul as an essence which differs from the body and is not dissolved by death."

Heart: I think it's important to include this one to show how it is used interchangeably in Scripture to reference the "soul" as well, as the Greek word "kardía" is translated to "heart," and among its definitions are: "the center and seat of spiritual life," "the soul or mind, as it is the fountain and seat of the thoughts, passions, desires, appetites, affections, purposes, endeavors" and "of the soul as the seat of the sensibilities, affections, emotions, desires, appetites, passions" and "middle or central or inmost part."

Spirit: "pneûma" has a long list of definitions, including the Spirit of God Himself, and even references "the soul" at one point (which is where I'm sure some of the confusion comes in with the spirit and soul often being used interchangeably), but they are distinctly different parts of us as Hebrews 4:12 attests, the soul and spirit can be divided by God's word.

But as it pertains to our spirits, I think these parts say it best: "the vital principle by which the body is animated... the rational spirit, the power by which the human being feels, thinks, decides... the disposition or influence which fills and governs the soul of anyone... the efficient source of any power, affection, emotion, desire, etc." The key difference between our spirits stands out to me as our spirits are the source of power behind what drives our soul.

In short, our earthly bodies (which will be made new one day, too, into heavenly bodies, according to Philippians 3:21 and 2 Corinthians 5:8) temporarily house our souls (the core of our being, the heart from which we live, think, feel, and choose) and spirits (the "breath" that powers or directs our souls and, therefore, bodies). They are all intertwined and constantly engaged with one another. Proverbs 17:22 (NIV) accurately illustrates how interdependent these parts of us are, saying, "...a crushed spirit dries up the bones." When one part of us suffers, our whole being suffers.

Body (+ Nervous System)

I'm not sure where we got the idea that our bodies and their needs were irrelevant to us now as "new creations in Christ," but as we've been exploring in this chapter, clearly, that is not what He intended. On the contrary, the verse "...your body is now the sacred temple of the Spirit of Holiness..." (1 Corinthians 6:19, TPT) is a strong testament to the sacredness of our bodies.

This body-denying theology sure didn't come from God, though, as many wrongly credit it to the Bible. Ephesians 5:28-29 clearly points out how ludicrous it should be, the idea of anyone ever hating their own body. It might as well read, "Duh, obviously one should nourish and cherish their body because that's exactly how Christ cares for His 'body' (the church)." This should be enough for us to realize that healthy "body positivity" was originally a biblical concept.

But perhaps the misguided notions were further spread under the assumption that since our bodies are indeed temporal, whereas our souls and spirits are eternal, our bodies are somehow "less than" or not equal to our invisible, eternal aspects. However, I'd like to blast that notion right back to the loony toon realm from whence it came, as we don't have to look far to see how much care and attention to detail goes in to even the most temporary of God's creations. Like the "well-dressed fields of flowers" that wither the next day, why even bother to create such beauty if it's not lasting, one might ask?

Because our God delights in and finds joy and glory in such details of His creations, and as that reference indicates by comparison to the flowers of the field in Matthew 6:28-31, how much more will our heavenly Father tend to our physical needs, such as the detail of what we eat, drink, and wear, as the passage continues. He uses that passage to put into perspective how we should not be consumed with worry about these temporal realities but also to assure us that God sees and knows and intends to amply provide for them. *Not* to disregard them.

So then, if our bodies and their physical needs are of such importance to God, then the way many have insisted on modeling or encouraging us into suppressing, denying, neglecting, and bypassing the needs of our bodies is unequivocally tragic.

These "perfectly, wonderfully made" bodies are the visible, tangible part of our whole being; they are beautiful vessels made in His likeness that bear us up and carry us through this life. These resilient, glorious, and good creations that *are* us are as precious, worthy, and essential to tend to as our souls and spirits.

If someone is cold, hungry, tired, or being chased by a bear, a word of encouragement or attending Bible study with you is obviously not what they need—not right now. The way God honors and responds to our physical needs is what should be modeled in His church (which we explore further when discussing the original church model in Chapter 10).

One of my favorite stories that demonstrates this beautiful truth so inspiringly is the story of the prophet Elijah during a most intense survival season when Queen Jezebel was out for his life. After running far away in search of safety, he came to the end of his rope, collapsing in the shade of a solitary tree, crying out to God in sheer exhaustion and defeat to just take his life before falling fast asleep. I love what happens next:

"Suddenly an angel shook him awake and said, 'Get up and eat!'

He looked around and, to his surprise, right by his head were a loaf of bread baked on some coals and a jug of water. He ate the meal and went back to sleep.

The angel of God came back, shook him awake again, and said, 'Get up and eat some more—you've got a long journey ahead of you.'

He got up, ate and drank his fill, and set out. Nourished by that meal, he walked forty days and nights..."

1 Kings 19:4-9a, MSG

The above story is one of my favorite stories that shoots holes in the often religious notion that our bodies are somehow "less than" other aspects of our being. As we can see from the fascinating retelling above, God's response to Elijah's evident emotional, mental, and physical distress was not to tell Elijah to buck up, pray more, fast, or that he should "just" trust the Lord more—which are all fantastic examples of common spiritual bypassing language. Nor did God send Elijah a worship song on Spotify to "lift his spirits"— while that is a lovely form of encouragement, it is supplemental to but never in place of immediate physical needs being met. Nor did God reprimand him with a convicting sermon to help motivate his spirit. God responds appropriately with practical compassion, tangible provision, and restoration for this scared and exhausted man's good body.

His response was to provide cool, shaded shelter for him to rest under.

It was to let the man have a nap.

It was to give him freshly baked bread and water for fortification and hydration.

But he didn't stop there. He lets weary Elijah take *another* nap. Then, the angel of God wakes him to eat and drink even *more* to get him ready for the next part of his journey.

Not only that, He sent His own embodied presence to deliver this sustenance. Many Christians believe that when "the angel of the God" is mentioned in Old Testament scripture, it was Jesus' way of engaging with humans before his incarnation in the New Testament. How amazing is that to think about? That all of the thousands of years before Jesus came to earth, he was already here interacting with us. Immanuel, "God with us," engaging us, meeting actual, practical, and physical needs.

Notice there is no cursing or condemning, critique, or body-shaming when it comes to Elijah's very real needs to find safe shelter, sleep, eat, and drink. He is not reprimanded for needing a break, not even shamed for wanting to give up on life itself in his moment of exasperation and desperation. On the contrary, *his needs are validated by the very presence of the Angel of the Lord, who hand-delivered the needed physical provisions to support and sustain his cherished life.*

God did not drive him to keep going past his limits, ignoring his very real, very normal human needs as we so often do to ourselves and to each other. In all of God's limitlessness, He designed humans to come with limits. Boundaries and needs were His ideas, so of course, He honors them. It's us who seem to struggle to follow suit.

I love how Whitney Hopler adds the cherry on top to what we can learn from this Elijah illustration of how our physical needs are intertwined with our emotional and spiritual well-being:

> Just like a parent taking care of a beloved child, the Angel of the Lord makes sure that Elijah has everything he needs. The angel follows up a second time when Elijah doesn't eat or drink enough the first time. As any good parent would point out to his or her children, it's important to address hunger and thirst, because those needs should be fulfilled in order to be strong enough to handle stress. When Elijah's physical needs are met, God knows Elijah will also be more at peace emotionally, and better able to trust Him spiritually.[16]

Looking beyond the demonstration in the story of Elijah of God-honoring His word, which promises to meet all of our needs, we can look to His provision of manna and quail in the wilderness, making water flow from a rock in the desert, providing oil and flour for the widow in need, or through Jesus's first miracle: turning water into wine for the wedding guests. I love how that example displays His delight to meet physical needs not even for the sole purpose of our survival, but in cases like that, for our "thrival" as well! It was an instance where it was purely for the joy of the guests and to preserve the dignity of the hosts, who would have faced public humiliation for running out of wine. From feeding the hungry crowds of followers during His ministry to causing His friends to catch loads of fish they needed for their livelihoods/businesses, the list goes on and on. His deep care for our bodies is the bar for which we should aim.

But what about the invisible things happening inside our body that are directly linked to the sensory intake coming into our bod-

---

16 Hopler, Whitney. "The Angel of the Lord Wakes Up Elijah." Learn Religions, Sep. 10, 2021, learnreligions.com/angel-of-lord-wakes-up-elijah-4031784.

ies through our reflexes and emotions? What about the automatic responses that happen as fast as a synapse transmission? How does this invisible but foundational system come into play with the whole of our beings? I still find it wild that I've yet to hear mention of this foundational part of our physiological make-up—the nervous system—mentioned in a church before. Besides an elementary overview in science textbooks, there'd been virtually no mention or awareness of the nervous system until the last few years. Thank God for continuing education by whatever means we encounter it.

I first heard of researcher Stephen Porges's Polyvagal Theory in one of my spiritual direction sessions with K.J. Ramsey. She gave me words and imagery from this theory that helped me better understand and visualize what was taking place in my own body, soul, and spirit simultaneously on the many occasions I'd been exposed to emotionally unsafe environments that caused my nervous system to become dysregulated. It was groundbreaking to me. To be set free from the cycle of beating myself up for responding in one of the survival modes such as "fight," "flight," "fawn," or "freeze" allowed me to see myself through a compassionate lens rather than a critical one. I'd previously kicked myself for not responding "better" or doing "more" under extremely stressful and some traumatic circumstances across my life. Like a deer trapped between oncoming traffic and a tall fence, nobody is criticizing the poor deer for doing her best to navigate an unsafe situation without a clear way out or through and without support. And the deer is just glad her instincts kicked in and helped her get to safety, even if it wasn't graceful, or there was a shortcut she missed, etc.

In the incredibly enlightening yet sobering (and potentially triggering) read, *The Body Keeps Score*, the author describes some of what's so deeply important from Porges' insights through this theory:

The Polyvagal Theory provided us with a more sophisticated understanding of the biology of safety and danger, one based on the subtle interplay between the visceral experience of our own bodies and the voices and faces of the people around us. It explained why a kind face or a soothing tone of voice can dramatically alter the way we feel. It clarified why knowing that we are seen and heard by the important people in our lives can make us feel calm and safe, and why being ignored or dismissed can precipitate rage reactions or mental collapse.17

Similar to the Trinity design of three parts making up one, our nervous systems are made up of three main "branches" that Polyvagal Theory illustrates as three different tiers on the Autonomic "Ladder":

- **Ventral Vagal Complex** at the top (regulated/connected/ where we want to be most of the time/where we are most connected to ourselves, others, and God)

- **Sympathetic Nervous System** (where we slide down the ladder next after reaching out for social support from alarming sensory input—from a loud noise to a subtle negative shift in someone's body language—and not receiving a response, activating our "fight or flight" modes)

- **Dorsal Vagal** (the lowest rung of the ladder we slide to if our attempts at fight or flight fall flat and we perceive being trapped, which leads to a hopelessness/helplessness which leads to shut down/mental collapse/dissociative responses as a last resort/attempt to keep oneself safe in the face of inescapable threats/danger, perceived or real)

---

17 Van der Kolk, Bessel A. *The Body Keeps the Score: Mind, Brain and Body in the Transformation of Trauma*. Penguin, 2020.

While other resources can delve deeper into these complex functions of our bodies which are crucial for self-awareness and understanding others intimately, it's essential to acknowledge that our spiritual well-being cannot be separated from our physical. Neglecting our bodies and nervous systems leaves us struggling with dysregulating narratives and presents a very real hindrance to our emotional and spiritual capacities, such as being unable to rebuild trust or overcome worry.

We can tell ourselves a lot of other truths but without engaging the truth of our bodies in real, practical ways to start experiencing that truth as our new reality, we end up with a lot of hopeful but weary travelers, desperate to know why—despite their deep belief in God's goodness and truth—they find themselves constantly on a loop, a cycle of old, struggling with something that they cannot seem to wrap their minds around on how to get themselves to "just calm down," "just be happy," "just rest," or "just trust" when that is no better than telling the terrified deer in the headlights to "just move" or "just calmly hop over the fence."

We don't know how to get there, and we don't know how because we don't understand how our whole being is designed—with systems integrated and aspects from body to soul to spiritual aspects intertwined. "Faith without works is dead" is the verse often taught in the context of backing up your words with actions, usually in the context of ministry. To actually go out and *feed the poor* rather than just pray for them. They are hungry. Help meet a physical, practical need to back up why this faith that we speak of is so very real and true, producing the fruit of an abundant life.

But what if the "poor and needy" are also the parts of *you* that need an actual hug, a hot meal, a nap, or a therapist to help navigate? We can learn how to listen to our bodies and help meet their very valid needs. We can learn how to recognize need in others and offer comfort, support, love, and encouragement in tangible, physical forms to help nurture each other's good bodies.

It's time for the church at large to start educating themselves, as well as educating those they have been entrusted to guide and encourage, with the truth of this integral, foundational operating system from which our entire body subconsciously operates. If we could nurture the whole being, starting with essential bodily needs—which include an understanding of how our nervous systems are trained, dysregulated, and how to get back to a state of regulation—we'd be treating on the deepest level, "the wounds of His people."

It's not that we can't get there and heal by the power of the Holy Spirit alone—it's that it would be lazy to assume He would give us bodies to tend with care like a garden and then have us abdicate that amazing responsibility and refuse to partner with Him in this endeavor.

We wouldn't witness a person suffering from bipolar disorder and say that their erratic behavior while manic was a moral issue. Likewise, there are a myriad of systems happening subconsciously without our body, from hormone balance to neurons firing (or not) to nervous system dysregulation, often as a side effect of trauma. In my past experiences, some would sadly deem mental or physical illnesses as "sin issues" when they have nothing to do with morality but rather biology in an imperfect world.

I believe we're just beginning to scratch the surface in the research world about their inseparability as it pertains to the well-being of our whole beings, but I'm excited about the breakthroughs made so far. I hope that the church will start humbling and educating themselves and start their own conversations about the fact that our bodies have a brilliantly intricate nervous system running throughout our core, connecting from our organs to our brains, perfectly designed by our loving Creator like an information intake, alarm system, and emergency response team to help keep us safe.

Many of us (and I'd venture to guess, most of us) have dys-regulated nervous systems, if not traumatized ones that we were never taught how to re-regulate, self-soothe, co-regulate, and other things that we *can* learn to help restore deeper wholeness from the inside out. Even if we've lacked the knowledge and support until now, there's no time like the present to start equipping ourselves and each other with truth that needs to be circulated until greater degrees of freedom are felt from head to toe.

Soul (Mind, Will, Emotions)

When differentiating the body from soul and soul from spirit, I found this description of the soul most helpful:

> With our soul, we can substantiate things in the psycho-logical realm. In fact, in Greek, the word translated as *soul* is *psuche,* which is the root of the word *psychology,* the study of the soul.

> In the Bible, we can see that our soul is composed of three parts: our mind, our emotion, and our will... Our soul has the ability to know, understand, love, hate, choose, and refuse, allowing us to substantiate the psychological realm. Our soul is our very person, and it expresses our personality.[18]

As we saw in our brief history in Greek above, "heart" is an-other word commonly used in Scripture to reference our soul—the center of our being, the place from which we think, feel, process, and choose, which all involve our wildly amazing minds.

---

18 "What Is the Difference between the Soul and the Spirit?" Bibles for America, 9 May 2023, https://blog.biblesforamerica.org/difference-between-soul-and-spirit/.

As the brain is to the physical body, the mind is to the intangible soul. It's the stage our thoughts dance across and the sanctuary in which the Holy Spirit's "still small voice" often speaks to us through thought, imagination, and even dreams. Our minds are vital "portals" through which we see and perceive our inner and outer worlds, and as such where mental health plays a crucial role in our wholeness.

We are entrusted with a mind to steward, meaning we must protect, sharpen, and fuel it with what is beneficial. This understanding illuminates Proverbs 4:23, "Guard your heart with all diligence, for out of it is the wellspring of life" (NHEB). This verse emphasizes the importance of tending to and safeguarding our minds, as the quality of our lives flows from what occurs in them. While the mind is where our emotions are cognitively acknowledged and processed (though as we learn to pay attention to our bodies, we'll often find that our bodies process emotions through physical sensations), it is also where we learned along the way to criticize, deny, and suppress them—habits we likely learned under survival mode situations, that we can now recognize as counterproductive and no longer serving us, as we aim toward greater wholeness.

Wants, needs, and feelings are essential, God-given gifts meant to enrich our lives! They are a vital part of our wholeness that, by no means, have to dominate us. When these aspects rule over us rather than support us, they become obstacles to our well-being. But when they inform, support, guide, and add depth of meaning through *feeling* our lives, that is how they were so beautifully designed to be a part of us.

Lest you've been told otherwise, even if you're the one who's told yourself a false narrative, here's the truth: your emotions are part of the perfectly and wonderfully made whole of you. When you experience pleasant emotions as a byproduct of goodness such as love, joy, and peace—they are gifts! They're meant to be savored, shared, and enjoyed thankfully. When you experience difficult emotions as a byproduct of suffering, pain, or discomfort—they are still gifts that testify to our wholeness and, therefore, our *goodness.* Like signs, our more difficult or unpleasant emotions point to something that needs tending to. And you, m'dears, are worth tending to.

Ignoring and denying our emotions is not tough or holy—rather, it is denying truth which sets you free. *"Well, how you 'feel' about something isn't always what's true about a situation."* I've heard THAT argument a few too many times in support of denying or holding in feelings in question. But that argument misses the point, which is that rather than holding your feelings in question, you simply hold your feelings first.

Feel them. Sit in them. Attune to them. Listen to them. The truth is that you are experiencing them, so acknowledging them is a beautiful demonstration of the verse about truth that sets you free (John 8:32). Does it mean every emotion gives you true information about the situation? No. But is the emotion real? Yes. So you hold it with tenderness: listen to it, process it. Maybe pray about it. Safely express it. Like getting to know someone, you ask yourself questions about it to help identify it (name), learn about where it's coming from (origin or event), and what brought it on (trigger). Like clues helping you inch closer to cracking a case, you keep following it. With curiosity and kindness, you befriend it.

Honor your emotions. Follow them home to the depths of your vast inner world. Trust the God who made you goes before and behind you. He is there with you and for you. If you can, take a trusted friend with you on the exploratory journey inward. No shame. No judgement. You are not weak for exploring the roots they lead you to. You are, in truth, brave—fierce beyond measure for facing and learning to constructively steward the uncomfortable and often un-charted truth you may discover there.

Our will can be thought of as the decision-making, action-tak-ing, directional "rudder" aspect of our person. It is where the "rub-ber" of our thoughts meets the "road" of the path we're on, where our thoughts and emotions are no longer in the vetting process but have been allowed to proceed and become desire. It is when we can follow through to support our good desires, and hopefully, our will leads us toward aligned action.

It doesn't mean our "will" will always come about since we don't always have a choice in things and definitely don't have con-trol over lots of things. But it does mean that we have aligned with an intent. By focusing our attention in a particular camp, we are throwing our hat in the ring, choosing a side, and standing for or against a thing. It helps align our prayers toward the thing for which we are choosing faith in the face of not actually having a choice to bring something about or prevent something ourselves. We pray that our wills would be aligned with God's and trust Him to bring it about in His way and time.

You can see how the focus of our thoughts in our minds and the emotions we experience can be incredibly powerful in inform-ing what we ultimately will. Which makes it even more crucial that our wills be in alignment with God's so that we are partnering with Him. We can't always know His specific will in any given situation, but we can know a lot about His will when we know His heart (thus, His soul/core), which is why walking closely with Him is not only vital but so very special. To become intimately familiar with what is on His heart and mind? To know and want in your heart and mind what you've come to know God wants, too? How incredible is that?!

When we're seeking Him with a genuine heart modeled after Jesus's own, the prayer of our life being that of the Lord's own, "not My will, but Yours be done, on earth as it is in heaven"—that is what it means to "surrender" or yield to God's will. We might not always have all of the details about it, but that is where our trust in His goodness and faith leaps to follow where He leads. If our will truly is that His will would be done, then we can't go wrong. He promises to provide wisdom when we ask for it in faith. He promises that His plans for us are good, to prosper us and not lead us into harm. We know that "He doesn't desire that any should perish," so we can know His will is for life, for everyone. We can know that He desires mercy, not sacrifice (Hosea 6:6), and align our wills to desire such as well. As you dive deeply into His Word and draw closer in relationship with Him, you truly do start to experience the manifestation of the passage, "We have the mind of Christ" (1 Corinthians 2:16). You start wanting what He wants, thinking like He'd think. Being moved in love or compassion or grief over the same things as God the Father was what moved Jesus to tears many times during His life here. The sweet harmony that comes with being attuned to His heart and will is one of the most incredible forms of feeling close to God I've ever experienced.

Spirit

Now that we have a general foundation for understanding how our spirits—while not our souls, but directly connected to them as the propellers as the source or the wind that powers them—let's look a little closer at this transcendent aspect of our being. I loved this description from the Bibles for America that focuses on the communicatory function of our spirits with the Holy Spirit:

> Our spirit enables us to substantiate the spiritual realm. In particular, **it enables us to receive and contact God Himself**... God being Spirit means His substance is Spirit, and our spirit corresponds to God. Just as we have to use our

ears as the proper organ to substantiate, or experience, sound, we must use our spirit to contact, fellowship with, and worship God.[19]

While it can be tricky to articulate in words things so other-worldly as one's spirit, a simple way to think of this aspect of your being is the only part of us that is not bound by earth, space, and time. Like the verse in Ephesians that says (in past tense, not future) that believers are, in effect, already seated with Jesus at the right hand of God in the heavenly realm? That is true. And it is also true that our spirits are embodied here on earth. Presently. Because our spirits are a part of His Spirit and as such, eternally connected to Him.

When Jesus said that He had to go back to heaven to be with the Father so that something better would come? He was talking about His Holy Spirit. Life with the Holy Spirit is supposed to be even *better* than life with Jesus walking alongside us here on earth in the flesh because His Spirit transcends time, space, and realms. It is ever-present and indwelling us always. The Holy Spirit was sent as a "helper," a "counselor," and "companion" (John 14:16). Ephesians 1:13 (ESV) says that we are "sealed with the Holy Spirit." He's within and surrounding us. An ever-present Friend, Protector, Provider, Power, and Guide.

Like the verse above says, the Holy Spirit will move in "impulses," and you'll often feel these like promptings or nudges or a "wink" of sorts in your spirit. I'd describe "hearing" the Holy Spirit as something deeply resonating with me. It might be a verse I read that hits me so specifically in that moment. It might be the sunlight suddenly landing on my hand, like a gentle kiss. It might be something someone says that sounds like an echo confirming something

---

19 "What Is the Difference between the Soul and the Spirit?" Bibles for America, 9 May 2023, https://blog.biblesforamerica.org/difference-between-soul-and-spirit/.

He's been trying to tell me. All I know to say is when it's Him, you'll begin to recognize it, and eventually, you'll just know in a very personal way. Don't discount or write it off. Engage. Lean in. Ask more questions. Watch Him blow you away with more specific, creative replies!

Engaging with the Holy Spirit, allowing Him to speak to your spirit, is how you'll begin to recognize and operate on a new wavelength, in new heights beyond what you've known before. Everyday things may move your spirit, activating your mind and emotions in a new way because a similar sensation or emotion resonates with something you've experienced in the natural realm. Things will manifest in a supernatural way that your spirit will recognize, and it seems to be a learned practice (or unlearning what we were taught, at times) to allow our spirits to truly animate our souls and bodies, allowing us to fully experience the richness God intended for our whole beings to walk in, and to truly have all lines of communication open with Him.

As Romans 8:14 says, "The mature children of God are those who are moved by the impulses of the Holy Spirit" (TPT). When we embrace our whole, integrated selves, we are able to recognize the way in which we were designed to be able to connect with God through our spirits, which will often translate as meaning or resonance in our souls or even a sensation in our bodies. When we believe that is our good and God-given design and understand how the parts of our whole work together, we can learn to *allow* ourselves to be "moved" by His spirit and engage with Him in new ways we might have never known we could encounter Him before. Or, to open the door to new possibilities, invite *Him* to encounter *us*!

Part 2:
ENCOUNTERED
Who and how God really is

Chapter 4

His Proximity To Us

"So we could seek after God, and not just grope around in the dark but actually find him. He doesn't play hide-and-seek with us. He's not remote; he's near."

Acts 17:27, MSG

"I am with you now, even close to you..."

Isaiah 43:5a, TPT

Near

The first time I can recall profoundly experiencing the nearness of God was when I was about 9 or 10 years old. Up until that moment, the verse-verbiage I'd been raised on, such as "God is always with us," "He never leaves or forsakes us," "When we call, He answers," and "when we draw near, He draws near to us, too" were things I read, professed, and believed by choice in my head—but I can't say I'd known what the manifestation of them felt like in my heart.

Despite the very clear verses testifying to the opposite, I retained such an impression of a far-away, "high and mighty" God up on a throne somewhere in the sky, in an unreachable realm, who kept tabs on me, sure, but whose nearness would fluctuate like an orbiting planet. Sometimes you can see it, sometimes you can't. It depends on a lot, such as the weather, the time of night, the rotation of the earth, you know? Perhaps you have to have just the right combination of factors to be able to really *experience* it.

At this moment in my life, our growing family of seven (including five/eventually eight kids) was temporarily living next to the construction site of our eventually-to-be home. We were in a single-wide, two-bedroom mobile home. My dad, having a degree in construction management (before becoming a conference planner for the ministry we joined, which is what moved us to Arkansas when I was an infant) and being an all-around brilliant handyman, had taken on the project of building our family's home on five hidden-gem acres that we would come to lovingly call Jonesland. It's a place that has held so many memories and adventures for our family and friends—a land worthy of its own book someday.

The mobile home that held us those transitional years was a humble little abode, with her modest mauve/borderline blush corrugated metal siding. It was the most affordable pre-owned home on wheels my family had been able to spring for when moving out to the land when I was seven. My parents had taken the secondary bedroom as theirs, creating a bunk room for us kids out of the primary, with two twin bunk beds and one hand-built toddler-sized bunk bed. What was more impressive was that I'd taken up piano lessons, and the only place for my electric keyboard was also in this small bunk room. Oh yes, and a single tall dresser all of the girls shared. The boys' clothes were stored primarily in the bedside table chest which was, of course, in the bathroom. It was an impressive space planning feat before I even had my design education to truly appreciate it.

There's so much about my unconventional childhood and growing up there that I loved. Being homeschooled provided time freedom, which allowed me the incentive to complete my subjects in half a day so that I could fish in the pond or ride my horses (yes, through her hard-earned babysitting money and sisters chipping in from their savings, this horse-girl's dream finally came true around age 12) with the other half of the day. Though I've spent the better part of my adult life identifying and dismantling the toxic ideologies I was raised with throughout my youth, I am grateful to have more "goodness and mercy" from my childhood to hold on to as I've learned to process and grieve the harmful theology that never should have been a part of it.

I've approached this with a posture of grief and lament over the injustices we all suffered at the hands of religious abuse rather than blame or anger toward my parents, as they were the initial victims of the deceit that swept us all in with its wholesome, harmless-looking, "biblically based" family values. Like the story of the frog who didn't know he was in a boiling pot of water because he had acclimated to the temperature as it slowly warmed up, my big-hearted parents were unaware of the harm in which we were swimming for many years, and as such, so were us kiddos.

I had been raised to that point to believe and trust in God, sure. To be a religious "good girl" and check the "quiet time" box off of my list for the day, which was the phrase used for any time of Bible study and prayer. Nobody was talking about how to actually *know* Him. And the only thing I'd heard in regards to experiencing him was to be wary of the Pentecostals who relied too much on their "experiences" with Him. Oh, and also to be afraid of experiencing God's anger and wrath. It never occurred to me until writing this sentence—the ironic hypocrisy behind distrusting actual *good* experiences of God but wholeheartedly embracing theoretical *bad* experiences of Him.

I don't think the legalists actually knew or had experienced His nearness in life-changing, visceral ways. I think if they did, they were too afraid to believe what they couldn't fully explain. I think we all miss out on a lot when we don't operate in a capacity of child-like faith and wonder. It makes sense to me now why Jesus empha-sized childlike faith. Fear can really be a faith-blocker.

But on this particular night of my story, faith won out with a sweet little victory over fear in a moment that allowed me to expe-rience God's felt nearness in a way that changed my understanding of His proximity to me.

On a usual night of sleeping atop bunk #2 in our dormito-ry-style room, I had woken in the night absolutely terrified from a nightmare. I cannot even remember what it was about, only the feeling of absolute petrification from fear. Like a dutiful big sister, I didn't want to risk waking my surrounding siblings by audibly re-leasing a wail or climbing down the squeaky metal ladder to get up and go find my parents. So I laid there in bed beneath the covers, feeling very afraid, upset, and unable to calm down or go back to sleep. I thought of God, and I thought of praying, which made me think of my Bible, which would, of course, involve descending the squeaky ladder. Too risky, I thought. The only resource I had close by was a book that I'd tucked near me before I'd fallen asleep. In keeping with my rather "old fashioned" lifestyle in which I may as well have been Laura Ingalls Wilder (*Little House on the Prairie* was one of the few TV series we were allowed to watch), I was deep into the pioneer prairie-day life of the fictional "Sadie Rose" series.[20] Suddenly, I remembered there was a Bible verse somewhere in a chapter I'd recently read in there. That would make do for some comfort, I thought. I shone my book light carefully on the pages in the corner of the dark room full of sleeping siblings and scoured the pages back to where I'd seen this bit of scripture. Lo and behold, I found it. It read:

---

20 Stahl, Hilda. *The Sadie Rose Series*. Crossway Books, 1992–1995.

"So do not fear, for I am with you.
do not be dismayed, for I am your God.
I will strengthen you, and help you;
I will uphold you with my righteous right hand."

Isaiah 41:10

I couldn't even tell you what the verse was in reference to in the story, but it was something that Sadie Rose had clung to in a desperate moment, and by golly, if it was good enough for her, it was good enough for me. She was, after all, my fictional prairie girl hero (next to Laura Ingalls Wilder, who was my real-life prairie girl hero).

I read it again, slower this time. Like a deep inhale, the words seemed to calm my heart rate. I reread them, saying them to myself in my head like a mantra. I felt something beyond calm. I felt a *presence*. It felt like God was *near*. Like He was somehow in those words, saying them over me, speaking them for *me*. I remember smiling and tearing up. In that moment, my knowing broke out beyond the bounds of my head and into my body, through my spirit, and my whole being knew that I wasn't alone. God was *with* me. And for the first time, I *felt* it.

I hugged my book with those alive words close to my chest, letting the comfort of the closeness of God and those promises wrap around me like a warm blanket, and fell back asleep shortly after. But that moment branded me for the rest of my life, as the moment that I first remember Scripture being the conduit for communication between heaven and earth—between God's heart and mine. It was a means through which God became real, present, and near to me in a felt sense. I felt like He was giving me that verse to hold on to, and thus, to this day, I've clung to that very passage as my "life verse."

Seeking After, Feeling Toward

It would be many years after that encounter with the very near presence of God that night that He led me to my life verse—many years of continued fear-based patterns of an on-again, off-again, close-to-and-far-away feeling from God—before I had enough miraculous encounters with Him to let the too-good-to-be-true-seeming truth that He is in fact, *always* near to me, become my everyday reality. But I look back at those years and see clearer than ever now that He was in constant pursuit of my heart and revealing Himself to me in small ways daily. Sometimes, I would recognize with wonder what was happening, while other times, I dismissed it out of habit—trained to distrust myself and my feelings, and, as a result, disconnect from what I now realize was God trying to interact with me.

But on days that I could get out of my religious, good-girl head full of fears and tune in to the whole of me, that's when I'd have these beautiful God-encounter moments when I'd feel Him especially close.

There were times in my teen years when I would slip out the door of our then-moved-into, hand-built-home in the dusk and even dark hours. Something about the night air seemed to "call" to me. I'd wander down to the horse corral and delight over my two sorrel beauties—both dreams come true for this horse-crazy teenage girl who hoped, prayed, and saved all her babysitting pennies to realize the dream now made real in the form of Surprise, a young, green broke gelding shared with my sisters, and Ruby Lee, my very own 13-year-old feisty mare, and ticket to escape it all when I needed to.

I'd braid their manes, sit on them bareback, or climb up on the edge of the corral fence. I'd savor the wind sweeping over me, dancing through my hair. I'd gaze up at the moon and the stars.

I'd walk along the edge of the pond, climb up in a tree, look up at the vast night sky, and talk to God about things quite casually and comfortably. Sometimes I'd even sing. I didn't know exactly how or where it bubbled up from at the time. I just chalked it up to me being a "free spirit" and creative at heart, that nature pulled me in, lifted my spirits, and made it easier to feel connected to my Creator. I didn't know at the time that that is exactly how He designed it. I hadn't yet found the following passage that explains this nature-as-demonstration-of-the-Divine so very well:

> "For the truth about God is known to them instinctively; God has put this knowledge in their hearts. Since earliest times men have seen the earth and sky and all God made, and have known of his existence and great eternal power."
>
> Romans 1:19-20a, TLB

I now know that that was the Holy Spirit, speaking to and meeting me in my spirit, beckoning me to come outside and spend time with Him; not out of duty, out of delight. He's pursuant and persistent like that. If we pay attention, we will notice that there's a draw or pull, a force like gravity, a deep longing that eventually moves us to action and interaction with the Divine.

That's Him. The seeking after, the feeling toward? It's not all on us—it's not one-sided.

He seeks after, feels toward, and longs to be near us, too. He longs to be near us even more deeply than we have the capacity to long to be near Him because what good we experience here on earth is the ripple effect and mirror of His perfect likeness. Like a parent missing their child and calling it "separation anxiety," this deep desire to be near the object of our affection is a mirror of how deeply He longs to be near us, as so beautifully illustrated in God's decree in the below passage:

"Oh! Ephraim is my dear, dear son,
my child in whom I take pleasure!
Every time I mention his name,
my heart bursts with longing for him!
Everything in me cries out for him.
Softly and tenderly I wait for him."

Jeremiah 31:20, MSG

In response to being sought after and felt toward by Him—even when we're not yet aware of that in our spirits—our seeking after and feeling toward that Acts 17:27 (NLT) speaks of, "His purpose was for the nations to seek after God and perhaps feel their way toward him and find him—though he is not far from any one of us"—is a natural *response* to His seeking us. Like a game of Marco Polo, He initiates, we engage.

Since the emotion-suppressing, leery-of-charismatics (and, I believe, deeply insecure and fearful) fundamentalists led me to believe what was contrary to the Acts 17 verse, I sadly didn't know at the time that I *should* seek "feeling" close to God, rather than just knowing and believing things. I now know that this flawed way of thinking squashed the catalyst that allows us to have a felt sense of God's presence here with us beyond the knowing and believing, thus tragically causing many to miss the richness and delight of feeling seen, known, and loved by God in a personally *experienced* way.

God designed the whole of us, and as we explored in Chapter 3 about the emotional spectrum being a part of His good and creative design, I believe they function at their best when in this divine capacity for communicating with our Creator.

Our feelings are tools of communication His spirit moves through, and our imaginations the instrument on which He plays, the page on which He writes, or the canvas on which He paints. We *are* His sanctuary. Our whole being is where we engage with Him.

I've felt His presence enough times now to know that it is the sweetest, richest, most awe-inspiring experience and that this is the kind of constant communion we were designed to have with Him. It's a symphony so inspiring you don't want to be deaf to, a painting so deeply moving you don't want to be blind to. It's a perfect fall day in the warm golden sunlight and fluttering amber leaves against a crisp blue sky that you don't want to sleep through.

Isaiah 57:14 (TPT) reads, "Yahweh says, 'Let the people return to me. Build! Build up the road, clear the way, and get it ready! Remove every obstacle from their path.'" I picture one of the "obstacles" that needs removing in allowing us to "return" to Him in a deeply felt, transformationally experienced kind of way, is the obstacle of having our imaginations and feelings discredited and condemned. I'm here to help remove that boulder in your way and to invite you to reconnect your faith to your feelings, and to allow Him to ignite your imagination once again with the vibrancy it held as a child.

How in the world did fundamentalist thought leaders think we could live out a "childlike" faith without big feelings and expansive imaginations, hallmarks of being a child, after all? And however, are we supposed to "feel our way toward Him" like we explored above if we fear, discount, discredit—or worse, disconnect from our feelings?

We have been told all the livelong day that "He never leaves us," but knowing that in our heads or believing that in our hearts are different than *knowing* by experiencing the feeling of His very near presence.

For example, we can know in our hearts and believe in our minds that the Grand Canyon exists, but that is a whole different reality to live in than the reality that comes after having stood at the edge of it, experiencing its awe-inspiring and vibrant grandeur for yourself. Once you've experienced it for yourself, when someone speaks of it, you chime into the conversation with a whole different kind of convinced enthusiasm, of having been *moved* by it.

The same goes for knowing about and of vs. feeling and experiencing God firsthand. You can't unsee or unfeel it. And the more you stop doubting your feelings about times you thought God was speaking to you or you felt like He was especially close in some particular moment, the sturdier your faith about what experiences God's presence is like becomes. It's a synergistic, up-spiral of faith and feelings intertwined.

What the conservative evangelical fundamentalists were afraid of when they tried to caution us from our own feelings when it came to our relationship with God was to not become so reliant upon them that we allowed our faith to falter in dry or difficult seasons when we for whatever reason, seem to "feel" God less. While their intent may have been good, their methods were still flawed, and they "threw the baby out with the bathwater," so to speak, depriving us of the vibrancy intended to be experienced in relationship with God.

Just like our earthly relationships go through seasons (think "honeymoon phase" in romantic relationships, "empty nest phase" in parent-child relationships, a "busy season" in friendships…) where feelings of closeness to the object of our affection may fluctuate from season to season, we don't allow a feeling of distance to define the relationship, or decide that that person in our life doesn't exist or must not care so much about us after all. Why? Because our knowing of that person's character, our history in relationship with them, and our previous interactions sustain us through the ebbs and flows of feelings and interactions.

The same goes for our relationship with God then, and the "fundies" had nothing to fear. It's like we were told to live in black and white and refuse to acknowledge a rainbow when we experienced one, for fear that when the rainbow faded away from the sky that day, our faith would be so rocked that we'd abandon it altogether. We are meant to allow experiences of rainbows and sunshine and the array of color in everything from wildflowers to the changing leaves bring us joy and sustenance that bring us to a deeper connection to the Creator of it all so that it would have lingering effects that fuel our faith even after the sun sets and long winter days (spiritually speaking) set in.

The church seems to have done a great job at large to convey the messages that we're to "seek" Him (first, with all our hearts, etc.), but I would suggest we have barely touched the surface, much less plunged in, to the way in which we *do* that, which cannot be breached apart from our feelings. Rather, we must intentionally attune to them, thus, "*feeling* toward Him," as Acts reveals.

How will we know when we've reached Him? If you allow yourself to believe your feelings when seeking Him with all your heart, you'll know when you've found Him. Jeremiah 29:13, "You will seek me and find me when you seek me with all your heart," is a promise.

More than that, I believe He'll meet you in a deeply personal way that you'll experience the keen sense in your spirit of *being found* by Him.

Discovering

On a quiet day in the woods, kneeling beside the creek that had become my "secret place" in that season of sweet spiritual growth and deeper discovery of God's nearness and heart for me, I was reading in the Gospels about the life of Jesus. He'd become so personal to me—truly, my dearest friend. I had a deep desire to have been there with Him, one of His disciples in the flesh. His friend, just like Mary and Martha got to be. A gut-deep ache and sense of longing swept over me to just be near Him. I began crying and praying, *"Jesus, I know that You are here, and believe that You are close to me. But I wish so much that I could see You or feel You. I wish You could reach out and touch me, be that real and near."* Just then—the most miraculous thing happened—I felt a gentle tap on my shoulder. Then again. My heart leaped as I tried to understand what was happening. I spun around to look and see who had snuck up behind me alongside the trail and placed these gentle taps on my skin—only to find raindrops resting on my shoulder. I gazed with wonder as I suddenly realized it had begun raining just after I'd asked to feel Him. I began laughing through my crying as I looked up at the sky and embraced the continued tapping of raindrops now on my face and hands, realizing what He'd just done. He'd touched me just as I'd asked—tapping me on the shoulder through raindrops. It gave a whole new meaning to this lovely passage:

> "Let us strive to know the Lord.
> His appearance is as sure as the dawn.
> He will come to us like the rain,
> like the spring showers that water the land"
>
> (Hosea 6:3, HSBC).

Presence. In its Latin origin, *praesentia*, it literally means "being at hand."[21] We sense (which is the second half of the word!) presence before we even see who or what is present.

The way we so often experience the presence of another is in easily recognized manifestations, such as eyes locking, a hand laid

---

21 "Presence, n." *Oxford English Dictionary*, Oxford University Press, 25 October 2024, https://www.oed.com/dictionary/presence_n?tl=true.

gently on your shoulder, or the sound of laughter joining in with your own. We recognize and know when we're suddenly not alone with our own thoughts and experiences. We sense when someone else has entered in *with* us. And that is a literal translation of one of God's names, "Immanuel," which translates as "God with us."

But how do we realize and recognize God's presence with us? What can experiencing God's presence feel or look like?

The short answer is that it can vary for each person, as the way He speaks, I believe, is so very personal to each of us. However, I believe there are enough shared experiences of ways that His children have individually and collectively "heard" Him. I believe that as we share stories with each other and read stories of our former brothers and sisters in the Bible sharing accounts of times they spoke with, heard, felt, or "saw" Him in some way, we become encouraged and even more convinced of our own encounters with God.

A book I've come to reference as a dictionary for supernatural occurrences of sorts, *God's Prophetic Symbolism in Everyday Life*, give a great introduction to the issue I've faced my whole life and how God changed my mind about it:

> Often believers will question whether God still speaks to us in this day and age. When this question arises, they are often referring to the audible voice of God. God can speak to us audibly if He so chooses; however, when it comes to hearing God's voice outside the traditionally accepted means, my experience has been that it is typically through something that gains your attention because it is unusual or out of character. We are not cookie-cutter Christians; we are unique beings, and therefore God will speak to us in ways that are unique to our spiritual makeup.[22]

---

22 Thompson, Adam F., and Adrian Beale. *God's Prophetic Symbolism in Everyday Life: The Divinity Code to Hearing God's Voice through Natural Events and Divine Occurrences.* Destiny Image Publishers, 2017.

If that isn't the truest thing! I believe that, just as Acts 17:27 says, "He has done this so that every person would long for God, feel their way to him… and find him—for he is the God who is easy to discover!" (TPT), the personal ways He speaks to us are meant to make it easy for us to discover Him.

God started speaking to me in one of those "unusual" ways at the age of 16, only I didn't recognize the occurrences as His voice at the time. I remember thinking it odd that, while in the midst of some major life transitions (including the tragic ending of the failed courtship-turned-rogue-dating-turned-near-betrothal relationship from the cult-ish church, leaving that church and accepting the invitation to visit the step-down church's youth group), I kept mysteriously encountering the number 747.

It would happen so ordinarily and unexpectedly that while it would catch my attention, I'd write it off as coincidence. But for a series of several weeks during that most intense and heart-wrenching season, it felt like almost every time I looked at the clock, it was exactly 7:47 a.m. or p.m. Perhaps the change or tax on a receipt was $7.47. Or the last three digits of the license plate on the car that pulled in front of me happened to be 747. Whatever the case, I felt seen through that number, like it was a very particular sequence that, for some reason, was "following" me.

But again, the environment I was in at the time had me religiously doubtful of anything out of the norm of tight-laced legalistic ideology. While I was in the beginning of emerging from that, I was still afraid or ashamed of my own thoughts at times. I was intrigued. It felt like a positive "sign" of sorts, but I eventually shoved it down and dismissed it enough to all but forget about it.

It wasn't until about a decade following that season that this creative message from God would resurface in my life, loud enough at a point that I was open enough to finally recognize it as Him.

Ironically, again, I was at another major crossroads in my life, just coming out of the most personally, relationally, and spiritually tumultuous season of my life that I'd later come to call my "quarter-life crisis" and into what I've come to call my "spiritual awakening" (more on that in Chapter 7).

During this time, I sought the Lord for wisdom on what to do or not to do in specific situations regarding my life, relationships, and even business, asking for His direction. As I was crying out for guidance, protection, and direction, so desperately wanting to do the right thing, wouldn't you know, that same number sequence began appearing again! I would try to force it out and not look for it to make sure I wasn't "reading into things." It didn't matter because He got louder, and 747 became a common number I'd encounter again and again. I noticed I'd more often see it at the exact moment I was praying about or thinking about the things I was trying to navigate. I'd almost arrived at a decision, and suddenly, a car with a 747 on its license plate would pass me. I'd pause a show or film, and the timestamp was at exactly 7 minutes and 47 seconds. Each time, my jaw would almost drop. My spirit was stirred, and I began to realize this was intentional.

This was *God*, somehow speaking to me in this creative message. Sure enough, as I began to settle on a decision and take steps in the direction I was feeling led in, often the thoughts in my heart at the moment this sequence would appear again. The tension in my life began to subside, the light became clear at the end of the tunnel, and He gently led me through gracefully and to calm waters and safe harbors in the ways I was praying for. I began to smile when I'd see the number, correlating at that point as a "God wink" to me, a confirmation or little reminder that He was with me, guiding every detail of my life. To this day, I still see it multiple times nearly daily, and I have lovingly come to call it "my" number and one of God's direct lines to me.

It was only then I could look back at the first time in my life that had occurred over a decade prior and realize that that, too, was God showing up and being present with me, guiding and directing me through the most intense situation I'd experienced up to that point in my life. I was overcome with awe, so deeply grateful, and downright tickled at the mystery and creativity of it all.

I didn't know about *this* side of God. Nobody ever told me about *Him* in church. They'd told me signs and wonders were basically dead and gone with biblical times. But as I was diving deep into Scripture during that time of spiritual hunger and growth like I'd never known, I tore up the Bible looking for evidence that God no longer spoke through signs, wonders, miracles, vision, dreams, prophecy—and I couldn't find anything supporting what I'd previously been led to believe. Rather, I found the contrary—evidence that God is "the same today, yesterday, and forever" (Hebrews 13:8) and that "nothing was impossible with God" (Luke 1:37).

I found stories from the Old to New Testament displaying signs and wonders as a way He confirmed His presence and helped others believe when they were struggling. From the story of Gideon asking for the Lord to confirm His voice through a "test" of laying out the fleece, one dry against the wet morning dew, and one wet with dew in contrast to dry morning grass—to doubting Thomas needing to see the scars in Jesus' hands to believe it was really Him. One of the most direct references to God speaking through miraculous means is in Isaiah 7:11, when the Lord literally says, *"Go ahead—ask for a sign from Yahweh, your God. Ask for something big, so miraculous that you will know only God did it!"* Ahaz, who God was speaking to then, said that he would *not* ask, or "test" the Lord. So Isaiah pipes up and rebukes him, saying that it's bad enough to try his patience, let alone try the patience of God. "The Lord Himself will give you a sign. Behold—the virgin will conceive and give birth to a son and will name Him God Among Us," he goes on to prophesy. God wouldn't have Ahaz's attempted "nobility" in refraining from asking for a sign. He basically said, "Fine, I'll choose the sign then." And thus, the most miraculous sign in history was promised—Jesus's incarnation.

Jesus's only time of rebuking those asking for more "signs and wonders" was when He was being taken advantage of when people just wanted him to do something fantastic to prove something or entertain them. But that is *not* the heart we are coming from when we are genuinely seeking to know Him up close and personal and honestly seeking His direction in our lives—and He knows the difference. He delights to reveal Himself to us, to "reward those who earnestly seek Him." His heart is postured toward the humble in spirit, and He promises to answer when we call, and that when we "seek Him with all our heart, we'll find Him."

It's just that sometimes we don't realize *how* we will find Him. He may take us by surprise with His unconventional, creative, and unexpected ways that He captures our attention and speaks to our spirits, and we'd do well to not "quench the spirit," but rather learn to be "moved by the impulses of the Holy Spirit."

I didn't mention this phenomenon I was experiencing to anyone at the time. I feared ridicule and being questioned about things even I couldn't fully explain. I just held on to it quietly between myself and God. It wasn't long, though, before more numbers started "appearing" before me. If it's happened to you, you know what I mean, in that you absolutely cannot avoid and have no way of commanding these numbers to or from you. I'd just be going about my day, and suddenly, there it would be.

The neat thing was that He'd seem to only introduce a few new ones at a time. Eventually, they became like clues, and I'd start researching and even began to discover some were tied to certain verses He'd highlighted to me that were speaking to something specific He was teaching me. It was absolutely miraculous and became something that added joy to my days and deepened my communion with Him as my thoughts were continually turned toward Him when I'd pray about or ponder these things beyond me.

Like God can't be contained within four walls of a building (like a church), He's too grand and wondrously communicative and creative to have spoken anything and everything He'll ever want to say between the covers of the Bible. He'll never contradict it, but He will speak millennia full of additional expression confirming and elaborating on those truths and applying them to specific, present-day circumstances we need to hear His voice in and see Him move in. He will draw near and speak to us how He sees fit. We just have to be humble and open enough to believe it and have childlike faith enough to realize it when He does.

Beyond speaking to me through specific numbers and their correlations to various verses and meanings, I'd also begun to recognize Him speaking through everything from nature to dreams. Some were heavier, warning dreams about particular people or situations in my life that, to my dismay and also not surprising at that point, came to pass. Some were purely beautiful, joyous dreams. One, in particular, was about Jesus coming back, and I penned it all in detail when I woke up in tears, utterly moved beyond words with what I'd just experienced in the dream. The heavenly music I heard so clearly in the dream I couldn't even articulate with my pen or hear again once I was awake, but my spirit remembered, and my body burst into tears—my soul, knowing it was the most out of this world, glorious sound I'd ever heard.

Leading up to and surrounding the time of this most favorite God-dream that would ultimately hold even deeper meaning and solidify messages God had been speaking through other avenues,

I'd also been noticing an influx of butterflies in the most uncanny moments and ways.

Now, I've always liked butterflies. But never have I ever had so many butterfly encounters as I did during that time. I found myself literally surrounded by them during that season. Across many months, I would notice a butterfly fly directly in front of my windshield while driving down the interstate, of all places. I remember one day in particular while driving over an hour west on I-40, I would look to the left and the right, and it was as though butterflies were dancing like crowds cheering on a sideline. "What are you all *doing*, and, *here*?" I pondered. More than a few times, I would set out on the walking path to my "secret place"—a cherished, sacred little place in the woods I'd discovered with a wooden bench beside a creek where I'd go read my Bible and journal, pray and just spend time with God—and as I'd start walking, a butterfly or two would fly up to me, encircling and dancing around me. They'd land on me and stay with me as I walked. I was in awe.

I felt sheer wonder and delight over noticing that these things don't just happen; they are by Divine orchestration, and they are ways God is present with me. As I studied the spiritual meaning of butterflies, the best definition I came across was that they can symbolize no longer being earthbound, as a caterpillar once was. It went along splendidly with what God was doing in my heart then. I wasn't surprised a bit when, not long after that revelation, I was driving to the same "secret place" path one day when my "Discover Weekly" (aptly named) playlist on Spotify shuffled to a new Josh Garrels song, and wouldn't you know, the song was titled, "Butterfly ."[23] I started laugh-crying—the lyrics were so ridiculously on point with what God had been teaching me during that time and through the illustration of butterflies. It felt like a detailed letter from God

23   Garrels, Josh. *Butterfly. Chrysaline*, Small Voice Records, 9 Aug. 2019.

about exactly what He was saying to me through all of the butterfly symbols.

Back to that particularly revelatory dream, I'd journaled about it all:

Last night I had this first dream where I remember feeling almost in love and dazzlingly swept up in the Lord. It was night. I stepped outside in the drive, like a walk to come away with Him. As I looked up, smiling at the sky (Him), a strong wind swept from behind and swirled around me like a dance, and swept me up in the air, maybe 15 to 20 feet off the ground, and swayed and held me there again like a dance. I was giddy with delight, completely surrounded by the romance of it all. Leaves blew, my hair blew, stars glittered. He'd (through the force of the wind) set me down and then lift me back up again, like a ride or a father tossing his child in the air to let them experience the joy of flying for a moment. It was so real. He was so real. His presence, His Spirit in the wind that lifted me. I'm trying not to cry in this café just remembering the feeling of being with Him, raised with and by Him like that. "Since then, you have been raised with Christ; set your mind on things above, not on the things of this earth." It goes so hand-in-hand with what I've been feeling through what He's been showing me about not being earthbound, about "rising with new wings," like a butterfly in the Josh Garrels song, or like Lana Vawser's prophetic words recently about an approaching season of being called higher and lifted higher. And last night, after a day of discussing and asking the Lord to keep revealing meaning with these numbers He's showing me, I was researching and entered the search terms differently this time and was led to a Christian ministry I've never heard of before called "Pour It Out Ministries." The lady had written a blog post addressing how God speaks in numbers! I've never seen anything like this, and she addresses SO MANY of the same numbers I see! 747 was one of them!! She said it often means "to take off," and that "God is taking you higher and further."

Reflecting on these experiences, I'm amazed by how God's voice came through such creative means, unlike anything I've ever been told in any church. I felt like the psalmist, who says in Psalm 18:28, "God, all at once you turned on a floodlight for me! You are my revelation-light in my darkness, and in your brightness I can see the path ahead."

He communicates through Scripture, His "logos" (written) word, for sure. But as Romans 10:17 (NKJV) distinguishes, "faith comes by hearing, and hearing by the 'word' (rhema, or 'spoken') of God." And as we know about "speaking," there are countless languages, such as different tongues, sure. But think about it—even the audibly deaf speak through signing, and the visually blind hear through braille.

We've got to get out of the stale box of thinking God will only speak through the Bible or audibly. In the words of author Adriane Beale, "God will speak to you how you are primed and prepared to listen."[24] We are unique, individual beings. He knows each of His children by heart! He'll speak to us through the means He knows we'll "hear," and by that, I mean that will capture our attention and resonate with us. This may be through pictures, visions, numbers,

---

24 Thompson, Adam F., and Adrian Beale. *God's Prophetic Symbolism in Everyday Life: The Divinity Code to Hearing God's Voice through Natural Events and Divine Occurrences.* Destiny Image Publishers, 2017.

dreams, lyrics, people, gentle nudges in our spirit, or highlighting something loudly, through nature, Scripture, song, film—or another whole myriad of ways through which He can connect with us. His intent in all of this? To draw us near, sharing greater intimacy with us. *That* is how deeply He loves us and how deeply He longs to be near us, too.

I realize embracing this can be quite the jump, belief-wise. But if you feel that perhaps you've dozed off in the sleepiness of your old beliefs, perhaps the fresh air of a faith leap is exactly the jump that could stir you awake, as Scott Erickson so poetically paints:

> "Moving from...
> believing you must bring God to everything
> to
> witnessing that God is already waiting to be found in everything
> is the revival you've been waiting for."[25]

25 Erickson, Scott. *@scottthepainter*, Instagram, 5 July 2024, https://www.instagram.com/scottthepainter/p/C9CvEj9xina/?locale=my&hl=am-et&img_index=1.

His Posture Toward Us

"If you took the love of all the best mothers and fathers in the course of human history, all their goodness, kindness, patience, fidelity, wisdom, tenderness, strength, and love and united all those qualities in a single person, that person's love would only be a shadow of the furious love and mercy in the heart of God the Father addressed to you and me at this very moment."

Brennan Manning[26]

Broken Mirrors

We've heard God referred to in roles that we have here in our earthly relationships so that we can understand His posture toward us in practical ways we understand. I like to call these references mirrors, reflections on earth of "as it is in heaven."

Some examples would be…

God as our heavenly Father (1 John 3:1, Matthew 6:9a)
God comforts us as a mother comforts her children (Isaiah 66:13)
Jesus as our Brother (Hebrews 2:11, Romans 8:29)
God as our Husband (Isaiah 54:5)

---

26 Manning, Brennan. *The Furious Longing of God*. David C Cook, 2009.

God as our Father is probably the most commonly used mirror reference throughout the Bible, so let's explore this one a bit deeper to better understand.

In a perfect world, the reference to God as our Father *would* click and make perfect sense, be deeply meaningful, and allow us to feel endeared to and safe with Him as one should with a good father. But this breaks down for many of us in our bodies and minds when we've experienced trauma or confusion in our reference points being the exact opposite.

In all my growing up years in church, I could never grasp the *goodness* of that connection, thankfully not due to a bad relationship with my own father, but due to my impression of the role of fathers as needing to be "feared." In the patriarchal world I grew up in, fathers were allowed to be domineering, power-tripping, authority-lording figures. I just thought my dad was (luckily) the exception to many of the other fathers I was around. Many seemed to excuse their controlling, harsh, and frankly unloving behavior "in Jesus' name" because of how God had set them up as the "umbrella of authority" over their households. *cringe*

So the mirror gets broken. What's intended to be a beautiful reflection of how God is postured toward us and how He relates to us gets cracked and fragmented to where we can't even recognize what that relationship was supposed to look and feel like in the first place. From where some of us stand, it's been distorted at best and shattered at worst.

Some didn't have a father.

Some had fathers leave.

Some had fathers stay, but they were so absent they might as well have not been there.

Some lost their fathers before we could even know them.

Some had cruel fathers who misused and abused them.

Some had fathers who loved the very best they could and still left us with wounds warranting navigation and repair.

It makes sense, then, that when we've heard of this supposedly loving Heavenly "Father," it can fall short of moving us to the state of exuberant joy and absolute trust in this Being if we're basing it on a poor reflection from our primary experiences with any given mirror.

You may know that God loves you but feel unlovable because a critical mother highlighted your flaws and shortcomings and caused you to believe you were unworthy. Thus, it is difficult to imagine what "like a mother who comforts her children" feels like if your mother was not a source of safety and comfort for you. You may believe that Jesus has called us his "friends" but not be able to grasp the depth of the meaning if you've struggled to find truly good friends, rather, have only a reference to shallow connections, deep betrayals, or flaky friends who were well-meaning but chronic for-getters and fail-to-follow-through-ers. You may want to believe He loves you with an "everlasting love" like a lasting marriage commit-ment, but have reservations about what commitment even means anymore after your marriage crumbled despite your best efforts to keep it together. If you weren't "rejoiced over" by your spouse, then how passionately He feels about you likely doesn't resonate.

You see? Beautiful mirrors, but sadly broken in places for each of us due to our own unique experiences with and exposure to these parallel relationship references. The good news is, if we weren't giv-en great experiential references to these relationship postures, we can start replacing what we know by experience with the truth of His heart, of His original intention.

One of the most powerful ways to start piecing our broken mirrors back together is by considering family, friends, and partners who *do* embody the beautiful qualities these roles should carry. Like family that you choose, we can choose to search out what's true and cling to the closest examples we have here on earth, which will then help provide clarity in the reflection as we understand more of how God postures Himself toward us in these various ways of relating.

We can piece together like a beautiful mosaic or patchwork quilt, the best qualities of all the people we've experienced to make up a new mirror. Then, when we look into it, we will see more of the true goodness of God's heart toward us.

Like removing the arrowheads to start healing up our wounds and living more unhindered lives, this is an invitation to take another look as He helps patch up and repair the broken mirrors and points us to shining examples of what He intended so that we can come to a deeper understanding of how He postures Himself toward us as a perfect and loving Father, comforting and nurturing Mother, Friend that sticks closer than a brother, or Husband that sees no flaw in his beautiful Bride.

Let's "reframe" these mirrors, if you will, and picture for a moment the reality of God's perfectly loving posture toward us, as seen by way of the myriad of reference points around us.

Mosaic Mirrors

A few years ago, the church I was attending at the time did a fantastic study on Psalm 23, slowly sipping on and savoring the Lord as our Shepherd and all that entails, including our Guide and our Host.

It was another beautiful reminder of just how kind, approachable, and near to us He is. It painted a picture of Him here with us in everyday life and hacked away at all the stuffy, stale, and religious rigamarole that so often trips us up and keeps us from experiencing Him as He really is and instead, cuts to the chase the truth and of what matters: He is with us, for us, near us, toward us.

Think of the nicest, most hospitable, and generous person you know. That person who's always so thoughtful, kind, and really goes out of their way to make you feel welcomed, well cared for, and especially loved. I thought of my granddad, Fred. When we'd go to visit my grandparents or had the pleasure of them making the trek up from Dallas to visit us, he was always the one at the dinner table with a big grin as he passed you more rolls. More potatoes. More everything. *"Your plate looks a little empty there, Kathryn." "Please, have more!" "Did you get enough?"*

Whoever your person is—where do you think those traits came from? If we're made in God's image, then all our little bits of goodness and kindness are mere reflections and fractions of what He is capable of goodness/kindness-wise. Think about that for a moment. He is closer, more present, real, generous, kind, capable, and down-to-earth than my granddad. Than your person, too.

Something we did at church to help wrap our minds around the realness of His personality, heart, and presence in these ways was to close our eyes and "picture this" in literal scenarios.

What would He say to us if He had us over for dinner? *"Please, sit here beside Me! I'm so glad you could make it." "Here, have some more! I made this special just for you. There's plenty. Eat up!" "That last slice of cake has your name on it. I won't take no for an answer— please, enjoy!" "Ah, you noticed the jazz music?! I knew it was your favorite."*

What would He say as He carefully guided us through a dark valley or dangerous terrain? *"Here, take My hand." "Stay close to Me." "I've got you." "I know this is scary, but don't be afraid. I'll get you through this safely."*

Remember to think of Him like this because it's really how and who He is. I'm sorry if you had the wrong impression of Him. As you've come to learn by now, I did, too. For so many, many years. But ever since He scooped me up and out of all of the church harm of those distant and disillusioned years, He slowly thawed my heart and opened my eyes up to who He really is and helped me glue back together the pieces of my shattered mirrors. Now, when I see the best qualities in my people, I see Him. And when I see Him, I think of my favorite reflections of Him in my people.

He's strong like my dad, generous like my granddad, gentle and patient like my husband, fun-loving like my mom, down-to-earth like my best friend, cheerful, hilarious, smart, and creative like my brothers and sisters. He is all my favorite things about my favorite people and more, all combined and perfected. Because He's where their best qualities came from, anyway.

Familial Reflection

Perhaps God's most successful way of helping me catch a glimpse of His wildly immovable love for me has been through the crisp and intact mirror of my own ridiculously secure and unrelenting love for my child.

Being a mother to my 7-year-old little Liam has changed me in so many ways, but internally, perhaps the greatest impact has been the way it's deepened my understanding of God's love for us as His children. I'd heard the verse my whole life from Matthew, which poses the question if we, who are imperfect parents, know how to give good gifts to our children, then just imagine *how much more* our perfect Heavenly Father knows how to give good things to us. But I don't think I'd really grasped it until I experienced the inherent drive to absolutely protect and fully provide for my child at all costs. There is no "duty" about it—it's an insatiable desire to care for him born out of my love and adoration for this precious little being entrusted to me.

I continue to be "wowed" by the verse, "Or do you think that I cannot call on My Father and He will provide Me at once with more than 12 legions of angels?" (Matthew 26:53, HCSB), like a wakeup call to the reality that we can also call on our Father that same way, and that not begrudgingly, but with delight, He shows up. I think it's easy to forget that as God's children, we have all of heaven on our side, available to us. It's also easy to forget just how willing God, as our loving Father, is to come to our aid and provide what we need when we need it. Not just the bare minimum, either. What we need and *more*. Excess. Abundance. He lavishes His love on us as a good parent does for their child.

Any time I start to doubt or forget God's posture toward me as His "perfectly and wonderfully made" kiddo, I can look in the mirror of how I would respond to my son to see a fraction of the picture of how God is postured toward and responds to me.

If he was in a bind and asked me for help, there would be no need for explanation, no judgement towards or condemnation following—I would *be there* for him. As a good parent, it's a no-brainer. Of *course* my heart would ache for him. Of *course* I'd give him whatever I could and provide whatever he needed as best I could. So how, then, could I imagine a perfect and limitless Parent doing anything less? (Broken mirrors are how, of course, but you get the point.)

Correct—He doesn't. As one of my all-time favorite verses says so well, He does "*immeasurably more*" instead:

> Never doubt God's mighty power to work in you and accomplish all this. He will achieve infinitely more than your greatest request, your most unbelievable dream, and exceed your wildest imagination! He will outdo them all, for his miraculous power constantly energizes you.
>
> Ephesians 3:20, TPT

What happens if your parental/familial mirrors are fractured, though, making it challenging to see this posture reflected toward you or from you in your own life? You can take a tip from Jesus and draw on his liberating definition of family in Luke 8:20-21 (HCSB). Someone tells Jesus, "Your mother and brothers are standing outside, wanting to see You." And He corrects them by addressing those in the crowd with whom He's speaking to whom this applies: "My mother and brothers are those who hear and do the word of God."

In short, *you can choose your family* according to who is actually listening to and living out God's Word. And what is God's Word but Jesus, "the Word became flesh"? You can look to those living and loving according to what Jesus would do and draw from their life-giving examples as spiritual mothers, fathers, sisters, and brothers. And if it's about you embodying the reflection of Jesus in a familial way to present a clearer reflection of His posture toward others in whatever role you may relate to here, you can also choose and learn to become more of the parent or sibling that God is toward you!

Friendly Reflection

While I've experienced my fair share of sinking friend-"ships" that sure could taint my idea of how friends really are, I've had too many solid "ships" to let it. I hope the same goes for you, too. Because "there is a friend who sticks closer than a brother" as it says in Proverbs 18:24. It's referencing Jesus, I believe, but isn't that just the best cue to look at the friends in our lives that have faithfully stuck Jesus-level close to us—closer than relatives? I believe friendship is one of the most underrated forms of relationship. Not all of us will get married, and not all of us will have kids. Some of us don't have siblings either—but friendship? Now, *that* is a relationship everyone can relate to and the essential foundation other forms of relationship are built upon.

Jesus speaks of the greatest form of love being in the context of sacrificing one's life for a friend. In John 15, Jesus references that He confides in His "inner circle" of disciples because they are His "most intimate friends." True friendship is a deeply-rooted bond that, if well-kept, keeps souls in sweet, sacred unity across time and distance, picking right back up where they left off, responding to a need without demands for explanation, loving without expecting something in return. They have your back. They go to bat for you. They advocate for your well-being. They vouch for you and defend you to others if needed. They choose to stay connected. They share the responsibility in tending to the friendship. They speak up in love, with truth, even when it's hard. They support you and celebrate your joy. They walk with you through difficult circumstances. With true friends, it is not a burden but a privilege and joy to lock arms with you and help you get to higher ground.

I get teary-eyed thinking of the dear friends God has gifted me through the years and pivotal moments where they stood by me, sometimes when it felt as if no one else did. There have been countless times across my life I've been deeply affected and my soul shaped by their sincere, unconditional love for me.

They are the ones who rallied around me and stood by my side for 32 hours of labor and then scrubbed up to be in the OR for the emergency C-section delivery of my child.

They are the small army who simultaneously defended my wellbeing and carried the grief with me as I achingly and one day at a time walked toward the inevitable ending of the marriage I fought for years to keep alive.

They are the ones who reach out to schedule a regular happy hour for nearly a decade and counting to make sure we keep in touch.

They are the ones who want what's best for me, no matter if it's the unpopular opinion or the hardest path.

They are the ones who show up in practical ways, from bringing a meal to share to regifting me with household storage items they thought I could use.

They are the ones who invite me to their kids' dance recitals and include my family in other family events because, to them, we are as good as, if not closer, than blood relatives.

They are the ones who remind me of the best parts of myself that I can be quick to forget or discount.

I want to mention them all by name and tell you what I love about each of them! I want to detail how they've made me feel seen, valued, and wholly loved. How they reflect God's immense love for me back to me in a way that I could feel beyond just knowing it. "Lifers" reading this, you know who you are. Thank you, thank you—to each of you, from the bottom of my heart, for the ways your love for me has helped me see God's deeply abiding and always enduring friendship with me, too.

Romantic Reflection

It sounds oversimplified to say that if you've ever been "in love" then that might be a mirror through which you can see the reflection of God's deep, intimate love for you, but it's a good starting point for believing that in short: He's crazy about you. Don't believe me? Just listen to this poetry that represents God's heart for us:

> "You are altogether beautiful, my darling; there is no flaw in you... You have stolen my heart, my sister, my bride; you have stolen my heart with one glance of your eyes, with one jewel of your necklace."
>
> Song of Songs 4:7, 9a, NIV

This particular relational mirror, however, has been the hardest one for me to see reflections of His love clearly, as it represents perhaps the most significant area of damage to my soul throughout my life. Of the three committed romantic relationships I've had, only the present one—my second marriage—has been healthy and functional, as intimate relationships are designed to be. In contrast, the previous two—the courtship-turned-dating relationship and my first marriage (as an almost-child bride at age 19)—became primary sources of deep confusion, grief, and emotional trauma. These experiences warped everything from my self-perception to my beliefs about committed relationships and marriage.

Until God brought me into this new season and romantic relationship with my now-husband—whom I adore to pieces and finally understand the writer of *Song of Songs*' enthusiasm about—I did not have a great personal reference for this epic, love-story kind of romantic love.

For much of my life, I believed married couples had no choice but to remain married, whether it seemed wise to or not. While I grew to understand that my parents did not have to but wanted to be married—and I appreciate that they've worked hard through the years to create a life-giving marriage they truly enjoy—since they worked in a marriage ministry, I think I assumed staying married was part of the job. I didn't fully grasp the growth required for them to not only love each other by choice but also to remain *in love* after all these decades.

In addition to that, the strict religious environments I was immersed in for so long seemed to treat divorce as the unwritten eighth "thing the Lord hates" in Proverbs 6:16-19, rather than recognizing that the seven actions described in the passage—ironically—are often behaviors that can contribute to necessary divorces. Then there was the out-of-context, mistranslated, classic Christian go-to guilt-tripping translation from Malachi 2:16: "God hates divorce." As I personally experienced at that heartbreaking crossroads in my first marriage, the phrase strikes terror into those already afraid and doing their best to navigate tragic relationship and family situations many cannot fathom. For further enlightenment on the truth behind the misused verse, I'd recommend reading what Gretchen Baskerville[27] and Margaret Mowczko[28] have to share regarding the original texts and earlier translations. As they explain, this more commonly heard translation greatly departs from the original texts, which clearly communicate that it is the *man who hates* and *deals treacherously* with his wife—unjustly divorcing her in a way that would have left her destitute in that culture—that grieves God in the context of that story.

---

27 Baskerville, Gretchen. "18 Bible Translations of Malachi 2:16: Does God Hate Divorce?" *Life-Saving Divorce*, 16 Nov. 2020, https://lifesavingdivorce.com/malachi/. Accessed 8 Jan. 2025.

28 Mowczko, Margaret. "God on Divorce (Malachi 2:16)." *Margaret Mowczko*, 21 May 2016, https://margmowczko.com/divorce-malachi-2/. Accessed 8 Jan. 2025.

As a kid, it seemed to me that many of the couples I witnessed growing up weren't all that "in love"—especially as limited and Disney-fied as my childlike understanding of the term was to begin with. Couples in the ministry and at the churches I grew up in seemed really good at following rules, making compromises, and, in the saddest cases, tolerating each other. Which, as I now know, is also not the abundant life God has for us. So while I'd always heard that the most "romantic" book of the Bible, Song of Songs, was a love story parallel to Jesus and His "Bride," the church, I didn't really buy it or have a reference point for it for most of my life.

In addition to that, most translations had failed to help me really understand the heart of the message. I'd try reading it, but the words would sting with either a pain of longing and wishing I knew what it felt like to be so deeply cherished, to outright being grossed out over hard-to-relate-to imagery ("Thy neck is as a tower of ivory; thine eyes like the fishpools in Heshbon," anyone?).

It wasn't until a friend recommended The Passion Translation Bible to me a few years ago that Song of Songs finally got through to me, and when it did, it changed my entire understanding of this dimension of what Christ thinks of me and how He feels about me—not to mention helped me set the standard for what deeply loving, affectionate, intimate relationships can look and feel like.

Something about this poetic translation allowed the message to permeate my heart, and I was gripped by a sudden awareness of how intensely and passionately God loved me. I could almost feel His adoring eyes on me, and I was absolutely undone to the point of tears when I first read verse 4:9, about how *He* is undone by "one flash of *my* eyes."

This romance between me and the Lover of my Soul was never described to me in this way. I had some idea of how the reference to Christ and his Bride was supposed to be reflected in the marriage relationship on earth, but for some reason, I always saw that as the bride being in awe of her husband. I never saw that it was mutual. It's the other way around, where He, too, is in love with us.

I leave the Creator of the Universe breathless. I tried a phrase from the verse on in first person. "Me?" I thought. Uncanny.

I dove deeper:

My beloved reached into me to unlock my heart. The core of my very being trembled at his touch. How my soul melted when He spoke to me! My spirit arose to open for more of his touch...

Blush "Sweet... and spicy!" I thought to myself. Curiosity took over, and I devoured the whole book.

Moved to tears every time I would read another passage, I was overtaken by the understanding of the depth of this specific form of love that our world has short-changed and sold off as all physical. Sure, these two clearly had a healthy "love life," but beyond what we commonly stop at with intimacy being physical, this book shows the layers of depth we so often miss of true intimacy—there is so much awe and wonder at each other's inward beauty, deep-seated trust, and championing of each other's unmatched character. It took my understanding of "love" and "romance" to new multidimensional heights of the fullness of its all-encompassing richness.

As I dwelled on this love story I was now completely captivated by, I kept picturing this man, who represented Jesus, more and more clearly. I was seeing myself in the story:

Me about Jesus:

"No one speaks words so anointed as this one—words that both pierce and heal."

"His hands hold unlimited power, but He never uses it in anger..."

"Everything about Him fills me with holy desire!"

"Most sweet are the kisses of His mouth, even His whispers of love."

Jesus about me:

"Every part of you is so beautiful, My darling. Perfect is your beauty, without flaw within.

"Even hosts of angels stand in awe of you."

"Turn your eyes from Me; I can't take it anymore! I can't resist the passion of these eyes that I adore. Overpowered by a glance, my ravished heart—undone. Held captive by your love, I am truly overcome! For your undying devotion to Me is the most yielded sacrifice. The shining of your spirit shows how you've taken My truth to become balanced and complete."

gasp

The more I read, the more I fell in love with this passionate, engaged, pursuant Jesus, and the sweeter our times became together as I realized how very reciprocal this relationship was. I know this to be true: "I know my lover is mine and I have everything in you, for we delight ourselves in each other" (Song of Songs 2:16, TPT).

Seeing Him in this light had this unexpected effect of boosting my self-esteem, which, in ways I didn't realize, had been so torn down by the broken romantic "mirrors" in my life. Verse by verse, encounter by encounter, He was repairing what others had broken in me when it came to understanding my own value, worth, confidence, personality, beauty, wisdom, character, and so on. If I could captivate the attention of God Himself, if He sings love songs over me, then surely whether or not I ever found a truly good reflection of this kind of love here on earth, all the love I needed was already found in Him, just as Psalm 62 says.

I'm so grateful He did, in fact, have an epic love story planned for me on earth waiting just around the bend of Him leading me out of the barren places I'd stayed too long. As this book is published, I'll be coming up on celebrating my fourth wedding anniversary with Forrest, the love of my life. Some days, it still feels surreal that there was an encore chapter in my otherwise tragic romantic history. Forrest loves me in a way that mirrors the love of Jesus, which works like a reverse mirror. I was able to recognize the traits in him by how his love for me reflected what I'd come to know through Jesus. He is truly my best friend, safest place, and greatest love, and I'm humbled every day by how *"I am my beloved's and he is mine"* reflects our relationship too.

Having lived on both sides of this one, no matter where you find yourself, with no references, only tragic ones, or solid mirrors that truly help you understand the Divine's love toward you on a deep and true level—His fire for *you* burns bright, and He is pursuing your heart, too.

His Pace

"Don't be pulled in different directions or worried about a thing."

Philippians 4:6a, TPT

"Those who trust in Him will not act in haste."

Isaiah 28:16b, TPT

Tempos

Mrs. Van was an angel manifested as a piano teacher here in Little Rock, AR. I was one of the fortunate children whose lives were forever impacted by not only her musical expertise but her genuine care and practical life wisdom. She got me through my first relationship with the boy I thought I was going to marry by teaching me how to translate my overwhelming emotions into sound, teaching me to constructively steward my emotions through the keys. Angry? We'd slam the keys with all our might as we picked up the pace and let it all out. Sad? We'd let it flow through the somber speed of heartache that extended to my fingertips, erring to the minor keys in a major way until I felt better.

She was a "safe space" before I knew what a safe space was. Better than a bartender or therapist, her listening ear and timely advice were God's grace to me on a weekly basis, from ages 7 to 17—ten years of thinking I was just taking piano lessons, when in fact, I was also visiting a sage mentor. She was the wise old Grandmother Willow to my young Pocahontas free spirit.

Week after week, I'd walk into her sunlight-filled studio—a study converted to a music room on the side of her home, with its own brick-paved pathway and glass French door. She got to see more of my personality, bents, frustrations, and hang-ups in that one hour together a week than I'm sure most who saw me on a regular basis were ever privy to. Being faced with a challenge like learning an instrument when you opened your eyes on this earth thinking you should have everything figured out already and being shocked and almost offended when you realize you don't, exposed lots of opportunities for personal growth throughout my musical education.

One of the best things she ever taught me, in a practical sense, was how to slow down and focus. I'd often send myself into a tizzy and a tailspin over my approach to, well—life—often beginning too broad, a blown-up scale, biting off more than I could chew, trying to take in the infinite with my finite mind, all in one grand sweep. This is still how I can tend to overwhelm and paralyze myself, and even then, as a youth, she saw that about me. I'd launch off playing from the start of a new song I was just taking on, like a horse from the gate at the track, only to stumble and fall flat only a few bars into the sheet music. While I initially equated success with playing the song, she would equate it with deeply *learning* the song. *Then*, I could truly play it, sometimes even from committed memory, without the sheet music.

And so, she kindly showed me a way I still lean on often with other things I try to tackle or adopt in life. Using what we already had in front of us, sheet music, she would flip over a page already played or a page yet to be played, overlapping the pages and using the blank white space on the backs of those sheets as a blinder to block off all bars on the sheet staring back at me, leaving only the single bar I was to work on first, exposed. It's not that the rest of the song vanished, and my work was now minimized. It's that she'd put up boundaries where she knew I was "prone to wander." Out of love, she would help protect me from *me*, covering up the big picture and minimizing my perspective so that I could only see right. in. front. of. me. The next step. The next note. Where I could breathe, fixing my eyes only on the one bar I was to be working on at that moment until I'd played it over and over again and could play it with ease. Then, she'd adjust the paper shield slightly to reveal the next bar of music to practice next. I would repeat the same process, practicing the new bar and then adding it onto the previous bar in a bite-sized, manageable way that was truly building something, one bar at a time. Though the pace of her approach seemed slower, I accomplished more—learning and really coming to know the song. Before I knew it, I would actually be playing it and playing it well. The speed and breadth with which I'd tried to take on the song as a whole quickly had actually frittered away more time and wasted energy in frustration of being overwhelmed and constantly having to stop and start again with each derailing off the tracks.

While I did finally learn to slow down enough to actually learn to play piano well, I still wrestle at times with my seemingly inherent initial defaults: fast thinker, talker, and doer. Unlike my struggle with procrastination surrounding larger projects, when I execute a physical task even so small as pouring a beverage, you'd better stand a few feet away to be clear of the inevitable splash zone from my swift coffee slinging and milk spilling. "Fast" has long been a way of life for me, and that is all well and beautiful when it is simply a personality trait. But what I've come to wonder is, what part of "me" in those ways were perhaps shaped by cultural influence, what of the environment of my upbringing, and what truly remains as an inherent part of my zealous personality?

If that is you, too, it's worth pausing for a ponder because here's a question I think helps us distinguish between what helps and what hurts us: what part of your pace enables you to be more of the *you* God's created you to be, and what part hinders you from becoming so? The undercurrent in our world today is one that speaks to "faster" and "more" being equated with "better," so it's also worth pondering if our motivation for accomplishing the most, the fastest, is coming from a place of striving and earning, comparing and keeping-up, so to speak.

A generally more hurried pace (hustle culture, workaholism, celebrating over-achievers, commitments out of obligation, over-committing to the point of exhaustion) is often the model here on earth, setting the stage for us from a young age. In addition to that, many of us came to have it deeply ingrained due to negative re-inforcement of this model up close and personal through hurtful and even harmful experiences. Whether you were made fun of by petty peers or hurried along by harsh parents, critiqued by a difficult-to-please teacher, taunted by an impossible timer, or yelled at by a boss with uncanny, unrealistic expectations—it's likely you may have experienced some unwarranted form of being hurried along in this life that's contributed to the shape of your inner world in ways you might not have even noticed before.

Regardless of where it stems from—our outer worlds, inner worlds, or both—it doesn't take much venturing out of the world and into the Word to see that that pace, that sense of constant *urgency* to *do* and *be*, living from a state of worry that propels us to haste, is *not* one of those "on earth as it is in heaven" ways of doing and being. I am here, my friend, to help set you free from the shackles others may have made you scurry right into or the ones you wrapped around yourself thinking this was the way it was or had to be.

No more. We are free to live from rest, trust, and reliance on Someone who holds every count of music and every beat of our hearts in His hands. We are invited to link arms with Jesus, whose way is easier and lighter, and learn to adopt His pace, which I've come to call "the pace of grace."

Slowing down your pace may not be not rocket science, but it is counter-intuitive to today's world and much of what we've been exposed to thus far in it. So very often, the inferred dynamic notated at the top of the pages of God's metaphorical music is *adagio* (to be played slowly).

Jesus, being God in man-form, of course, already did everything and all of it well. He most likely didn't need blank-white-page-blinders to slow Him down or help Him learn. (Though there is a verse I love—Isaiah 7:15—that points to Him still learning as a child, that there's "a time when he's old enough to distinguish between right and wrong," which leaves me awe-struck over the idea that as a child, our ever-relatable Jesus still had to learn the very same things we had to! But I digress...) Gleaning from what is recorded about His time here on earth when it comes to His tempo (i.e., His approach, His priorities, His *way* of being, doing, speaking, thinking, responding) never ceases to amaze, and even soothe me.

He largely lived in a steady, patience-filled, worry-free way that took each day in stride and simply allowed for white space around the margins of the proverbial "bar" of music that was right in front of Him at each moment. He wasn't looking behind, nor too far down the page, but was fully present with what and who was in front of Him, living one bar at a time, one day at a time, as though there was plenty of time for everything and all of it. Time seemed to expand to contain exactly what it was meant to, and nothing was ever missing. What a beautiful contrast to the way in which today's culture has contrarily influenced our thinking at large, as well as the micro-level at which a hurried pace can trip us up due to our own experiences.

When I thoughtfully observe Jesus in His daily life here on earth, I have to pick my jaw up off the floor over the vast chasm between His way and my long-embraced way. Everything Jesus said and did, the pace at which He lived, ate, slept, prayed, traveled—there's an effortlessness between the lines of all He did. His underlying rhythm, this "pace of grace," sounds a lot more lovely than the commonly acceptable and often expected "rat race" used to reference our culture's contrasting norm.

Our pace (mental and physical) is important because it's the tempo in which we live, a common thread woven through every aspect of our moments. The pace in which we live affects everything from our relationships, such as our presence or distractedness when we are with our loved ones, to our literal physical nurturing, such as proper digestion from a meal slowly consumed rather than one scarfed down in a few bites. While "there is a time for everything" (Ecclesiastes 3:11), including times we must multitask, such as having to work from our laptops alongside watching our little ones who are being entertained by their iPad, as well as times we'll need to scarf down a protein shake or a bar on the way to a meeting. But what I'm suggesting is that even the way in which we do the many things we do can be approached from a different place of trusting, peacefulness, graciousness (toward ourselves and others) born of a sense of unhurriedness, even in moments when a dash of *accelerando* (faster) is called for.

Let's study a few times Jesus left everyone awe-struck over His preferred pace.

Against the grain

I think it is no coincidence that two of the most memorable examples of Jesus modeling a sense of unhurriedness were surrounding the same family. Mary, Martha, and their dear brother, Lazarus, were clearly some of Jesus' dear friends mentioned during His time here on earth. Perhaps in His all-knowing kindness, He knew they'd need this pace modeled on more than one occasion to take it deeper to heart. (Though I reckon this recurring example was meant to encourage far beyond the original recipients of the lesson, as it is still teaching us today!)

First, Luke 10:38-42 (TPT) states, "As Jesus and the disciples continued on their journey, they came to a village where a woman welcomed Jesus into her home. Her name was Martha and she had a sister named Mary. Mary sat down attentively before the Master, absorbing every revelation he shared. But Martha became exasperated with finishing the numerous household chores in preparation for her guests, so she interrupted Jesus and said, 'Lord, don't you think it's unfair that my sister left me to do all the work by myself? You should tell her to get up and help me.' The Lord answered her, 'Martha, my beloved Martha. Why are you upset and troubled, pulled away by all these many distractions? Mary has discovered the one thing most important by choosing to sit at my feet. She is undistracted, and I won't take this privilege from her.'"

Can you imagine? You're hosting an event in your home with a Special Guest who's going to say a few words to everyone. Your co-host, who is also your housemate, decides rather than help you with normal hosting responsibilities (greeting guests, offering refreshments, cooking, tidying, overseeing the crowd, making sure everyone has comfortable seating, knows where the restroom is, etc...) she's going to hunker down on the floor, right at the feet of your Special Guest, fixing her gaze on Him and soaking up every word He says. (I'll be honest—I'd be a bit miffed, too. We see you, Martha!) But instead of rebuking your co-host, He defends and commends her while being genuinely concerned about you and all your worries and hurries. In a subtle between-the-lines suggestion, He invites you to throw caution and social expectations to the wind and follow her example. Talk about a humility check and a contradictory call to adventure into the uncomfortable new territory of slowing down and even *relaxing*! But you can hear His deep care for you as He asks, "*My beloved… why, oh why are you so upset, troubled, pulled away (from Me) by all these distractions?*" You were giving these distractions something He so longed for—your nearness, your presence. Not just for Himself, though He delights greatly in your company, but because He knows what you *truly* need, what we all truly need. He longed for what would be best for you at that moment, which was to sit and soak up Life Himself.

Let's look at another example of Jesus slowing down the pace to the point of upsetting the norms, and in this case, seemingly unnecessarily to the point of being deemed "too late" by commonly expected standards. But as we find along the journey, "They will not be overdue a single day," as it says in Habakkuk 2:3 (TLB).

The second instance takes place in John 11:1-8 (HCSB). Essentially, Martha and Mary's dear brother Lazarus, who was a close friend of Jesus as well, became very sick—to the point of death. So his sisters sent a message to Jesus, "Lord, our brother Lazarus, the one you love, is very sick. Please come!" When He heard this, He said, "This sickness will not end in death for Lazarus, but will bring glory and praise to God." Here's the part that always confounds me: "Now Jesus loved Martha, her sister, and Lazarus. So when He heard that he was sick, He stayed two more days in the place where He was." Ahh! On the third day, He finally rallies his disciples, and they begin their travels to their friends in distress, Jesus knowing full well that Lazarus has already passed or "fallen asleep." He tells His disciples, "It's time that I go and awaken him." What an outlook, what a verse! He goes on to tell the disciples that this will give them a chance to see who He really is—to trust Him by what happens next.

When they finally arrived outside of the village where the sibling-friends lived, Lazarus had already been buried for four days. Mary rushes out to meet Jesus and cries out to him in her disappointment and grief, "My Lord, if only you had come sooner, my brother wouldn't have died. But I know that if you were to ask God for anything, he would do it for you." Jesus told her, "Your brother will rise and live." She replied, "Yes, I know he will rise with everyone else on resurrection day." Here's where it gets good—like His first tender moment to help Martha slow down and rise above the situation of the hosting scurry, Jesus offers her a more hopeful perspective once again, "Martha," Jesus said, "You don't have to wait until then. I *am* the Resurrection, and I am Life Eternal. Anyone who clings to me in faith, even though he dies, will live forever. And the one who lives by believing in me will never die. Do you believe this?" Then Martha replied, "Yes, Lord, I do! I've always believed that you are the Anointed One, the Son of God who has come into the world for us!"

Martha then goes to get her sister, and Mary then goes out to meet Jesus, who is "*lingering* outside the village" (TPT). Even his posture during such a pivotal, high stakes encounter, was recorded as a rhythm of rest. He could "linger" in such a moment because He fully trusted God was able to do "beyond all we could ask or imagine" (Ephesians 3:20, TPT), and He wasn't worried about the bleak looks of things. But despite having an emotional grip due to already knowing what would happen next, the thing that happens next is a beautiful pause for deep empathy, which I just love that He models making time for. He prioritizes His people, acknowledging the depth of loss they've endured, and focuses on being fully present with the grief of His friends. Rather than skip ahead to the next bar of music He already *knew* was coming, as glorious a moment as it would have been, His response was not, "Ladies, calm thyselves! I have the answer! Let's move right along to me raising your brother from the dead. Hurry up, let's go!" He takes the time even then, even with the solution in hand, to be present with them in their pain. By doing so, He lets them know they are seen and that they have time to fully be in that moment, acknowledging all of the pain and grief, sitting with their feelings. Jesus does NOT rush past or belittle big feelings. He welcomes them. He sits with us in them. *He feels them with us.* He takes the time.

Ready for this bar of a divinely beautiful moment?

Mary falls at His feet in tears, crying out, "Lord, if only you had been here, my brother would not have died." "When Jesus looked at Mary and saw her weeping at his feet, and all her friends who were with her grieving, *he shuddered with emotion and was deeply moved with tenderness and compassion.*" Moments later, this verse says: "Then tears streamed down Jesus' face." The story continues with Him asking Mary where her brother is buried, and they journey that direction, all the while still deeply grieving. "Then Jesus, *with intense emotions*, came to the tomb—a cave with a stone placed over its entrance."

In the next few verses (I highly recommend reading the whole story in John 11; it's one of my favorites), we see Jesus, at last, get to play the bar of music He's patiently been waiting to play; the one where He finally got to awaken His dear friend back to life through an astounding miracle that encouraged everyone who witnessed it, to believe in God.

Imagine that! You have a Best Friend who *could* do anything, be it walk through walls, teleport to you, or meet your need from afar. But instead of rushing to your side in your darkest hour, He waits, He lingers, and by all earthly concepts of time and life-or-death situations—He runs late. Very, very late. Too late. He *should* have hurried, you think. He could have prevented this gut-wrenching outcome and spared you this pain.

Yet somehow, because of who He is, He's right on time to accomplish something greater than prevention: He accomplishes restoration.

He makes everything right again and brings back what and who was lost by way of a miracle that fortifies not only your faith in His good heart for you but also has a ripple effect to encourage countless others for centuries after that instance. In the natural realm, it is so easy and natural to think narrow-mindedly. To not see beyond, limited from the possibilities of what could be, with Him. Trusting His pace and timing and turning our hearts toward adopting the ease and effortlessness through which He lived is one thing we'd actually do well to hasten toward.

He was, and still is today, one to stop everything. He makes the time, takes the detour, extends a hand, and gives a blessing, all while not sweating about it, putting Him behind, throwing off His schedule, or running late to the next obligation. Though time was a limited resource for Him, too, while here on earth, He still didn't operate by the world's ways of things. He lived from a higher view, remembering what we often forget about time—we do not own it. It originates from God, and what's gifted to us here is just that—a gift. But rather than being stingy with it from a place of scarcity or be misled into spinning His wheels thinking He could sway and control it, He lived with wisdom regarding time, and from a surrendered posture to God's all-knowing, overarching, superseding truth that God provides enough time for what actually needs to be tended to in a day.

We often miss that and try to cram too much, too many wants and well-intended goals, into the limits of what that day is actually meant to contain. Alternatively, we can take it for granted, perhaps frittering a day away on what does not need our time or attention at all, or at least not in the large quantities we may commit to a particular thing. But Jesus knew that the times and seasons are truly in God's hands and that it is only through a close relationship with Him that we will be able to discern what matters *most* in any given day or moment, to be able to give our attention to that which would have Him echoing what He commended Mary for, "you have chosen what is best, and it won't be taken away from you."

Origins

As we learned at the end of the above story, hurriedness, haste—and the sense of urgency that drives it—is often rooted in the panic of not-enough-ness. Fear. Anxiety. Scarcity.

And God knows, we've all been through some hard and hurtful experiences in our lives that have rightly warranted such responses. I hope you hear me when I say that there is endless, boundless compassion for that. So much room and space to name and grieve the seasons we've endured that may have as a result, taught us that we have to pick up the pace, fend for ourselves, trust few, rely on ourselves and so on, that may have contributed to our sense of hurriedness and unrest, a fear of slowing down, a worry over never having enough of a limited resource such as time.

Like a pendulum swinging back, it seems a generation of hoarders and workaholics followed the generation that went through The Great Depression. It makes sense—in a purely human sense, it really does.

But the thing is, we are not just human. From this world to the bodies we are in today and the limited resources like time that we are given while here are so very temporary; it's incredibly easy to forget that.

If that is where we stop—if the lessons we learned the hard and hurtful way that helped shape our hurried and worried pace, to our detriment, are what we allow to be our ceiling, we'll never see further than what we see in the physical, which may very well be limited resources that will never seem like enough.

But if we can hold in our heart-eyes to "fix our eyes not on what is seen, but what is unseen," we can burst right through the ceiling of the natural and remember all of the resources available to us by our birthright in Christ. When we hold to the truth that we have the entire wealth of the Kingdom of Heaven at the ready for us to draw from and a loving Heavenly Father who we can come before and ask for what we need, boldly and without hesitation—imagine what a different, more empowered, less worried, unhurried way we might live? Our paces are contagious and can influence those around us to either slow down or hurry ahead with us. I've found the most graceful pace will always carry the most weight, pulling us in the direction our soul was made for, like a flower toward the sunlight.

When I've been able to embrace the pace of grace, I watch with awe as the sense of hurriedness dissipates in the presence of a deep-seated trust in the remembrance of God's promises, which are part of my inheritance as His deeply loved and amply provided-for child. That allows me to focus on what's in front of me without racing back or jumping ahead but helps me remain steadily anchored in the present, where I find His moment-by-moment grace is always enough. As I've allowed Him to help me overcome my "default settings" I was partially born with and partially conditioned into, healing the hurriedness that comes from a sense of distrust and panic and slowing down the tempo to walk in step with Him, I've found time and again, His promises that speak to this struggle all prove true, and have been a constant source of encouragement in my journey to adopt a "pace of grace."

It's been through slowing down to His pace that the rest of the journey has become possible, as in my haste, I was rarely able to see and hear Him speak. At this slower and more present pace, I'm able to pause and pay attention to nuances throughout my days I'd have missed had I been living more hurriedly. It's through slowing down and learning to see as He sees and move as He moves that I've even had the time or attention span to receive breakthroughs and revelations that He knew I needed to be able to refute the lies I'd been living under with the truth He continued (and continues!) to reveal to me.

Part 3:
ENLIGHTENED
Uncovering the truth about some especially hindering lies

Grace > Sin

"To speak of sin without grace is to minimize our Savior."
                                          Nathan James[29]

"Remember this: sin will not conquer you, for God already has! You are not governed by law but governed by the reign of the grace of God."
                                          Romans 6:14, TPT

Missing the mark

"Father, forgive them! For they know not what they do." Those were His compassion-drenched words as Jesus hung on the cross, experiencing the full effects of sin.

Those words perfectly reflect the Father's heart toward humans in their sinfulness/brokenness, which is the part I think most people miss. I lacked the words for until He whispered that verse to my spirit as I wrestled with how to begin this weightier chapter. To me, His example in those excruciating moments is the bar that was set, to be the anchor to which we cling in the moments we are the most wronged by someone. To me, those are the same words we need to cry out on our own behalf when we are overwhelmed by the realization of our own failures.

29 James, Nathan. "Sermon on Grace." *Epoch Church*, 2017, https://www.epochchurch.org.

I wish that when we heard the word "sin," the next word that would come to mind is "compassion." Unfortunately, I think when we hear the word "sin," words that ring the opposite of compassion come to mind first. It still makes me cringe, like hearing the sound of an out-of-tune piano. I think this is because the majority of the time it's been used around or toward me, it's been to judge, condemn, guilt, or misdiagnose actions and situations. The way it's often used (more like misused) in Christian circles tends to imply that what someone did was willful, intentional, and knowingly wicked. While that can be the worst case, only God can truly weigh someone's heart and motives, so we remain inept at diagnosing someone's heart. At best, it's used when referring to an accidental offense or even a matter of differing opinion. So, using the same term to describe all three directions seems nonsensical, omitting room for nuance. It lacks awareness. It lacks understanding. It lacks grace. In truth, we cannot posture ourselves around sin the way Jesus did until we've understood grace. *That* connection is what was missing for the majority of my life.

After being falsely accused, berated, beaten, starved, humiliated, stabbed, pierced, and crucified—among other horrors—Jesus, of all people, would've had every right to correctly call out the sinful actions of His perpetrators in those moments, no matter the origin of their motives. Had He cried out even just accusations from the cross accusing them of their sin in His final moments of coherence, I might have believed that He was more concerned about sin itself, as many Christians seem to be preoccupied with. But looking closer at where His focus was placed instead, "Father, *forgive* them! *They don't know* what they're doing," had me pausing at the epiphany of what we've missed in this famed moment: He was focused on the "why" behind their harmful behavior, and the grace that would forgive and give them freedom from these offenses they didn't know they were doing. To behave as they were, He knew, they had to be shackled to fear, so very blind and in deep need. He saw sin as a prompt to compassion. We often see it and are prompted to repulsion. There is a sobering grief to be sown in the gap between how vastly different His posture and the common Christian posture toward sin. He made allowances for what they didn't know.

That is what we can be pretty poor at: making room for the "whys" behind our failures. Tuning into the heart, having compassion toward others and ourselves, and forgiving (giving ahead of time) that there's a blindness that needs sight in order to be made well. That is what gives heart to my belief that Jesus is far more concerned about our whole being's well-being—and that true sin, whether willful or accidental—is to be treated with compassion because it bubbles up from places inside ourselves we often can't see until harm has been caused. It's those places that initially only He can see—but calls us to turn inward and journey into Him—the places that need the most healing.

This is why, too, I believe the self-reflection and discovery prompted in therapy is aligned with Jesus' focus on helping us awaken to what we are still asleep to within ourselves, or "engaging with our stories," as therapist and podcaster Adam Young says.[30] Helping us *know* what we're doing—and *why* we're doing it—is absolutely key if we're to tend to the roots of harmful behaviors, and as psychology has proven (which supports the biblical concept), we cannot effectively heal apart from compassion.

All of this makes "sin" too small and flat of a word to encompass the emotional, mental, and spiritual work involved in understanding how our stories holistically shape up—from emotionally to neurologically and everywhere in between—that informs how

---

30 Young, Adam. *The Place We Find Ourselves,* March 2018-present, https://adamyoungcounseling.com/podcast/.

we engage with the world around us at present, successfully and through much failure. This brought me to a deeper look at the origin of the word. I love Addison Bevere's insight into the translation issue in his book *Saints*, where he elaborates on this point of ambiguity with the word for which our English language has just one (sin) used to describe the "many" Hebrew and Greek words that originally had different meanings, thereby "flattening the ancient words, losing important nuance." I love his elaboration on the issue:

> "The Greek word *hamartia* (translated 'sin' in Scripture) could have been used to mean anything from an involuntary mistake, to a serious offense against a god.

> This idea of sin is not as straightforward as we'd like to think, and that's probably another reason there is so much angst about it. Let's look at what the Greek and Hebrew words all have in common. In their commonality, we find the essence or central nature of sin.

> In their original language, **all the words translated 'sin' in Scripture convey the idea of missing a target**. Sometimes the target is clearly defined and understood, other times it isn't. But in either case, when the target is missed, there is a form of loss."[31]

And in the face of loss caused by missing the mark, time and again, Jesus models compassion, not condemnation. No matter how much we might want to once we realize that we, or someone else, missed the mark—once we're grieving the loss caused—we often scramble to try to redeem it ourselves, and if we can't, we blame and accuse in an attempt to alleviate the pain. But the truth is that none of us can erase or undo what's been done, any more than we can pour spilled milk back in the jug from the puddle on the floor where it landed. God knew this, and He has *already* cleaned up the

---

31   Bevere, Addison D. *Saints: Becoming More than "Christians."* Revell, 2020. Emphasis added.

spill *for* us in the God-amazing way only He can.

We can set the double roll of paper towels down. He has already cleaned up past and future milk spills. He knows that we can't. He doesn't ask us to fix it because He already did. He reminds us who we are because of who He is and what He's already done on our behalf. His calls such as to *"repent"* or to *"go and sin no more"* are *not* condemnations as we've often heard them—they were always the most hope-saturated and faith-filled *invitations* to *rise to who we really are.* To live aligned with the truth of our identity: co-heirs with Christ. As divine royalty. As perfectly loved and abundantly cared-for sons and daughters of a king. Of *the* King.

That is the truth we should be dwelling on surrounding "sin." Remembrance of how He resolved this issue on our behalf should set us free to start associating it with words like "compassion" and "redemption" rather than being stuck in the word associations we so often do. But it's hard to change the narrative around "sin" when many of us have grown up being taught to fear it.

Idolization & Weaponization

Among the anxiety-inducing, misleading messages surrounding sin ingrained in me from a young age was one that went something like this: "Sin is fun, sin is desirable, you'll want to sin, but you'll have to try very, very hard not to even though you'll always want to. That sinful nature, you know, gosh darn it. Hard to escape! Wish there was something we could do about it, but we can't." I remember being afraid of sin and everything surrounding it. Afraid of what it meant, afraid of what to do should I have the chance to participate in it—whatever the supposedly so-appealing temptation would have been. Afraid of giving in to it, afraid of never being free of "it"… whatever this, *it* even was.

As Matt McMillen often says in his man-made-religion-busting videos, "You don't *want* to sin. *They* make you *think* you want to sin because they call you a 'sinner' and then tell you not to sin. It makes sense if you don't think about it!"[32] (Ha!) And for the longest time, it seemed as though everyone around me lived as though Jesus had actually said, "It's not quite finished" rather than "It is finished." I didn't know at the time what I was functioning in (more like dysfunctioning in), but in this way of life, I was still living under the "letter of the law." And as Paul shares in 2 Corinthians 3:6 (TPT), "The letter (of the law) kills, but the Spirit pours out life."

Christians can be great at making an idol out of sin itself without even realizing it and not so great at understanding or explaining what even classifies as "sin," as we explored in the previous section. Even things that would fall under the category appropriately, they hyperfocus on avoiding so much that they seem to fail at fixating on the bigger picture. Which is that because of Christ's successful, *finished* work on the cross, sin should take a back seat when it comes to our focus.

Sin has way too much power credited to it. I may get flack for saying so, but the truth is, sadly, that many lovers of Jesus are still fearers of sin and have yet to experience true freedom from perhaps the sin they're actually blind to: *choosing to live in fear of sin itself.* The irony, beyond that being completely unnecessary thanks to Jesus's complete success at the cross, is that many do not even know how exactly to define this thing they live in fear of. Talk about a real boogie monster!

The good news is that there is a simple way to weigh whether or not something is deemed "sinful." The more challenging news is—it encompasses lots more than even the refereeing Christians

---

32 McMillen, Matt. "mattmcmillenministries.com." *Matt McMillen Ministries*, 4 Sept. 2024, mattmcmillenministries.com/.

who seem to enjoy pointing out others' shortcomings may want to admit. But Romans 14:23b (TPT) gives us a good guide by which to measure our thoughts, actions, motives, etc.:

> "For anything we do that doesn't spring from faith is, by definition, sinful."

There you have it, folks! So any time we make a decision from a place of fear, act unlovingly towards another, or doubt God's promises (there's that "sin" we so easily fall into), we're missing the mark.

The even better news that Psalm 139:5 so reassuringly reminds us is that He has already gone ahead of each of us into our futures and followed behind us to "spare me from the harm of my past" (TPT). He's taken care of it, so that we don't need to waste even a moment more dwelling on it. We can leave behind our "former identity," as Romans 13:14 puts it, but as the verse contrasts, rather be "fully immersed into the Lord Jesus." How amazing is that?

Don't give sin more air time in the program of your life than it deserves. Sin is a pebble to be stepped on or over in light of the vast landscape of our lives. While it can temporarily hold captive those who yield to it or willingly participate in it, while it's grievous to fall short and miss out on the best for us, it is not a permanent destination—we can choose life at any moment. Sin is powerless to have the final say, powerless to name or define us—because we have already been claimed and named by our Father.

To fixate on missing the mark makes a bit of a performance-based perfectionist out of us, which falls short of who we actually are. To fixate on sin, one must take their eyes off of Jesus. You'd go cross-eyed trying to focus on both due to the vast distance between the two. Our eyes weren't made to go in two opposite directions; rather, a singular focus held in our gaze. Christians need to realize this and choose whom they will serve—Jesus, who is Grace embodied, or their fear of mark-missing.

You are perfectly and wonderfully made. Let's not forget that. But we still face genuine mistakes, human error, and cause accidental harm in addition to the less common cognitive mark-missing. When we're legalistic about perfection, we'll extend little to no grace; instead, we extend harsh judgements toward ourselves and others that weigh and hinder our hearts—and theirs.

Here's a better way to understand this dichotomy:

Having a mean thought toward someone = being human.

Acting on a mean thought toward someone = sin/harm.

Experiencing normal human emotions such as anger, fear, and attraction = being human.

Channeling those emotions in unhealthy ways (for example, hurting someone with those emotions) = sin/harm.

The problem with generally mis-categorizing our humanness as "sinfulness" is it condemns the good way God made us. It has caused us to experience shame and feel condemned (both deception, as there is no condemnation in Christ Jesus), usually at the hands of accusations of others.

Let's take the emotional spectrum, for example:

Anger can be used for good, to inform that injustice has occurred and motivate someone to help implement changes toward what is right and good. Anger can also be used for harm, to inflict pain on someone who is perhaps the trigger to your anger in an attempt to appease the anger.

Fear can be listened to in order to inform steps toward safety, therefore motivating someone to help protect what is right and good. Fear can also be listened to in a harmful way, which, when yielded to, can dominate someone's life to the point they live IN fear and are often paralyzed from taking the next steps toward something good that God has for them.

Anytime we give an emotion God's place in our life, that is, giving more time, attention, or ear to it than we do to God—it can become idolatry, which is an actual sin. So it's not the emotions themselves, but rather *what we do with* the information they give us, that determines if our choices are for the best or cause harm (miss the mark).

Another way sin is misused is when what's actually occurring is a difference of conviction or opinion. This is what Paul addresses in 1 Corinthians 10 when he talks about each person adhering to their own conscience when it comes to matters of partaking in or abstaining from various food and drink. I'm sure, according to the understanding and convictions of some, the fact that I enjoy alcoholic beverages would fall under the "sin" category. I don't believe consuming alcohol is a sin, and I believe there's plenty of scriptural evidence to support that it's a gift to be enjoyed in moderation. But as long as I am not abusing and misusing the gift, which would cause harm to myself and to others, I am living according to my conscience on that matter of personal opinion.

Because of the ambiguity of the word as we know it in English and the tones it takes through various misuse and abuses of it woven into our stories, it can feel like a gray area. Even the times it is clear we are in the wrong, how we arrived there might be the gray part we aren't sure how to make sense of. I believe this is another reason it is deeply important we learn to engage with our origin stories—to help light the path to how we arrived at certain crossroads we wish we hadn't and be able to build new roads to never venture back to dangerous places again.

You may have your own story that comes to mind of what I'm talking about. To put context to it, I'll take you on my most vulnerable, clear mark-missing, hard story.

Before Grace

When I think back to the "stone ages" of my life, I see a rocky, barren, monochromatic gray landscape. This was my inner landscape before grace—everything was hard. Dry. I was always afraid of something or someone. More than anything, afraid of messing up—of missing the mark in any area of life. High-control religion, which by nature is void of grace, makes petrified and often prideful perfectionists out of us. It never ends well in this land.

Nevertheless, it's the land many of us, myself included, have journeyed through before awakening to the sweet, sunlit kiss of grace. In my mid 20s I was unknowingly in this oppressive era of my life before coming to understand and experience grace in a visceral way. As the saying goes, it had to get worse before it got better.

On my way to my own resurrection, I was unknowingly beginning a descent into emotional, relational, and spiritual death unlike anything I'd ever experienced. It wasn't a physical near-death experience but something that left me feeling like a shell of myself, living a zombie-like existence. Unaware of the mind-body-spirit connection and completely ignorant to the concept of mental health, emotional safety, and relational boundaries, I was on my way to becoming trapped in a cycle of depression and unhealthy coping mechanisms—all while berating myself like I'd learned to with the toxic works-based and grace-absent mindset that tragically permeated every aspect of my life at the time.

Before being fully submerged in this foreign darkness, I had a moment of unprecedented bravery. After several years of ongoing harmful behavioral patterns in my marriage at the time that were a constant source of distress to me, and following many attempts at confronting them, I approached my then-husband, gingerly suggesting we might benefit from marriage counseling. My courageous suggestion was met with a disbelieving laugh and invalidation that denied we had "marriage problems." I now have compassion for the delusion my now ex-husband seemed to be under at the time because on some level up to that point, it seemed I, too, had believed we were above having "issues" that couldn't be solved by trusting Jesus more. (Thanks, spiritual bypassing.)

But being shut down in my moment of brave honesty and without the confidence to push back through all of the subservient, submissive wife training thanks to the religious teachings I grew up under—I tried to "trust" and let it go. This left me feeling cornered in a place of quiet panic. I thought I was experiencing something but was told that wasn't the case. I reached out for support and was told it wasn't needed. Not knowing what to do, my nervous system quietly slipped from fight to freeze (though I was unaware of this and other would-have-been-helpful terminology at the time, of course).

Not long after that, I slipped into a season of denial, grief, and emotional numbness. Though physically present, I became increasingly "checked out" from my marriage and, in general, oblivious to the fact that this was a common subconscious response to emotional dysfunction or unsafety when your nervous system tries to dissociate in an attempt to protect you from a seemingly helpless situation.

I'm still not sure whether it is more accurate to say this happened in the midst of the above or as a result of it, but nonetheless, I soon became alarmed to find myself feeling attracted to other men—something I didn't know could be a natural occurrence even in healthy relationships. I thought there must have been something deeply wrong with me.

I felt immense shame and fear of my feelings, which, looking back, is no surprise considering how I was raised in environments that overall seemed to encourage the dismissal of feelings. Not only was I unable to shake the despair over my inability to fix my marriage, but it was further compounded by the new terror that arose inside of me regarding these unwanted feelings of attraction. Even more afraid of confiding in my husband for fear of my vulnerability being used against me, I bottled up these emotions. I was trying my best to navigate it all, while sinking deeper into isolation.

The more I tried to suppress my feelings, the more they festered, leading me further into what I didn't realize at the time was actually depression. The emotional and physical toll of my inner turmoil manifested as daily crying spells, which I quietly hid from everyone but my dogs. I was crying every day in secret, completely unaware that it could be a tell-tale sign of depression, yet concerned that this didn't seem normal or okay. I remember Googling questions like "Does it hurt your eyes to cry every day?" The emotional pain was unlike anything I'd experienced up to that point in my life or since.

After several months in this dark and depressed state, something interrupted my daily pattern of secret tear-fests: someone started paying attention to me. Too naive to recognize the red flags at first, I only focused on the fact that when this person spoke to me—seeming to take a genuine interest in my life with deep and thoughtful questions—I didn't cry that day. It felt like a lifeline, and I began to rely on their attention to feel okay. While I initially saw them as a friend, their view of me and my own emotional reliance on them became inexplicably twisted.

While I'd started to acknowledge my own discomfort and confront this person with what I was beginning to realize about emotional boundaries that had been crossed in what seemed to be increasingly inappropriate conversations, I still didn't have the words for it. All I knew was that I was in over my head, I didn't want to offend or hurt anyone, but I didn't want to go back to crying every day. I realize now that what further complicated me "coming to" sooner was battling my inner "good girl" at the same time, who'd been indoctrinated through religious teachings at such a young age that prioritized others above self and thus, trying to tiptoe around not offending, accusing, or hurting someone's feelings—even someone who did not have my best interest at heart. I found it nearly impossible to stand up to others—men especially, thanks to my patriarchal conditioning—and would cave under the guilt trips and silent treatments when I'd try to pull away emotionally, returning to try to smooth things over. Thus, I remained bound by fear of man even as I contemplated how to get out of the deep end of whatever this toxic friendship had evolved into.

It wasn't until my husband became suspicious of my increasingly detached behavior toward him that, just as I'd requested earlier that year, we finally ended up in marriage counseling—but now, for even more pressing and depressing reasons.

At first, the counselor listened to my husband unleash his feelings and accusations of me being "involved" with someone else. I felt myself sinking into the sofa, as far away from him as I could be on the other side. I felt misunderstood and enraged at the hypocrisy that, of course, *now*, he wanted to be here—when I'd so desperately wanted to long before that. It felt to me as though he waited until he thought he had something against me to finally make it a priority.

I was surprised by the way she validated his concerns while, at the same time, stood up for me. I'd seemed to fail so greatly at the times I'd tried to stand up for myself, and no one had ever stood up *for* me when I had taken part in the wrong. She seemed more concerned with getting to the root of *why* I'd ended up here, missing the mark as I had. For the first time in this situation, I felt seen, believed, and advocated for—while still knowing I wasn't in the right. It was… otherworldly. What *was* that? It gave me a spark of hope, of relief. Maybe someone could help light the way back out of the darkness I'd descended into.

I remember her communicating that while it was good he was finally realizing and admitting fault for the issues I'd tried to address in the years preceding this moment, the fact that I had been chronically dismissed, and the confusion and disconnect between what I was experiencing and what I was being told I was experiencing, had primed me for this point of crisis and compromise. She showed kindness and compassion toward the both of us, validated both of our grievances caused by the other, and held us both accountable for the areas we each needed to address. She exhibited grace and truth like I'd never known it before.

Grace, in any form, was so foreign to me at the time that I didn't know what to call it. But the way she responded to us both at that first meeting I could only liken to the faint remembrance of the feeling of wonder I'd experienced upon reading the story of Jesus intervening to mediate between the woman who was about to be stoned and her accusers who were put back in their place by Jesus with the words, "He who is without sin, cast the first stone."

It was through her gentle prompting and helpful guidance that the mutation of a relationship I'd somehow gotten involved in started to come to light in my own eyes, awakening me from the disillusioned stupor I'd sunk into. She handed me a sheet of paper that read much like a checklist to evaluate relationships and determine if they were forming into something unhealthy and inappropriate. My heart sank as my eyes opened. I realized with horror and despair that many of the items on the list sounded alarmingly similar to this twisted situation I was trying, but failing, to navigate. I felt sick to my stomach—my body weighed down by the truth my mind was beginning to grasp. Through nauseated deep breaths and hot, watery eyes, I made out more words on the page that these resonating symptoms all pointed to: "chemical reaction" and "emotional affair" struck me like a blow, knocking the wind out of my whole being.

I could have vomited right there on that wise old owl of a counselor's couch. "*This isn't me,*" I thought—"*how could this be me?*" No matter how many issues my marriage had, *this* was not who I was. No matter what other issues were present, no spouse deserved betrayal, accidentally or purposefully. *How could I have let this happen?* It felt like an out-of-body experience as I suddenly saw myself drowning in the deep end, despite all my best intentions with the foggiest memory as to how I'd arrived there. We left that joint session with her tasking me with a decision to make: either end whatever this "thing" had become or end my marriage. Despite the grievances against me leading up to my own failure, I was not about to become a person who ended something as serious as a marriage because of another person.

Tremendous Grace

Seeing my mistakes so clearly was excruciatingly painful and dreadfully disheartening. I had always prided myself on perfectionism, mistakenly believing that a spotless record and straight A's made me worthy of love and value. I operated under a law I hadn't even realized I was following: if you break it, you pay for it. If you can't pay for it, you suffer for it. The concept of "grace" applied was so foreign to me then. I was determined to face the music, to fix everything, even while trying to untangle what was truly my fault or the fault of another I'd allowed to go too far, lost in my own clouded, depressive state.

I couldn't bear the thought of having tarnished my record as a "good girl." I felt humiliated and ashamed, expecting more of myself. In a spirit of self-reliance, I was ready to put myself through a self-imposed purgatory, trying to earn my way back. But before I could completely exhaust myself trying to fix what only God could, I encountered God's grace in a way that changed my understanding of everything. Words fail to describe the experience, but Ephesians 1:5 in The Passion Translation captures it well as "his tremendous love that cascades over us would glorify his grace."

After being presented with a choice at that crossroads of the first meeting with the counselor, I truly did not know what I should do. I was at the lowest point of my life, and as if the embarrassment and shame of recent realizations wasn't enough for me to want to run away and hide, I was still desperately miserable at home and did not trust the man I was married to.

I considered denying my faith if that's what it took to be able to freely walk out on my marriage, which is, at the time, what I thought it would have required. I was still under the delusions that many Christians remain under: a belief that God hates divorce more than the treachery done to those who ultimately end up seeking it as a means to permanently draw boundaries that protect their safety and/or sanity.

But at that conflicting moment in time, a still small voice inside me prompted, *"You probably want to be sure you're doing the right thing before making a permanent decision that will change your life, right?"* I countered, *"But it looks like there's no one right way; I have to choose the best path for myself."* The Voice replied, *"For so long, you've believed My Word is truth—why did you stop reading it? It might be useful now."*

I realized that I had grown tired of the legalistic act of reading my Bible just for the sake of it, having seen hypocrites do the same. I decided I would only read when genuinely inspired, but that feeling rarely came. The Voice continued, *"While it's admirable that you don't want to be a hypocrite, you've missed out on years of times I wanted to speak to you. I long to encourage your heart and give you direction. I've been waiting for you to come back. You're always welcome with Me."*

After reasoning with God, I decided I couldn't, in good conscience, wreck so many lives out of sheer exhaustion without first seeing if He would guide me. I confined myself to the guest bedroom one morning, giving God a last shot, telling Him He'd better speak now or forever hold His peace.

And speak, He did.

I was, and remain to this day, absolutely astounded by this encounter with God that changed the trajectory of my life.

I didn't come out of that room until six hours later. I was shocked to realize this much time had passed, as it felt like only one hour to me. It was the strangest phenomenon of time standing still as though I'd entered Narnia through a portal in that guest room. I spent those hours fiercely tearing through my Bible, desperate to find life, truth, and guidance if it was there to be found. And found, it was.

I cried out of frustration, shame, and self-loathing. I no longer recognized who I had become—selfish, bitter, and cold. I wrestled with God from deep within my soul, feeling torn between good and evil, light and dark. Hebrews 4:12 talks about the Word of God being alive and active, dividing soul and spirit, and searching out the motives of our hearts and thoughts. It was true. That was exactly what I was experiencing.

The words I was reading were jumping off the page and resonating in my spirit like I'd never known, and it was somehow sifting through the story, dividing truth from lies, and revealing what had previously eluded me. It felt like a light beaming through the fog of my disillusioned, wounded heart. Words in the Bible seemed to light up, connecting like a magnet to my aching soul. Even verses I had read before but never fully grasped came alive. I highlighted everything that stood out to me, red ink now marking many previously pristine pages of my Bible. I could barely keep up underlining everything at the speed at which it was being illuminated. After six hours, my Bible was bleeding, this red ink highlighting truth across pages made from a tree—a sobering picture of "the Way, the Truth, and the Life" poured out for me, also bleeding across a tree.

I saw everything clearly for the first time, crying tears of horror and tears of relief. I was terrified of how close I had come to making irreversible decisions from that dark and desperate place, which at the time would have been for all the wrong reasons. I felt tricked, deceived by my own justifications. Everything I was reading shifted my focus from striving and proving to receiving. To simply surrender and let Him truly be the Lord of my life in a moment when I'd never felt so out of my depth to navigate the way forward was a sweet relief.

When I finally grasped that I could never suffer or self-condemn my way to making up for choices I regret and that "penance" (which we'll see below is so often confused with "*repentance*") was never what God was asking of me in the first place, I began to sink into the incredible grace that "cascades over me." Now, like Paul in 1 Timothy 1:13-14 (TPT), I can testify that "mercy kissed me... even though... I was ignorant and didn't know what I was doing. I was flooded with such incredible grace... full of faith and love for Jesus."

Embodied Grace

Still dazed by the life-changing outpouring of grace I had just experienced, I realized it might not stop there. If this invisible, supernatural Being would show up and speak to me for hours, changing my mind when I was stubborn, desperate, and thought to be beyond reach—maybe He would keep showing up. Maybe He was good for His word, unlike so many others in my life then. Perhaps He was worth trusting, and maybe He could save me—not by freeing me from my problems, but by sheltering me as I walked through and out of them, partnering with Him in the art of repair. Though the thought terrified me, I felt a steady resolve that He would be faithful to show me the way through, one day at a time, if I kept showing up.

In the months following, my "showing up" and spending time with Him was sporadic. But as He continued to reveal layers of my heart, showing me my deep need for His grace, wisdom, and direction, I began to show up daily. I decided to commit fully—to less noise and distractions, clearing time and space to "put Him first." For my visual learner's sake, I made it visible and actual: I got up every day and spent time with Him in His Word before touching my phone or opening my laptop, filling myself with His truth to navigate the day.

Each time I showed up, He answered my questions through His Word. Most mornings, I was brought to tears by new truths, humbled by His impossible love that hadn't given up on me despite my recent encounters with the worst version of myself I'd let myself become. My time with Him grew richer, sweeter, and more healing, and I began to thirst for it each day like I'd never thirsted for anything before. I can only describe it as a supernatural empowerment, opening my eyes to spiritual realities and allowing me to see and experience God like never before.

Verses like "All you thirsty ones, come to me! Come to me and drink! Believe in me so that rivers of living water will burst out from within you, flowing from your innermost being…" (John 7:37b-38a TPT) suddenly made sense.

It felt like I couldn't survive a day without that time with Him. He never failed to fill me with healing, hope, truth, wisdom, and insights. The verses about "daily bread" made sense, too. I realized that the byproduct of my time with Him was "bearing fruit" of the Spirit: I was becoming kinder, I found it easier to forgive, and anger toward those who'd harmed me turned to compassion and a fierce desire for them to be rescued from their self-made prisons, just as I had been.

Though my life was far from figured out, I had a quiet and steady peace and an unspeakable joy that welled up from inside me—not because my circumstances were ideal, but because I was smitten with this new Lover of my Soul, this One who could be trusted and who gently carried me through and showed me the way to go, choice by choice, day by day, as I tried to learn about Him and live as He lived. He was all the things He promised and more. He showed up exactly as He said He would, keeping no record of wrongs, sheltering the weary, and fighting for the defenseless. He was the one sure thing in my life, and I realized He was what I needed and had been missing all along.

I cannot express all the ways this consistent time with Jesus began to change me from the inside out into a renewed person. Friends noticed the change in me, saying I was "shiny," like a light was coming through me. Verses like "let your light shine before men" suddenly made sense. I was on fire with lightbulb moments, in the beginning of a "honeymoon phase" of my relationship with the Lord, which would continue unfolding in new depths and dimensions in the following years. Most people in my life at the time did not "get" what I was experiencing. They could tell everything was different—but it was almost foreign, as though they didn't know what to make of it. In ways, it felt like, spiritually, I was awake and running on six cups of coffee while others around me still slept soundly.

Maybe it's a foreign concept to you, too, like it was to me back in the BG (before grace) age of my life. Maybe you haven't had the greatest examples of what grace looks and feels like when extended to you or from you to others. Thankfully, even when we've been failed by systems and individuals around us, we don't have to look far to find stories of grace embodied in Jesus.

His compassionate approach toward those who had missed the mark and were being marred by the stones of shame and condemnation society threw at them is a vivid display of Romans 2:4 (HCSB): "God's kindness is intended to lead *you to* repentance." But that word repentance—that alone has been the source of such confusion among Christians! Like the word "sin," "repentance" has often been misused, burdening people with guilt and shame. This heavy interpretation of repentance has caused many, myself included, to view it as synonymous with proving one's remorse and paying "penance" for past mistakes. In contrast, when Scripture speaks of a "godly grief [that] produces repentance" (2 Corinthians 7:10), it's emphasizing a transformative, redemptive process rather than one rooted in self-condemnation.

Here's where I think we went wrong: the original Greek word often translated as "repentance" is "metanoia," which actually means "a change of mind." Unfortunately, the Latin Vulgate influenced many English translations, leading to a focus on "penitence" or acts of penance, which implies a need for self-mortification to atone for sin. You can almost smell the works-based ingredients in it. Yuck.

In her insightful blog, *Here's the Joy*, author Rebecca Davis shares more on the background of the aforementioned poor translation. During his study of the Latin translation, Martin Luther questioned whether John the Baptist's call to "do penance" truly reflected the original intent of the Greek text. He discovered that "metanoia" didn't involve acts of piety but rather a fundamental change of mind and heart.[33] Davis has become one of my favorite authors on the subject, further highlighting in book four of her *Untwisting Scriptures*[34] book series how this mistranslation has led to much confusion. She refers to another expert on the topic— Treadwell Walden, author of *The Great Meaning of Metanoia*—who lamented the replacement of "metanoia" with terms that convey the notion of penitence. Walden argues that "metanoia" represents a profound transformation—a change in mind, heart, and life—that the English term "repentance" fails to capture. Walden further explains that "metanoia" was intended to be an "upward call of God," a message of hope and transformation. Unlike the burden of penitence—which demands suffering for wrongdoing—"metanoia" is about allowing God's grace to bring about a deep, internal change, leading to a transformation of one's entire being.[35]

Isaiah 55:1 (NIV) invites us to "come, all you who are thirsty, come to the waters," offering God's grace freely. This reflects the true meaning of "metanoia"—a hopeful, grace-filled invitation to transformation. Davis encourages us to reinterpret passages like Acts 26:20 not as demands for deeds but as calls to embrace a new way of thinking and being, producing the 'fruit consistent with repentance.' This is what we should seek in ourselves and in those who have hurt us: genuine evidence of a changed mind, heart, and

33 Davis, Rebecca. "Why 'Metanoia' Is So Much Greater Than 'Repentance'—And Why That's Important." *Here's the Joy*, 1 Oct. 2023, heresthejoy.com/2022/02/why-metanoia-is-so-much-greater-than-repentance-and-why-thats-important/.

34 Davis, Rebecca.. *Untwisting Scriptures to Find Freedom and Joy in Jesus Christ. Book 4, Wolves, Hypocrisy, Sin Leveling, & Righteousness.* New Morning Press, 2022.

35 Walden, Treadwell. *The Great Meaning of Metanoia.* Thomas Whittaker, 1896.

way of life. True metanoia isn't just lip service; it's a deep change that brings about transformation, hope, and new life. That's what He came for: "I came that they may have life and have it in abundance"(John 10:10).

I'm sorry that so many have treated you and me as though it were otherwise. As though we had to claw our way back into their good graces with humiliation and self-flagellation to prove our commitment to make up for our failures by being stripped of dignity. That is not grace. That is punishment, works-based, letter of the law living. It's beyond unnecessary—it's cruel and opposes Jesus' way. Because grace embodied doesn't humiliate people; He always protects their dignity. John 8:3-11 is my favorite illustration of this truth:

> Then in the middle of his teaching, the religious scholars and Pharisees... brought a woman who had been caught in the act of committing adultery and made her stand in the middle of everyone. Then they said to Jesus, 'Teacher, we caught this woman in the very act of adultery. Doesn't Moses' law command us to stone to death a woman like this? Tell us, what do you say we should do with her?'

This is my favorite part, a Jesus "mic drop" moment:

> Angry, they kept insisting he answer their question, so Jesus stood up and looked at them and said, 'Let's have the man who has never had a sinful desire throw the first stone at her.' And then he bent over again and wrote some more words in the dust... Her accusers slowly left the crowd one at a time, beginning with the oldest to the youngest, with a convicted conscience. Until finally, Jesus was left alone with the woman... He stood back up and said to her, 'Dear woman, where are your accusers? Is there no one here to condemn you?'... She replied, 'I see no one, Lord.'

> Jesus said, 'Then I certainly don't condemn you either. Go, and from now on, be free from a life of sin.'
>
> John 8:7, TPT

Go and be free from a life of sin. What words! What a commissioning, completely void of condemnation, completely saturated with the heralding of freedom. Grace is a cease-fire call—a line in the sand. Guilt will never produce what grace will because Christ Himself is Grace, embodied. I was awestruck that I had now encountered Him, amazed at the profound impact it was having on my life.

The Grip of Grace

One of the greatest gifts that a wise old counselor gave me back in my darkest days—when I felt trapped by death and swallowed by shame on her office sofa—was a practical understanding of how grace worked on my behalf. She repeatedly emphasized, to penetrate my penance-based mindset, that after a grave mistake, what matters most is turning around—'metanoia'—and the long-term fruit that testifies to transformation. She explained that true repentance is not about confessing every mistake to the world but about genuinely turning from harm and moving forward in grace. She also warned against sharing my deepest failures with emotionally unsafe people who might use them against me.

I tried to follow her advice, but even with only a few people aware of my regrets, rumors still spread. Others would approach me with "the whole story" they had heard, which was often distorted like a game of Telephone. This filled me with shame and the urge to explain myself. I've learned the hard way not to oblige when others want to poke and pry. I hope you, too, know that you do not owe others your stories, nor do you need to trade in painful pieces in an effort to satisfy their curiosity or to buy their "good graces". Good graces, by definition, can only be freely given.

Over time, I learned a harsh truth: no matter how much "fruit consistent with repentance" appeared in my life, and even though Jesus offered me forgiveness once and for all, some people would never allow me to move past my mistakes. They would continue to judge me by my worst moments, using them against me as a permanent record.

While Jesus offers grace and the freedom to move forward, the world—especially some Christians—often tries to trap us in our past. This is the tragedy of a world that knows little of the transformative, liberating grace Christ paid for. While it's hurtful when others meet us with judgement rather than grace, may we come to embrace it as a reflection of their lack of understanding rather than an accurate assessment of our heart, taking the opportunity to extend grace to them instead—forgiving them, because they just do not understand what they're doing, sadly remaining in the dark to the way of Grace.

No matter where you've been, what you've done, what you've allowed, who you hurt or how you were hurt, or who now holds it against you: it is no match for the powerful grip of grace that now holds you and me, my friend. I wish more Christians woke up daily remembering how securely they are held in grace as contrasted so clearly in Romans 5:17b:

> "Death once held us in its grip, and by the blunder of one man, death reigned as king over humanity. But now, how much more are we held in the grip of grace and continue reigning as kings in life, enjoying our regal freedom through the gift of perfect righteousness in the one and only Jesus, the Messiah!" (TPT).

God meets us in our messes, often in the most impactful ways where He otherwise wouldn't have had our full attention. He is the Author of your story, the Artist of your life, and He is known for making beauty out of ashes. Never be afraid to look up, for it is only ever enemies of your soul who would have you look down and wallow in shame and despair that is no longer assigned to your account. Look up as an act of defiance to the darkness that dares to try and keep you in its grasp. I promise you, you will be met in the warming light of His gaze and held in His strong grace-grip. Contrary to the world's system, there are no hoops to jump through first, no prerequisites to be met, no degree of suffering, pain, or proving to be descended to first. For the humble heart and "metanoia" changed mind, there is nothing left for you but grace, and anyone who tells you differently is tragically misinformed.

I've heard the argument against some being "too grace-focused," which I'll summarize as: they seem concerned that if we partake of "too much" grace, enjoy it too much, or become too reliant on it, it makes us complacent towards sin, and we'll take advantage of it and use it as a pass to sin. To those who hold this concern, I would counter with my own concern that if this is their take on it, then perhaps they've yet to truly accept God's grace and let it be fully unleashed in their heart. Because the way grace works is not to produce behavior modification, but it goes after so much more on a deeply heart-transformative and life-motivation level.

Grace will give you new heart-eyes to see as He sees, align your heart to want what He wants, and empower you to live out of an overflow of thankfulness precisely FOR this unmerited favor now cascading over your life that you've done absolutely nothing to deserve. You cherish it, treasure it, and live empowered because of it. A byproduct of being deeply affected by grace is like Romans 6:6 (NLT) says, "We are no longer slaves to sin." There is no such thing as too much grace.

He's been waiting for you to lift your head, open your eyes, and step into the free-falling, cleansing, refreshing, freeing grace. It was bought and paid for, reserved with your name on it thousands of years ago for you to partake of, perhaps in this very moment.

Grace washes over you and fills up everything from the gaping gaps to the small crevices you didn't even know were there in your life. It takes you by surprise and leaves you feeling a mix of anything on the emotional spectrum, from deeply humbled to over-the-moon overjoyed. Like having a late fee waived, a ticket removed from your driving record, being unexpectedly handed a week off of work, or having charges dropped and being released from prison—truly receiving the news that grace has already been credited to your account feels almost too good to be true. It's nonsensical by the world's standards—which, so often it is those "out of this world" concepts that make perfect sense in the Heavenly realm.

I still breathe a sigh of comforting relief when I read Isaiah 54:4a (TPT), "Do not fear, for your shame is no more. Do not be embarrassed, for you will not be disgraced." To me, it might as well conclude with, "You will be *graced*." So consider yourself "graced." Whatever comes against and contradicts that is deception.

Let yourself be graced like this, my friends. He's taken away all shame and all need to earn or prove anything. The hardest part for me was to believe that something that sounded too good to be true was completely, wonderfully true!

Chapter 8

Faith > Fear

"Do not yield to fear, for I am always near. Never turn your gaze from me, for I am your faithful God. I will infuse you with my strength and help you in every situation. I will hold you firmly with my victorious right hand.'"

Isaiah 41:10, TPT

(my life verse)

Fear

If you came across an old love letter from someone you knew of but didn't know well, you might find phrases that the intended recipient would understand—inside jokes, abbreviations, and references to specific moments or memories. Without knowing the people involved in that correspondence—their heart, their sense of humor, their intentions—it would be easy to take things out of context.

Text messages can leave so much room for different interpretations without being able to see someone's face, read their body language, and hear their tone, which helps give meaning and context to what they're saying (thank you for helping us resolve some of this, emojis!). In the same way, reading the Bible apart from knowing the sound of His voice (which becomes personal to you as He speaks to us all uniquely!) and the way in which He moves, it can be easy to misread, misunderstand, and take things differently than He intended them. If you read Scripture apart from an alive and active relationship with the Holy Spirit who illuminates and guides you through it, feeding you from it in real-time, you may be reading a history book at best and a rule book at worst. This was not His intent.

I think this happens often with the many instances across Scripture where it reads "don't fear" or "don't be afraid." I believe many of us have heard these admonitions in a rather harsh, commanding and corrective tone, rather than how I believe He actually intended it to be read. With how I've come to understand His heart toward us, I now hear it in His gentle and compassionate love, like this: *"Shh, it's alright, I've got you. You don't need to be afraid. Here, take My hand, I'm right here with you. I'll show you the next, best step."*

He doesn't say, "Do not *feel* fear." He created emotions for a good reason, as we explored in Chapter 3. They're our good and well-designed internal alarm system. He knows we'll all have reasons to experience very valid feelings of fear across our lives. So He certainly didn't mean, "Don't feel this emotion I created and gave you for good reason." Yet so many live feeling small and condemned when they experience "fear" at all, as though that must mean their faith isn't big enough to keep it at bay. On the contrary, being able to feel fear is a gift—it means that your nervous system and emotions are working—yay! But as you are in charge of what you do with the information fear gives you, fear itself does not have the final say over your life and decisions. So *it's what you do with fear that's at the heart of these calls to rise above fear.*

This is why I love The Passion Translation's description of the verse, differentiating that the call is to not *yield* to fear. To yield to something means to "surrender," "defer," or "give the right of way."

Other instances of this similar admonition across other translations read "do not *be* discouraged" and "do not *be* dismayed," as in, don't give in to, hunker down, embrace, and remain in. Because *being* is a state of *abiding* in. Of choosing to stay there. Of choosing to become the thing. In these verses, I hear the admonition as, "*Don't become something you're not; don't stay in a place you're meant to move through.*"

It makes much more sense that in love and detailed care for our well-being, He calls us not to surrender to or become fearful, as it's meant to be fluid emotion, something to prompt the next move. We experience fear. We involve Him in the why, what, and how of it. And then, we aim for our next move to be motivated by faith, not from fear. Our emotions have His signature on them, and the heart of them traces back to His heart. Our emotions can motivate us to move closer to God and to keep in step with Him. How cool is that?

The trouble with fear when we yield to it, is that it solidifies like sinking sand. That's when it's absolutely crippling, and we get stuck. That's what this verse is calling us to freedom *from*. We cannot live the abundant, victorious life He designed us to and paid for us to be able to walk in when we walk yielded to fear. We can't be moved to a deeper reliance on Him when staked in fear. It is a tent peg through our shirt, holding us to the ground when He's beckoning us to get up and walk with Him!

Something God spoke to me over a year ago as I was mulling over all of this. It is a phrase I repeat to myself often to remember to #yieldcheck how what I'm surrendering to has a direct correlation to what is being produced in and through my life:

What you yield to determines what your life will yield.

Because yielding means "to surrender and defer to," but it also means "to produce."

It's important to dig deeper beyond fear itself and be aware of what "fruit" it bears when it is given a place of permanence in our lives. Complacency, stagnation, worry, anxiety, despair, blindness, heaviness, are the first "fruits" that came to mind that can be born from the plant of fear. But by yielding to Him instead, we yield abundant, good, spirit-fruit.

"… then you'll become fruit-bearing (yielding) branches, yielding to His life…" Colossians 1:10, TPT

It's worth stopping to consider what we're giving the right of way to on a large scale in our lives, which can be traced back to the micro-scale of small moments each day yielding to certain thoughts, emotions, beliefs, and distractions. May we yield to Truth and Goodness so that what our days and lives bear is also true and good.

Ensnared

One of the most potent and absolutely entrapping forms of fear I've personally wrestled with throughout my life has been the "fear of man," as mentioned in Proverbs 29:25, which will always "prove to be a snare"—or, more practically put, the fear of other people's opinions about me. Fear's thick and gnarly roots in that area, which ran deeper than I ever realized, were finally pulled up like never before several years ago during a tumultuous season of major life transitions.

From a long-time-coming, gut-wrenching, but needed separation from my first husband to reuniting once more against my better judgement, to sadly but necessarily filing for divorce months later… to dating again soon after, to ultimately remarrying not long after that… I "upset the apple cart," as they used to say, in my small, conservative Christian "corner" of the world.

I knew that I had stayed in moment-by-moment, constant communion with the Lord during that season—knowing He was the only source of strength and provision to help me navigate what no one should ever have to face. It was only by His guidance that I was able to permanently move forward from a marriage that, for over a decade, had been a constant source of pain, confusion, grief, and nervous system dysregulation—leading to the intensification of my autoimmune disease amidst the unrelenting stress of that environment. The union had come to stand in opposition to the values and beliefs I held dear. As I grew in understanding my own worth and 'belovedness' in God's eyes, I was able to let go of the lies that had kept me there for too long, stepping toward sustainable freedom and healing.

Some days, I was still shaken—oscillating between the "what ifs" and the doubt that threatened to drown me—and the confidence in God's hand leading me through the uncharted territory of that transitional year. Sign after sign confirmed my next steps, guiding me through and out of that personal "Egypt." I wholeheartedly believed these were the doors God was opening in my life, though the timing was unexpected and stretched my faith to new heights. It felt like a rapid display of His promised recompense to "restore to you the years that the swarming locust has eaten" (Joel 2:25, ESV)—a way of redeeming lost time and propelling this newly single mama and her young kiddo into a whole new season of restoration.

But, as it's the Lord who looks at the heart and "man" who often only takes in the outward appearance, others can be quick to make assumptions and pass judgements. Thus, many around me kept the "rumor mill" churning in that season, which ushered in many lows, and I felt fear of being the target of gossip, unsolicited "advice," and scrutiny from others. I wasn't letting my fear of man do the choosing when it came to my actions, but it was all I could do to process it enough to keep from being overrun with anxiety throughout that season. I was distraught over what others were thinking, which stories they'd heard, how misunderstood I was, and who might be judging me. I kept getting fragments of opinions from people too distant to understand the full context. I felt compelled to explain, defend, and prove myself to everyone. After exhausting myself this way, it took some wise friends repeatedly speaking the truth to finally penetrate the roots of my fear. That truth was along the lines of the below mantras I still cling to:

You don't owe anyone an explanation.

You don't need to be afraid of what they think.

You are not called to please man but to please God.

Letting go of people-pleasing is a continual practice, but one that pays life-changing dividends and is absolutely worth pursuing. When God shows you something that does not make sense to them, you will need to "choose this day whom you will serve." And as Paul so wisely points out, "Am I now trying to win the approval of human beings, or of God? Or am I trying to please people? If I were still trying to please people, I would not be a servant of Christ" (Galatians 1:10, NIV).

I still have to remind myself sometimes, but I have learned and taken this truth deeply to heart:

The expectations of others are a sure measure by which to mismeasure God's timeline, good plans for, direction of, and call on your life.

Trust me—you do not want to miss what God has for you. The only way I know to miss it is by shrinking back from stepping where He's leading (and even then, in His vast grace, He has a way of working everything together for our good). Aligning yourself with what the crowd around you is beckoning—rather than with His specific, unique, and unfolding plans for your life—is an avoidable tragedy. No matter how well-meaning others may be or how much they say they care about you, love you, and don't want you to make a mistake, many deeply loving, well-meaning people advise from their own experiences or try to direct you based on fears they haven't yet worked through. As my dear dad wisely says, "We all receive incorrect advice from good-hearted people." This is why people cannot be our compass.

I didn't realize how long I had lived for the approval of man, but it began so young and was so deeply ingrained in the behavior-focused, fear-based religious institutions I was a part of. I longed for approval from everyone: my parents, pastors, peers, teachers, bosses, friends, boyfriend, husband, in-laws, clients, and even acquaintances on social media. The crowd from which I was forever approval-seeking only grew as I did. It was an epidemic that felt like a normal way of life to me. To not rock the boat, to defer to others' comfort and preferences, to not cause upset or offend people was taken to an unhealthy extreme and masked as "loving others" and "putting others before self." The verse about considering others as more important than yourself (Philippians 2:3) was taken completely out of context, jacked up with steroids, and instead of loving others, bred self-abandonment (different than humility and servant-heartedness), dishonesty, pearls being cast before swine, compromise of convictions, and other grievous fruits of being trapped in this "fear of man" snare.

I traced back the path to the way by which I'd arrived here in my early thirties when I should have been perfectly capable of confidently making my own decisions I believed to be in the best interest of me and my child. Perfectly capable of recognizing the Lord's leading in my life. Yet here I was, convinced in my own mind and heart of what He was doing and where He was leading, yet absolutely haunted by the fear of man as I made those best decisions. It didn't have to be that terrifying, but because of my past of living in this snare, it was. Thankfully, this life upheaval was the uncomfortable catalyst that allowed for the major excavation of those ensnaring roots.

I began to realize a large part of this life-long struggle of people pleasing was due to the religious authoritarian climate of my upbringing. Childhood development specialists harp on the natural process in early childhood of developing autonomy or a sense of self apart from others, namely your caregivers or other consistently present people in your life. This process should have been happening for me around the time that Christian thought leaders of the time like, Dr. James Dobson and Bill Gothard, were teaching parents (mine included) that a child resisting parental directives was born out of sinful defiance and a rebellious will that needed to be broken—rather than what is actually at play in most cases: that it is developmentally normal and good that children will experiment with limits to learn where boundaries are, what they do have a say in, and so on.

At a very young age, perhaps it's what outfit they feel like wearing, or what flavor of ice cream they want—small and good practices in autonomy! But as children get older, if they are not entrusted with proportionally appropriate and greater degrees of healthy independence and self-trust, deep-seated fear of stepping out of line is bred. An over-reliance on others to make decisions develops, and it is difficult for them to even feel okay about the ones they do make. Normal processes I should have been growing through to develop an appropriate sense of autonomy were stunted by being misdiagnosed as a spiritual issue. "Honor your father and mother" has been weaponized to guilt developing individuals back into line, or in the words of Gothard, back under the "umbrella of authority."

So, here at this crossroads of my adult life, I realized that's what God knew it would take. Without something as socially controversial in the deeply conservative Bible Belt setting in which it was in, I don't know that these fear-of-man, people-pleasing, co-dependent roots ever would have been exposed and hacksawed away to set me free.

As relational beings, we are designed with a deep need and desire to be loved, accepted, and included by others. It's not just something we want; it's something we *need* to feel emotionally safe, secure, and attached in meaningful relationships. This is a good, God-designed aspect of being human! But there is a difference between feeling securely attached in a healthy relationship to others while maintaining your God-given individuality that He's entrusted you to be responsible with and accountable for, and the insecurity that results in abdicating that responsibility by measuring your choices by what others expect of or want you to do so as to stay in good standing with them, which forms co-dependence.

It's natural to want to stay with the herd to avoid being cut off or isolated. But God designed us to be unique even within our "pack." We need our differences, perspectives, strengths, and even opinions to make up His body. We can't all be the same joint, ligament, or tendon. We must lean into who He's calling us to be, even if it means upsetting others who don't understand, since their callings, past experiences, and convictions will likely differ from ours.

Basing our decisions on what others think or what will make others happy rather than God is actually a form of idolatry, giving human opinions more weight than God's voice in our lives. It's also a form of low-key manipulation, driven by a fear of rejection, therefore trying to choose what will produce the most likable outcome rather than the most honest one. People-pleasing often stems from trying to avoid the discomfort of conflict and staying connected to others. But it hinders us from looking inward and discovering our true convictions, separate from anyone else's, as well as creating radio static-like interference in our communion with God, and we need that closeness with and clarity from Him to stand firm when the time comes—to know deep in our bones the "whys" beneath the hills we're bravely willing to die on, even if that means alone.

Oh, to be like Paul, who said with such boldness: "I'm not the least bit concerned if I'm judged by you or any verdict I receive from any human court... The only judge I care about is Him!" (1 Cor. 4:3-4, TPT). God's opinion is the only one that truly matters. As one of my favorite pastors and theologians, Peter Hiett, often reminds me through his sermons, "God *made* His judgement, and His judgement was *Love*."[36] So if we need not fear the opinions of others, and Jesus—who came not to judge but to save us—holds no condemnation for us, then *who* are we afraid of? *What* are we afraid of?

When fear is allowed beyond a feeling and is made into a dictator, it becomes a giant, distracting ruse intended to hinder us from our God-dreamed-up destinies. And we have the choice to surrender to and serve it at the high price of missing out on the life He's already paid for us to experience. When we're living for an audience of one, *the* One, we, by default, have less capacity to be concerned about what other people think. You can only truly focus well on one thing at a time, hence, the root of the word "priority": "prio," meaning "one." So by default, if your eyes remain fixed on Him and what *He* thinks of your decisions, how they align with *His will* and far surpassing *good* plan for your life, you, by default, will only have the ability to see others' opinions like a faint haze in your peripherals.

---

36 Hiett, Peter. *Relentless Love: Sermons.* The Sanctuary Denver, https://relentless-love.org/sermons/.

Speaking from recent and ongoing experience, it's a far less scary way to live.

Faith

If fear is what holds us back and paralyzes us from action, faith is the activator for growth, the catapult that launches us forward into the life for which we're designed.

Faith is defined as "complete trust or confidence in someone or something,"[37] and "trust" is defined as "a firm belief in the reliability, truth, ability, or strength of someone or something."[38] Like amino acids as building blocks to protein, faith truly is the most essential foundation to our spiritual lives, allowing us to step deeper beyond the shallow bounds of a purely cognitive belief system. Like James 2 reminds us, unless our faith is active—living by what we believe—it's fruitless. When we're faith-deficient, we just can't function as we're designed to. We quickly sell ourselves (and God) short by living a half-life that doesn't dare to step beyond what can be fully explained. If you require all of the details and a full, tangible explanation up front before you choose faith, you might be agreeing with or approving of it, but would it really be "having faith"? Because the essence of faith is complete trust and wholehearted belief, even if you don't see the "how" or "when" yet. Hebrews 11:1 (NHEB) puts it so clearly: "Now faith is being confident of what we hope for, convinced about things we do not see." Even if you don't have all the answers, you know what's possible because all things are possible with God, and that is enough for you to leap by faith into where He's calling you.

Even if things look grim on the surface, you can choose by

---

37 Oxford Languages. "'Faith' definition". *Google*, https://tinyurl.com/4pn5kfss. Accessed 22 Oct. 2024.

38 Oxford Languages. "'Trust' definition". *Google*, https://tinyurl.com/zseuk5pp. Accessed 22 Oct. 2024.

faith to see beyond the present natural reality and into a heavenly one, standing in alignment with God's will for it to be "on earth as it is in heaven." You can have an active, participatory role in partnering with God and His heavenly hosts to usher heavenly realities and solutions to Earth. It's *that* powerful because it's a gift *from* Him, and *He* is that powerful!

While we can be great at beating ourselves up for being "ye of little faith," getting down on ourselves and wishing that we had more faith won't solve our problems or increase our faith. That's because faith isn't something we muster up like a magician pulling a rabbit out of thin air—no. It's like picking up a Christmas gift with your name on it from under the tree, unwrapping and embracing it as your own now, new as it is to you. *Choosing to accept the gift of faith is an act of faith itself.*

God delights to give us the desire of our hearts, so if you desire to have more faith, I guarantee you, ask Him, and it won't be long before you find yourself up against decisions and opportunities that will press you toward the edge of your comfort zone and give you the opportunity to grow in faith, stretching your arms out further in childlike anticipation as you reach to pick up your gift. Another way to think about it is that we can really only ever be faith-deficient if we're already full of something else. That's where fear "full" and doubt "full" come from. When we've ingested too much of things we weren't designed for, it makes us sink, and puts us out of commission. So by choosing to fill up instead of faith, we, contrarily, become faith-full!

Fast forward from the aforementioned season of uprooting, social upheaval, life transitions, and ultimately rerooting to where I am now learning to "bloom where I'm planted," I am living proof that only He knows the plans He has for each of us. I wholeheartedly believe now that those plans are indeed to prosper and not to harm us (Jeremiah 29:11). I shudder at the thought of staying where I was. Many advised it would be "best" for me to remain in my former marriage. I knew God knew the details that many did not and was asking me to pick up my mat and walk out in faith away from that situation.

From the moment I took a shaky leap of faith and said "yes," I have followed His path one day at a time. In return, He has done nothing but protect, heal, restore, grow, and build my life in the most abundant ways—though not without growing pains—transforming me from the inside out.

Everything others warned me about, such as the regrets I would have if I pursued divorce—proved to be misguided. Someone even cautioned me that if I proceeded with the divorce, I would lose my joy and that God's presence would leave me. I remember crying about that in my old room at my parents' house during the emotionally grueling separation the year preceding the divorce, but God's Spirit quickly met me there, replacing those lies with truth. He reminded me of the scriptures, *"I will never leave you or forsake you"* and *"In My presence is fullness of joy."* If His presence is always with me, then I can never lose my joy since it comes from Him.

He truly does "reward those who earnestly seek Him." I am now living amidst a harvest of good fruit from that season when I chose to walk by faith—no matter how scared—into the unknown with Him. There are many precious gifts He's since woven into my life, but the most extraordinary is being entrusted with a miraculous love story: getting remarried to the purest, truest, most gracious, and kind soul I've ever known. I'm thankful to call him my best friend, business partner, husband, and bonus dad to my kiddo. I could fill another book about him and all the ways and reasons for my deep love, but in short, I wouldn't trade sharing this life with him for anything in the world.

Looking back, if I had listened to others' daunting cautions against leaving my former life in the time and season God called me—exactly when and how He led—I would have missed this next chapter. It has been sweeter than I ever imagined, a safe container for healing and a catalyst for growth beyond what I thought possible. I'm also deeply grateful to have healed to a place where I can foster a collaborative co-parenting relationship with my ex-husband, working together to ensure our child grows up surrounded by an over-abundance of love and support from both families. There's simply no place that God's grace cannot reach and His compassion cannot conquer, and no amount of history or differences could dim the brilliant light of love that we share for our precious son.

When we follow Him, there can only be life. When we follow others, it might not always lead to immediate death, but if it's not confirming what He's already told you, it will be less than God's best for you, and trust me, friend, that risk isn't worth taking.

Take the best path—His path for *you*—no matter how hard, new, or scary it may seem at first. Only He knows what's truly best for you. His heart is *for* you, His plans for you are *good* and can be trusted, and you will only get there by way of uncomfortable, unpopular, stretching faith. "For we walk by faith, not by sight," and when you "trust in the Lord with all your heart," He really will "make your path straight."

Chapter 9

Rest > Striving

"Since God loves us so completely, we don't have to work hard to get love from everybody else. I mean, we can if we want or we could just relax into God's love. We don't have to prove ourselves to anyone. We don't have to perform. Or pretend. We don't even really have to explain ourselves to people so they will get us. We can just rest in God's love and experience joy."

Maggie Johnson[39]

Striving to Earn

I've always liked games. Board games. Card games. My favorite game as a child was Monopoly, and to this day, I still love it. Sometimes, I feel that I missed the foreshadowing signs that I would've loved a career in real estate. (Ending up in interior design and short-term rental property ownership as a profession is a close relative, though.) The only trouble was, as a kid, there'd be a point in almost every game where I would have a meltdown when I started to lose or when someone else won. My zeal for fun and for winning would take a hyper-competitive turn that felt completely overwhelming, and much to my embarrassment, would often end in a tantrum

---

39   Paulus, Maggie. *Facebook*, date unknown.

that would land me in time-out or worse, my big sister whom I absolutely idolized, refusing to play with me anymore. This struggle with competitiveness-gone-awry continued on into my adulthood, which, yes, proved to be of even further embarrassment. The last time I recall actually shedding tears over losing a game was over a game of mini golf in my mid-20s. I know. Like I said, embarrassing.

But it wasn't just with games.

A similar perfectionistic drive often surfaced in my schooling, from elementary school age tear-fests when I'd fail at a math speed drill test through college when I couldn't seem to stop stressing and studying for four years straight with very little downtime for fear of "slacking off." I didn't know how to say that I did my very best on an assignment unless I'd spent virtually every hour I could between when it was assigned to me and when it was due dedicated to the assignment. It showed up in my work, from being half of a duo with my big sister as the most sought-after babysitters in my teens, going the extra mile to plan a thoughtful craft with the kids and clean the house once they went to sleep, to being a star employee at the restaurant I worked at through college, to my first job at an interior design firm right after school, to stressing myself out with unrealistic demands as I stepped into the world of entrepreneurship, beginning my own design firm in 2013.

In the last decade, as I've pondered, wrestled, and struggled to understand what was *with* this inherent *need* to do and be the best at whatever it was I was doing. From much honest and deep reflection, angst-filled prayers and gentle answers, and years spent with great therapists, I've been able to get to the root of much of it and what is the common denominator between these hyper-stress-inducing aspects of my life and, of course, it overlapped and intertwined with the religious dogma I grew up around. The long-held subconscious beliefs driving me in those ways went something like this:

If you keep striving toward being good and being good at things, you're a "good" person. Others will give you gold stars for your efforts and accomplishments. Good people are well liked, well loved. Well liked and loved people are safe. Ergo, by striving to be good, you will be relationally and emotionally secure.

If you *don't* strive hard enough to be good, you will, by default, fail. Failing means you are bad or bad at the thing you tried. Bad people and people who aren't good at things are a disappointment. They need work, they need help, which is a burden to others. Disappointments and burdens are not liked and loved by others. Ergo, by failing or not striving with all your might, you're bad at things at best and a bad person at worst, which will render you relationally and emotionally insecure.

In short, my striving mentality was subconsciously motivated by a desire to be safe, accepted, and secure (all human *needs*) that manifested as hypervigilance to "be good," which makes sense as the fundamentalist belief systems have a way of turning absolutely every tiny thing into a moral issue that is, in turn, a reflection of your value and worth. It was a panicked search to earn and prove my worth to others and to feel worthy myself. Behind that was a desperate search for love, approval, and safety—born out of not understanding that my worth was inherent and did not rise or fall with my accomplishments: that I was loved for who I was, not what I did.

It's still an upsetting, mind-boggling thought process and reality to untangle. *Where* did this come from? *How* did I internalize subconscious messages like this from such a young age, carrying it with me unidentified for over two-thirds of my life to date?

The ins and outs of our psyches, personalities, and our individual experiences and perceptions that shape us definitely play a part in how we grow up interpreting and engaging with the world around us, but I can tell you exactly where I was soaked in these messages on a consistent basis: the influences of the churches, ministries, and attached communities in which we were involved in those formative and impressionable, developmental years.

Perfection and good performance among families and individuals were prized in our circle. Not outright, of course, but it felt like a kind of invisible currency that the homeschool families with "quivers full" of children traded in, which I can only imagine now as a parent, the pressure that must have put on all of the misguided parents also trying to be as "good" as the family on the next row up, keeping up with the so-and-so's so as not to be excluded, new content for those rumor mills, or as it went at that small rural church—shunned by others.

I remember my mom's detailed beauty routine with my sisters and me every Sunday morning, with curlers in our hair from Saturday night to our matching dresses and shoes. I believe a part of it was the joy of having a gaggle of girls to dress up and the fact that matching clothes were, in part, a practical choice, making it easier to locate us in crowds. But part of it seemed frenzied and stressful, as though we had to measure up to some unspoken expectation appearance-wise. When it came to church, I remember getting so many compliments on how darling we were in our matching outfits, perfect porcelain doll ringlet hair kissed with grosgrain hair bows. My parents were often praised for having such well-behaved, obedient kids. Nobody, not even I, was aware that I was obedient because I was genuinely distraught by the thought of failure, punishment, and the disappointment I felt when such normal "horrors" of being a child occurred. As you can imagine, I didn't let myself get in trouble often. We'd get complimented on how respectful and polite we were all the time. The "yes ma'ams" and "yes sirs" were a sure way to get additional admiration. "Good" behavior was a hot commodity in my world and went right along with a heaping helping of corroborating theology to solidify the system for me.

Somewhere between the pulpit and the playground, I was constantly influenced by an ideology I'd only later come to identify as spiritually, emotionally, psychologically, and, therefore, relationally harmful. They didn't understand the truth. And therefore, neither did I. I ingested concepts that terrified me instead. I remember a lot about how disappointed God was in us, how we were born inherently evil, and about the wrath and punishment of God. I was taught how we all fall short, so God had to make up the difference. I always felt like I should tell Him I was sorry for being such a chore. It sounded like I was a lot of work and quite a disappointment to Him before I could even form words. To please Him, it seemed I needed to be absolutely perfect, constantly confessing every remotely "unchristian" word or thought, and be devoted to a daily quiet time like my life depended on it.

I've maintained a strong relationship with my parents despite the realizations I've come to in adulthood, and I'm grateful for the chance to have open conversations with them about parts of our upbringing that were challenging for me and some of my siblings. They, too, have grieved the deception and misunderstandings that were present in our religious environment—one that aimed to protect but often relied on control and fear. We were all doing the best we could with what we knew at the time. After working through anger and grief over those experiences, I now feel deep compassion for my parents. Becoming a parent myself helped me realize how hard it is to feel like you're doing it "right," even when you're doing your best. I'm thankful that, with grace, we've found truth, freedom, and even closer relationships with each other, made possible by the grace we've discovered since then.

But with that being my normal reality at the time, you can bet I tried my *darndest* to be not only good but perfect. I was usually on high alert to dodge the bullet of more disapproval and consequences by authority figures around me. I share all of this with you to connect the dots of where my striving to be "goodest" and best to earn love and approval really began. It's the only way I could be in "good standing" with those around me, so it's how I got the idea that striving for God's love and approval was what I was supposed to do, what pleased Him, too.

Somehow, they'd skipped over all the passages that specifically express His heart for the *exact opposite* for us.

What they encouraged and celebrated was behavior modification rather than heart transformation. They were, in effect, constantly attempting to re-crucifying Christ. All of the striving and good behavior to earn brownie points with each other and with Him was inadvertently a way of saying His sacrifice at the cross on our behalf wasn't enough. In the words of Paul in Galatians 2:21 (TPT), "For if keeping the law (perfection) could release God's righteousness to us, then Christ would have died for nothing."

That's the issue with legalism—it is based on striving and earning, which runs counter to everything Jesus did at the cross. It's trying to add to what He did. It's a resistance to full reliance on Him and a continually exhausting self-reliance act that will only run you into the ground. It's like saying it *isn't* finished—when Jesus whispered definitively as His last words that it most definitely *is*. There's nothing more to add to His gift because Jesus' life *was* the most perfect beyond measure, and He laid it down. For us. So that we could finally, at last, once and for all and all at once, be made perfectly new, spotless, and clean records with new, soft, teachable, willing hearts. He is grieved by sin, yes, but never from a place that makes Him turn away in disapproval; rather, in a way that has Him move near to us to rescue and help us get back on the path He paved for us.

Striving to earn His love and approval will never work. Because He loves you just as much today as the day as He did before you existed in the flesh when you were merely a dream in His heart to bring to life one day. We all get caught in striving for different reasons, but this one for emotional security is one of the biggest ones I see as a major hindrance to our living in the freedom we were designed for.

The other biggest form of striving I've had to rest my way out of in recent years, and can still be prone to revert to in my most forgetful moments is one that tends to be driven by a search for more tangible security to meet more physical and financial needs.

I bring you…the hindrance of striving to survive.

Striving to Survive

Our survival instincts, while part of God's good design for us to help keep us safe and live through dire situations, were intended to be a temporarily accessed skill rather than a long-term state from which we live. Yet so many of us run ourselves ragged, not understanding that we're doing it to ourselves unnecessarily. God knew we'd have a tendency to get stuck in this mode that wasn't meant to be a sustainable way of living, which decreases our quality of life from truly living and thriving like He intends to so much less— merely surviving.

I think we get stuck in survival mode when we live forgetful of His promises to provide and forgetful of all the times He's provided for us in the past. Either that, or we remember them, we just don't wholeheartedly believe it and want to "help" Him just in case He forgets.

I've wrestled with these trust issues, and if you do too, I want you to know they are very valid, as they often stem from the broken mirror reflections we looked at in Chapter 5 of others who made us promises they didn't keep, or failed to provide for us in some way at some point along our lives when that was their responsibility. The panicked feeling of being forgotten, left hanging, unable to provide for ourselves, and not having those who are responsible for us able to fully provide for us when it comes to our basic human needs in the natural world will really do a number on our nervous systems. It can take some time to heal from—to repair—with evidence of the times we had enough provision, the times others came through for us, and we felt safe and taken care of.

But in time, we really can learn that we don't need to live by those old hesitations from trust breaks with others that drove us to a hyper-independence of "I'm fine, I can take care of myself." We have a loving, amply supplied Father who delights to give good gifts to His children and promises to provide for our every need. The more we start to trust Him, ask for His help, and pray for specific provision, the more we build a new track record for our nervous systems. We really can be at rest. We can trust Him to provide for what we truly need.

In Matthew 6, Jesus gives us perhaps His most memorable admonition on the subject of worrying about our basic survival needs:

> Don't worry about your life, what you will eat or what you will drink; or about your body, what you will wear... Look at the birds of the sky: They don't sow or reap or gather into barns, yet your heavenly Father feeds them. Aren't you worth more than they?
>
> Matthew 6:25-26, HCSB

I love the way the Message phrases this next part as Jesus continues to enlighten us in verses 30 through 32:

> ... don't you think He'll attend to you, take pride in you, do His best for you? What I'm trying to do here is to get you to relax, to not be so preoccupied with *getting,* so you can respond to God's *giving.* People who don't know God and the way he works fuss over these things, but you know both God and how He works.

Gah! If we know God and how He works—if we can hold on to remembrance of that, we won't find ourselves getting caught in the survival mode trap, fussing over "these things."

Outside of its designated time, we'll be trying to face the events of tomorrow within the bounds of today's graces. We'll drain today's resources by pulling in tomorrow's tasks. He promises "new mercy each morning" that is specially marked to meet the needs of that day. This is why the "one day at a time" saying honor our own limits of time, energy, and resources that we're entrusted to steward each day. Honoring our limits is to honor God's design, timeline, and allows us to thrive from a place of deep-seated trust and reliance on Him rather than merely trying to survive as we spin our worrying wheels and absolutely wear ourselves out.

What is fascinating about the often counterintuitive ways of God (such as thinking of heavenly things first in order to watch earthly provision manifest, which can feel out of order or out of our natural order) is that when choosing to live and work from a place of rest, trusting rather than worrying, with His supernatural power energizing and fueling our days, we will often find ourselves accomplish more than we might expect. I've come to call it "heavenly math," when the time and energy felt shorter and used less exertion than I'd anticipated, but I was able to get further on my to-do list or just felt a full day go smoothly in general. I notice a distinct difference in how much "mileage" I seem to get out of a day when I'm really in tune with Him, staying connected and conversing with Him in my spirit throughout the day, versus when I have had a very "fleshy" day (you know, those extra earth-bound days where you lose sight of the call to "fix your eyes on things above, not on things of this earth.") But even so, He designed our good earthly bodies and minds, knowing what they'd need to thrive, and setting up the standard of a "day" to contain just enough of what we need and keep out what would be too much, if we can only let those things loose from our hoarding hands and runaway minds at times.

The illustration I come back to again and again is that of His constant day-to-day provision for the Israelites during their 40 years on their way to the Promised Land. The rhythm with which He put the provision of manna in place for each day will forever be a plumb line to help me realize when I'm stepping out of trust and reliance on Him and reverting to a state of striving from a God-forgetful place of just trying to survive—when we were made to *thrive*!

Let's journey back for a moment to thousands of hangry Israelites wandering through the wilderness around Exodus 16…

First, the Lord spoke to Moses, telling him that He would provide bread from heaven for the people. Each day, the Israelites were to go out and gather just enough for that day, and in this way, God would test their obedience. On the sixth day, they were to gather twice as much as usual so they would have enough for the Sabbath—the day He'd set aside for them to *rest*.

When the dew evaporated in the morning, thin flakes like frost appeared on the ground. The Israelites, not knowing what it was, asked each other, "What *is* it?" Moses explained that it was the bread God had given them to eat. He instructed them to gather as much as they needed—about an omer for each person in their household.

(Which, Google told me, can be equated to about 43 chicken eggs or 15 cups of barley. That's quite a bit of manna!) Some gathered more, and some less, but when they measured it, everyone had just enough. On that first day, Moses warned them not to keep any of it until the next morning. However, some did not listen and kept some overnight, but sure enough, it wasn't meant to last into the next day; thus, it smelled and became infested with maggots. Gross.

So, each morning, they gathered what they needed, and by midday, the remaining manna on the ground melted away. On the sixth day, they gathered twice as much, and when the leaders reported this to Moses, he reminded them that the next day was the Sabbath, a day of rest dedicated to the Lord. They were to cook and prepare what they needed, and whatever was left over should be kept until the next morning. This time, the leftover manna did not spoil. Miraculous! Moses told them to eat it on the Sabbath, as there would be no manna on the ground that day. Despite this, some people still went out to gather manna on the seventh day, but they found nothing. The Lord questioned Moses about their continued disobedience and reminded them that the Sabbath was a gift, which was why He provided enough manna on the sixth day for *two days*. So, the people rested on the Sabbath, and they named the bread "manna."

One read through the above story, even I get frustrated at the Israelites for not catching on quicker. Until I realize how often I *am* the Israelites. Ah!

He went to the extent to meet their very real need for nourishment with Old Testament DoorDash and put limits on what and when they could gather so that everyone would always have exactly enough, not too much or too little, never be overworked and underfed, and even planned it so that they wouldn't have to lift a finger one day out of the week, providing a special grace for the manna to keep overnight just that one day out of the week, to allow them time to REST. But still, some of the people still went out to gather on the seventh day. *facepalm*

Can you relate? I often wonder what drove those "some of them" to hang on to the leftovers till morning 6 days out of the 7 when it wouldn't keep, or to go out ready to gather more on the day they were intended to be resting, though He'd told them that day's portion would be given the day before. But then I realize it was likely the same tricks and traps that drive me if I fall asleep at the wheel of my spirit and kick me into my hurried and anxious survival overdrive: Scarcity (what if I run out?), fear (what if there's not more tomorrow when I wake up?), worry (what if I'm still hungry later?), efficiency (maybe if I could just gather ALL that I need for a week all at once I'd have more time for XYZ), control (maybe I could finally feel caught up or get ahead by working on my day off). Perhaps you have something to add to the list from your own experience.

But God, in His beautiful, unfailing pace of grace, created a plan that provided more than enough, exactly when it was supposed to, how it was supposed to—all they needed to do was trust Him and gather from a place of rest and reliance on Him. He had it all taken care of for their good and His glory—all they needed to do was follow through on their end when He called them to rest and to gather. We overcomplicate it unnecessarily when we work from a place of striving rather than rest.

A fun side note to that story that's worth mentioning, too: manna wasn't the only kind of food He provided. That's right—God knew His people needed more balanced macros than that and provided protein in the form of quail that would cover the camp in the evenings in between the manna that would fall in the mornings.

So the next time you wonder if God forgot something or is resigning you to "live by bread alone," take a step back outside in the evening. He likely has a fresh quail dinner (or the equivalent of what you need to be fortified) with your name on it.

Being at Rest

In taking note of the myriad of ways in which He provides for our needs, both emotional and physical, we begin to combat the hindering and unnecessary tendency to strive and can begin to settle into the sweet state in which we were designed to live from: rest. It's what He promises and longs to give us, as we're reminded by His gentle invitation to rest in Matthew 11:28-29 (NIV):

> "Come to me, all you who are weary and burdened, and I will give you rest. Take my yoke upon you and learn from me, for I am gentle and humble in heart, and you will find rest for your souls."

How do we "rest in God," though, practically speaking? The best way I've come to understand it is that we're resting in the finished, perfect, and complete work of Jesus at the cross on our behalf, so we can cease striving to measure up, store up, and keep up, and simply fall back into the ironclad promise that He is, and has, taken care of it.

Isaiah 26:12 (TPT) says it beautifully,

> "Lord Yahweh, you will establish peace and prosperity for us, for all we have accomplished is a the result of what you work through us."

Does this mean we're lazy, purposeless beings? Many aspects of many religions would like you to think so to keep you on a loop of the endless hamster wheel of *doing* rather than *being*. It's the classic Mary and Martha story contrast. The world and so many would have us believe our value and worth comes from what we *do*. But all He's ever asked of us is to *be* who He's created us to be and to be present with Him, like Mary exemplified, "choosing what was best" by simply *being* with Him—sitting at His feet.

So, quite the contrary. What He's done by "doing all our work for us" is to free us up from fretting about and wasting precious time on what we could never have come up with a solution to, to liberate us to use our one, wild life, the health, ideas, love, energy and other gifts and resources He's entrusted to us—everything—to splash like overflow from the full cup He's poured for us. We live purposefully now from a place of ease and trust, as a celebration of His love and grace, a song of thanksgiving back to Him. We "work" now toward the collective and unique purposes for which we were created! We can do all of this from a state of total and complete rest in our right standing with Him, which makes way for our unity with each other and is never short of the grace that multiplies, provision that abounds, and needs that are promised to be met—all because He has taken care of the need to strive anymore, ever again.

Collective purposes would include, first and foremost, to know and love Him and to be in constant communion and close relationship with Him. To make Him known by way of our love toward others. To encourage one another to love and do good deeds. To steward what He has entrusted to us in the form of unique gifts and resources for the enrichment of ourselves and others, for our good and His glory.

Unique purposes would include our individual callings and missions. "He knows the plans He has for us to prosper us and not to harm us, to give us hope, and a future." Our paths and callings, His "plans" for each of us, are like a unique treasure map and an invitation to adventure with Him into the great unknown He's designed for us to discover with Him, as it unfolds a little more a day at a time. Among my callings and purposes is writing this book, for example! It's been a total faith leap and trust fall to answer the call that He placed on my heart some years ago, even giving me the book title so far back I can't remember how or when; it was just… there, in my heart. I'd think of the book, and I'd hear the title like it was picked out a long time ago by someone other than me.

May we each have "ears to hear" and let this out-of-this-world reality sink in and take root in our heart's ground; that we may begin to truly live from this place of resting in our unchanging right standing with Him that allows us to take a deep breath, lay aside the burdens of striving "men" have saddled us with, and relax into His perfect love and abundant provision.

Finally, as we learn to rest in this boundless love of God, we can come to know what it feels like to be truly, securely, cherished, and *held*. Not because of a darn thing we've done. But because of who we are to Him, who He is, and all the things He's done on our behalf.

Being Held

In most of the Christian circles I've been in, there's a well-meaning but still confusing and incomplete admonition to "cling to Christ" or "run after God." It always struck a chord of panic in me. "What does that even *mean*?" I often wondered in my younger, more spiritually traumatized years. "What if I don't do it *enough*?" "How do you even *do*… that?" "What if I forget?" "How will I know I'm holding on, and what if my hand slips? What if I'm not running fast enough? *Why* is He hard to keep up with?"

Those well-meaning calls to action regrettably made God seem intangible, indifferent, and tough to keep near. As we've been exploring in this book, that is an absolutely inaccurate image of our passionate and pursuant God. At worst, it's vague, misleading, and terrorizing. At best, it's a mere fragment of what's meant to be an effortless response to the far surpassing and awe-filled reality that is this:

We have a God who clings tightly to us.

He watches over us day and night, never sleeping. His detailed care and concern for us goes down to the hair count on our heads. He delights over us with singing. He quiets us with His love. He holds on to us. He never lets go. He never leaves us. Never forsakes us. He promises all of this, with very clear promises like this:

"You always have My presence. For haven't I promised you, 'I will never leave you alone, never! And I will not loosen My grip on your life'" (paraphrased from Hebrews 13:5b, TPT).

And all of this—not begrudgingly to do us any favors, but because He *wants* to. Because He *loves* to! We're His precious children. He doesn't let go of us any more than I'd ever take my eye off of, disconnect from, turn my heart from, run away, or hide from my Liam love. Yet that's how we've often been influenced to think of God. Elusive. Unwilling. Put out. Out of reach. Hard to please. Easy to displease.

Dear friends, I hope you're seeing and believing by now that these ideas of Him could not be further from the truth we were created to rest in and live from.

He is *already* near.
He is not going *anywhere*.
He longs to be close to you.

Yes. You.

The truth is it works much like the way I wildly adore my precious Liam love, down to still slipping down the hall some nights, checking to make sure he's still breathing when he's sleeping, always aware of his whereabouts, always looking out for his well-being, delighting to provide anything he needs, never getting enough time with him, never able to snuggle him close enough or hold him long enough, treasuring every detail of him, heart exploding over everything from how he speaks to how he skips and dances, always at the ready to defend and protect him, kiss every scrape, and dry every tear.

My lovelies. Believe deep in your bones with me—*that* is a mere fraction of the way God feels about you. And that fact has *absolutely nothing to do with your effort.* It has everything to do with the fact that you have always, and will always, be precious to Him. That's the kind of revelation of His love that will melt your heart, help you breathe a sigh of relief, and hunker down into the secure love that holds onto you. That rest, trust, security? *That's* what enables us to *want* to love and cling to Him, too, from a place of natural longing.

The way we're told in 1 John 4:19 that "we love because He first loved us"? It is that exactly. We hold on to Him as a response to realizing and trusting that He's already holding on to us. He will love and cling to us without ceasing—regardless of if we do.

Be free, my friends. Cease your chasing and clinging from a place of striving, and rest in this: you are already held fast by a God who *adores* you, who's promised to never let you go.

Breathe. Relax.

Sink into that embrace.

Being proverbially held allows us to cling to Him from rest. May we discover with relief that we are already fully supported by His embrace, and say along with the bride to her bridegroom in Song of Songs 2:6 (TPT), "His left hand cradles my head while his right hand holds me close. I am at rest in this love."

Part 4:
EMPOWERED

*Who we really are and how we
can live more on earth like it is
in heaven.*

Identity & Relationships

"Devotion to God is not about a loss of self, but rather a true understanding and full recognition of the person God created you to be."

Mark Batterson[40]

Who You're *Not*

On a normal day, upon falling down the social media rabbit hole of someone who liked something or was suggested to me on social media, I came across a stranger's profile. She looked like a sweet girl, and I could tell immediately she was a believer like me. Except, wait—she was a believer, but instead of like me, like who I *used* to be—identity-confused. Her Instagram profile bio began with, "*A sinner in need of a Savior.*" My whole body cringed. I've seen and heard it so many times. I've *lived* it.

This message reads like a "help wanted" ad for believers who are living their lives as though Jesus didn't really die on the cross or didn't finish what He said He did. It's as though they believe-ish. Yet live asleep to the identity that He came to give us. I wanted to tell her, "Good news, lady! He already came to save you and said it

40 Batterson, Mark. Foreword. *Saints: Becoming More than "Christians."* by Addison Bevere. Revell, 2020.

was finished, ergo—you are no longer a 'sinner' (though you will still sin) and you're no longer in need of a Savior, *you have Him!* Newsflash: He's arrived! His saving efforts were effective! The wait is over, the search can stop. You've been made new!" It's like "B.C." and "A.D." There's a "before" and an "after." It's like choosing to still live in the Stone Age when it's the 2020s outside.

"Identity amnesiacs"[41] is a term Paul David Tripp has used to describe believers who view their identity through horizontal substitutes (such as their work, relationships, etc.) rather than remembering who they are vertically—their true identity in God. To be God-forgetful momentarily is something we will all do at times or for seasons. We are human and can be forgetful. We can lose sight of the truth and need our perspective refreshed. But to live in an identity-confused state daily and indefinitely, though, is a tragedy I hope to help resolve! Why would we choose to live from a mindset that He died to free us *from*? It's like little orphan Annie waking up each day in her new home at the Warbucks mansion, still living from a place of unworthiness of being adopted into such finery, and choosing to put on her worn old frock from the orphanage, ignoring the glorious wardrobe her new dad already bought and paid for and hung in her sprawling closet. Verses that have been taken out of context and run amok to the detriment of so many of us have been the ones surrounding the "self."

Scripture has much to say about the "old self" and the "new self," putting off the "old man" and putting on the "new man," but it's unfortunately been thrown around and woven in and out of context and timeline, weaving a tangled web of confusion. If it's been hard for you to keep up with, too, you're in good company.

I think there's also some hesitation that works against those

---

41 Tripp, Paul David. "Getting Identity Right." *PaulTripp.Com*, 6 Feb. 2013, www.paultripp.com/wednesdays-word/posts/getting-identity-right.

who might want to believe but feel like they'll lose themselves in the process. It sounds scary. It sounds hard. To "die" to self. To "deny" yourself. There's a sound of loss in the sentiments, and I've seen that deter some from taking hold of the news, not realizing that the thing they're afraid of losing is simply something that got in the way of their *true, divine* nature. By dying to the "old self," you are not losing, but *gaining*, your real self! In a practical sense, remember, the old self was compromised. So it is not that you become not-you, but *more* of your real, true, amazing, God-dreamed-up self.

Was the "beast" in Beauty and the Beast still his same personality essentially, when he was under the curse that transformed him into a beast? Yes, sort of, just—angrier, more bitter, a little scarier to those who couldn't see his heart, who he truly still was underneath the outer skin. But the "beast" self hindered him from being who he truly was—a human prince. So to deny denying your old self would be like the beast choosing to remain in his beastliness for fear of "losing" himself when transformed back to his original self. Who wouldn't want to be set free from a curse, to transform from what shrouded you and get to become who you really are underneath it all? It's still you. But it's the truer, freer, lighter and more *alive* you.

I believe many churches do a poor job of explaining our true identities in Christ, which is why it's hard for people to let go of the only "self" they've ever known. Some churches, like the ones I grew up in, fail to convey the truth of shedding the old self and distort it entirely. In some circles, "denying oneself" is taken to such unhealthy extremes, encouraging people to stay in unsafe situations under the false belief that it pleases God or that they somehow deserve such suffering. This warped view often leads to feelings of worthlessness, causing self-neglect and allowing mistreatment from others more easily. But selflessness is humility, *not* enablement of harm. To belittle ourselves is to deny the truth of God's Word. We must reject this harmful mindset and embrace the inherent worth, goodness, and belovedness God created in us and intended for us to discover in ourselves. "Love your neighbor as you love yourself" holds a key truth: we are to first learn what it means to love, care for, and hold self-respect for ourselves before we are truly able to love, care for, and respect others to the same degree that we have learned to embrace ourselves.

Who You *Are*

These days, it seems all too rare that I get uninterrupted, face-to-face time for heart-to-heart talks with some of my dearest friends. Amidst various map distances, raising vibrant kiddos, supporting them in their extracurriculars, and many of us working more than full time, it takes much intention on both parts to make time stand still long enough to get together and prioritize staying close.

Among the world's most shining examples of fullest-plate people who still manage to be consistent and intentional friends is my childhood friend Luke (mentioned earlier in this book). As he spent so much time with my family growing up, helping build our house, he became like the big brother my siblings and I never had. To this day, he endearingly calls me "sis." Luke is one of the few who has stayed with me through all of life's seasons—both lows and highs—truly exemplifying Jesus' "friend that sticks closer than a brother" kind of love. One of the sweetest ripple effects of our life-long friendship is that our boys were born less than a year apart and are now going on eight years of being best friends, too. All the more reason that we make a point to get our families together regularly.

On one such and particularly festive Christmas-time visit to their home in recent years, the sun had just set on that mildly chilly December evening. Luke and I had stepped outside onto the sprawling front porch of his farmhouse, built with his own two hands, to take in the Christmas light display he and his three kids had created. From up at the house, which graces the hilltop of their 11 rolling acres of rural beauty, you could still faintly see the panoramic view of the valley in the distance below us. An impressive display of Christmas lights ran all the way from the county road, up their gravel drive, and twisted in and out and around all of the trees that lined the edge of the field in front of the house. Like true kids at Christmas, we were lit up with excitement over the lights, glowing brighter with joy than the lights themselves. I forget who said it first, but we were thinking the same thing at that moment: "I miss Lauren."

Sweet, angelic, graceful Lauren—Luke's wife of 17 years and mother of their precious children—tragically lost her life to mental illness a few years ago. Lauren had grown up with us in the fundamentalist church of our youth, the one heavily influenced by Bill Gothard's IBLP teachings. While mental illness can be a standalone battle, I've always held an extra dose of righteous anger on her behalf toward the traumatic religious teachings and experiences that surely exacerbated her struggle. While the place through which we all met had caused us all a great deal of suffering even after we'd navigated our way out of the webs of lies, I knew she suffered more than I could fully grasp. I always appreciated our vulnerable conversations when it came to our shared experiences there. I ached with her and for her, and she with me. And now I will forever ache with Luke over the loss of her from this life.

As we stood there missing her and wishing she could be with us in more than spirit to enjoy the array of Christmas lights, we reminisced about what a beautiful soul she was and continues to be now to the fullest extent in her new body in Heaven. We recounted in detail more things we loved about her: her gentle voice, her kindness to all she encountered, her creative spirit that could paint, play music, and just about anything else inspiring. And yet, he recalled how she often couldn't see her true self. The wonderful qualities we still remember her by and always admired her for, she struggled to see or believe about herself. She was quicker to simmer in insecurities, sometimes even wondering why people even liked her. "No way!" I responded. "She was so amazing, though!" I wish *she* could have seen what we see in her. And I believe looking in the eyes of Jesus face to face now, she sees herself more clearly than ever. And yet, I knew exactly what he was talking about. I thought for a moment and sighed a knowing sigh, "What's sad but true is, I can actually relate to that more than I wish I did."

I shared with him about a recent meltdown moment I'd had where my insecurities swelled to a towering wave that crashed down around me, leaving me completely disoriented. "This may sound silly," I'd squeaked out through tears at the time to my saint of a husband, Forrest, who's gently journeyed with me through much inner healing these past couple of years, "but can you remind me *why* exactly you like me again? Like, for some reason, I just can't think of anything good right now, and all I feel and see are the things I don't like about myself that I'm frustrated with." He'd proceeded to share with me character and personality traits that were true, aiding in drowning out the lies and quieting the insecurities.

We all *need* people who will speak into our lives and remind us of what's true about us, and we all need to learn how to ask those people, even if it feels silly, for reminders when we need them. It doesn't mean it will fix our insecurities, heal our illnesses, or solve our problems, but it is a reinforcing balm to our sometimes shaky sense of self—especially when we are coming back from a self-esteem deficit, as is often the case for trauma survivors. Luke listened to my also relatable story, shaking his head at how much more prevalent this type of short-sighted, contorted vision about ourselves must be, and the way taking hold of the truth seems slippery to our grasp.

He brought up one of my little sisters who'd recently made a victory social media post, sharing about how far she'd come in recent years in seeing herself more clearly and feeling free to be who she really is. She shared transparently about her own insecurities, doubts, and negative self-talk she used to tell herself, shortcomings that seemed like largecomings in her own eyes at the height (rather low) of how she saw herself critically. She celebrated her breakthroughs in every area from body image to spiritual walk, realizing how delightfully loved she is by the Divine. Luke said he'd messaged her after that post, saying that while growing up with her, he'd had no idea she felt those negative ways about herself. He, being one of those people in both of our lives, reminded her of who she truly was all along, commending her and calling out the gold in her, encouraging and building her up, affirming her in the truth she was now finally embracing about herself.

We reminisced about our shared roots in that fundamentalist church, grieving the harm it caused but also feeling grateful that we gained each other through it. I've often told him, "If it meant having you in my life for life, I'd go through it all again!" I've often felt isolated, thinking the off-base ideas I internalized about God, others, and myself were unique to my experience, as though the confusion was somehow my fault. But hearing similar stories from others puts things in perspective, realizing how very not alone I am in these struggles. He reminded me how he, too, grew up with insecurities and false notions about himself, which I found hard to believe given how incredible he is. Yet, if none of us—neither he nor his wife, nor my sister nor I—were immune to identity struggles and doubts, it's clear that none of us are immune to the lies about who we truly are.

Our identities have likely been under attack since the Garden of Eden. If Adam and Eve doubted who God was and what He said was best for them, then surely their understanding of who they really were came into question as well.

I can picture Eve now:

"Well, I guess I am ignorant then—maybe he's right. Maybe I'll be wiser if I eat this fruit."

"If God is keeping this from us, then He must not really love us after all. I guess I'm unlovable..."

"Maybe if I hide, it will be okay. I'm such an idiot. I should have just listened to God. I'm so gullible—I always screw things up, gah!"

And don't you know the sneaky snake knew exactly what he was doing? It was like a rigged game of Jenga. All he needed was to pull that first block, and everything would come crashing down. Not just the blissful unawareness of evil, which they were shielded from by abstaining from that particular tree, but also their clear and correct view of themselves in light of who God is and who they were in Him.

The enemy of our souls knew that one lie could spark an identity crisis lasting for millennia.

No matter how you came to believe what's faulty and dismiss (or perhaps never have been told) your true identity and automatically inherited traits as a child of God—a creation of His good hands and fruit of His redemptive grace—it's time we get back to who we really are. Dear friend, in case you've forgotten or never been properly introduced, I'd like you to meet your wonderful, amazing, God-inspired, and indelible true self that's hidden safely and securely in Christ Jesus, unable to be altered:

A literal saint (Romans 1:7)

God's home (Ephesians 3:17)

God's beloved (2 Corinthians 6:18, Galatians 4:7)

Perfectly, wonderfully made (Psalm 139:13-14)

An image-bearer of God Himself (Genesis 1:27)

Precious and honored in His sight (Isaiah 43:4, TPT)

Flawless (Romans 5:1, TPT, Song of Songs 4:7)

Energized by His miraculous power (Ephesians 3:20b, TPT)

Competent and able (Philippians 4:13, 2 Corinthians 3:5)

Completely, wonderfully free (Galatians 5:1 TPT)

Bold (Proverbs 28:1)

Empowered (2 Timothy 1:7)

Beautiful (Song of Songs 4:7)

Confident (Ephesians 3:12)

Captivating (Song of Songs 4:9 and 7:1)

Delightful (Psalm 37:4)

Rejoiced over (Zephaniah 3:17)

Victorious (Romans 8:37)

The list goes on and on. For starters, He tucked love notes about who you are and how precious you are to Him in His Word. Then He continues to speak echoes and variations of that same truth today and every day through His "now" words that He speaks to our hearts through everything from illustrations in nature to parallels in life circumstances, through song lyrics or lines in a book or film, to words of encouragement that come from those around us. If we have ears to hear, we'll be met with irrefutable evidence of who we are and who we are to Him. Those truths become our new reference points for how we can see and value ourselves.

Let who you're *not* fall away like the leaves in due season. Now is the time, the season for letting go of what's dead—be it your religion, your identity, or other things you thought were real but have let you fall clean through to the cold, hard ground, where you're now met with this reckoning of what's true.

In your sifting of what's true of you and not, here's another all-encompassing measure I've found helpful time and again when I've been tempted to "wear" something ill-fitting or hold on to something that is no longer a part of my identity, and was never in the first place. The wise Jolene Miller, in a sermon she gave at The Sanctuary church in Denver, said this: "If it doesn't stick to the resurrected Jesus, then it doesn't stick to you."[42]

> Guilt? Would roll right off His back.
> Shame? Not a chance.
> Too thin? Too fat? Hilarious.
> Too loud, too quiet? Preposterous.
> Bad at this or that? Unimaginable.

What have you believed about yourself that you don't need to allow to stick anymore because it doesn't stick to Jesus? Only who and what He is, and who and what He says of you, truly defines you. It's time we claim our true identities as sons and daughters of the King, rise up and run the race like the royalty we truly are, throwing off everything that hinders, which, in this case, would be our old, false identities.

The Lens of Love

Learning to see myself in light of the Truth and embrace my new, restored identity has been an ongoing, slow process. I'll never forget

---

42 Miller, Jolene. "Cliffsnotes on the Seven Letters Taking Stock at the End of the Year." *Relentless Love*, 31 Dec. 2017, relentless-love.org/sermons/cliffsnotes-seven-letters-taking-stock-end-year/.

the moment, during my spiritual awakening that followed my quarter-life crisis, when I realized that God had been doing a deep work in my heart in regards to how I saw others around me.

Before this transformative experience, I didn't even realize it was "normal" for me to view others around me with anything from a neutral, detached, negative, or inappropriate lens. I might pass judgement on those who seemed obnoxious or rude. I might feel inferior, embarrassed as I compared myself to pretty or seemingly put-together people. A smug attitude might be cast toward someone I felt superior to. I might indulge in a moment of objectification, staring a bit too long at a particularly attractive person. While the above observations might be relatable and even sadly considered "normal," back to our Beauty and the Beast analogy of our true selves being restored to their original design—the above is actually so abnormal to our original design and only normalized where our "old identities" reign. It's a tragedy to miss out on a restored perspective because it's completely lovely and life-altering, as I came to experience that transformational day.

I'd walked into Boulevard Bread that morning, which is my favorite local café in Little Rock. I ordered a coffee and a bite of breakfast, and as I wasn't going to be there long before the workday's events, I sat at the small table in the corner of the bakery portion, where you can still see the bakery display case and people-watch as others come and go through the double glass doors. It also held the inspirational view of the old farm table around which the line winds, full of local items such as fresh produce, bean-to-bar chocolates, as well as other goods. I couldn't even tell you now if I was getting a head start on work at my laptop or reading and journaling at the time—all I know is as the door swung open and as I looked up as a reflex, I started to notice each stranger that came through the door, and stepped up to the counter, in a different light. I don't know how else to explain it except that I was very aware that people were suddenly *precious*. Adorable, even. Cute. Sweet. Well-meaning and *good*. Trying their best while battling insecurities the same as me and as you. Suddenly, defenses were down, and this unfamiliar adoration for others quietly overtook me. I sat dumbstruck in the corner.

There was a woman who looked slightly older than me who stepped up to order, and as she did, she tucked a piece of smooth and shiny red hair behind her ear and fidgeted, tugging at the hem of her colorful wool skirt. She looked sweet and unsure, hopeful but nervous, as if she were off to a job interview or a first date. "*Aww…*" a thought came to me that continued something like this, "*You go, girl—whatever it is, you're off to conquer today, you look great, and you got this!*"

I didn't catch myself after this first moment of noticing, but shortly after that, I watched a man who looked slightly younger than me, sharply dressed with nicely-gelled hair, place his order, and as he did, I couldn't help but take in the way he held his leather laptop bag that hung from his shoulder with such care, how serious of a professional he looked while still so youthful. He looked as though he, too, had taken extra care of his appearance today, as though he was trying not to break the mask of "fake it till you make it." A similar note of encouragement for him popped into my head, "*It's okay, you've got this—you're doing a great job, and I'm sure whoever needs to realize that, will. I'm not your mom, but if she were here at this moment, I feel like she'd want you to know she's so proud of you.*"

Tears began to well up in my eyes as I noticed small details about these strangers ordering coffee, suddenly overwhelmed with encouraging thoughts toward them. I almost felt like I should have run across the café to tell them, and these days, I likely would. But then it was so new it caught me off guard. "What is *happening*?"

I thought to myself. "I don't even *know* these people!" It was as though God's voice inside me whispered back, *"But I do."*

Each person in front of me was suddenly *dear,* and I was hit with a stark awareness that they were cherished. God was teaching me to see through the eyes of His heart, and it moved me to my core. With this perspective, I couldn't have compared myself to or judged that shiny, red-haired, and cutely dressed woman because I was too preoccupied feeling proud of her and rooting for her. At that moment, she was like my sister. And I couldn't have swooned over that well-dressed young man, because I was full of thoughts his own mother would have had. He was someone's son. At that moment, he was my brother. Absolutely life-altering.

My struggle with comparison seemed to deflate like a burst balloon.

My struggle with lust seemed to drop dead at the door of my heart.

When we can see those around us through God's love, it becomes impossible to hold negative or degrading thoughts toward them. Truth is stronger than lies, and once revealed, it shifts the lighting of how we see going forward. Seeing others as reflections of His glory, equal to and just as precious as me, melted away my former, sometimes small-minded way of thinking. At that moment, I could no longer view them any differently than how God does: dearly loved and worthy of all of the dignity in the world. It was a distinct, transformative shift. Like chaff in the wind, old patterns of thought drifted away, and the golden wheat of seeing people through the lens of divine love remained.

Just as "no man can serve two masters" and "sin can't conquer you because grace already has," you can't be consumed by two ways of thinking at once. There can only be one way you default to subconsciously in an instant out of habit, and that day, the old faulty train of thought derailed, and a new, grace-filled way of seeing others was set in motion that continues to run on my default tracks to this day.

Obliterating Objectification Culture

Just as I discovered that my old perspective on innocent bystanders was influenced by my previous "old self" mindset, it wasn't long after that that God began to reveal more about the dysfunctional way I was brought up to view how men and women related to each other.

As you've likely gathered by now, the hyper-conservative, evangelical fundamentalism, and purity culture I was immersed in deeply affected every area of my life. This topic, which still causes harm in churches and relationships today, weighs heavily on my heart. I mentioned earlier the strictness of the fundamentalist church I attended, where there was no youth group to avoid "gray areas" between boys and girls. It was the same church that had me, at 11-12 years old, wear a men's size X-large T-shirt in a Christmas skit to "hide womanly shapeliness" and avoid being a "stumbling block" to men. They enforced gender-segregated Sunday school, pushed courtship to prevent romantic "stumbling," allowed only side hugs, and discouraged girls from wearing clothing with chest graphics or details for similar reasons.

What all of these messages had in common between the lines and in undertones of condemnation could be summarized as something like this:

> Men are threats to your purity, and in engaging with them, you risk being tarnished in some way. Women are threats to men's purity and, at no initiation of their own but simply by having bodies, cause any tarnishing that might oc-

cur. We are all reduced to body parts strung along like puppets by uncontrollable desires in a relational terrain set up for our failure, with risks and pitfalls lurking behind every interaction, so we should assume worst intentions, be extra awkward around each other, and remain on guard and alert at all times.

Pretty life-giving, am I right? I wish I was exaggerating. Even as I sit here 20 years after escaping that cult-like "church" environment, the feelings of having those messages ingrained in us are as fresh as the years of my brainwashing and indoctrination into such grievous, unbiblical nonsense.

I wish I could say that that church was the only environment in which I experienced those messages and that I was hearing truth in other realms that held more weight, but sadly, similar ideas were being modeled for me in circles outside of that church, yet instituted by another ministry. I remember thinking it was odd when we had to get a babysitter just so that my mom could ride with my dad to the airport to pick up a woman flying in for something related to his work with a ministry. I later learned there was a ministry-wide rule that married men and women should never be alone together to "avoid the appearance of evil" and prevent temptation. Even in the high-control ministry environment I was used to, I remember thinking that surely, a marriage ministry of all organizations would have figured out a better way to avoid relational pitfalls, right? One that didn't assume people would abandon all moral reasoning at the first chance, perhaps? But instead of focusing on internal measures of cultivating and fostering goodness, it seemed to me that much like the church we attended at the time, they, too, created an emphasis on outward appearances.

What those holding up banners for external and excessive measures like this miss by going to such unnecessary extremes, is that hearts aligned with Love will only want what's best—what's *loving*—for others and for themselves. When your heart is in functional order, motivated by and for Love and all that it encompasses, you love others and only allow yourself to be truly loved by others. You don't want, nor would you allow, what is sad, tragic, and damaging. You want to protect, uphold, preserve, and champion those you love. And you know they want the same for you and recognize that they treat you the same way, too.

Contrarily, when your heart is in a dysfunctional and disillusioned place as mine once was in this relational realm, then setting up an external parameter to avoid "appearances" would be as good as the efforts of the two little pigs who built their homes with straw and mud that didn't stand a chance when the "big bad wolf" came around. Or like the verse about the "man who built his house on the sand" instead of on the solid rock. External measures not only fall short but seem to have a way of inviting trouble themselves, as it seems, to plant ideas that something is supposed to happen without these thin measures and weak attempts to set you up for "moral purity."

So guess what we should be focusing on in churches and communities?

Soul health. *Emotional* health. *Mental* health. *Spiritual* health. *Relational* health. That is the best measure of protection against most catastrophes these days, to focus on the good we want to grow into, *not* making creepy weirdness more weird by acting like that's normal and bound to happen without our feeble house of cards "protecting" us.

Think about it this way: if non-Christians or "unbelievers" have healthier opposite-sex interactions and friendships and a more natural ability to treat each other with decency and respect than "believers" in the Living God do, something is terribly wrong, and in this case, I guarantee Journey would change their lyrics and urge them to "*do* stop believin.'"

Those who go after these feeble external measures—and to this day, I sadly still know some who operate under this faulty thinking that is not aligned with God's heart, nor how Jesus treated the opposite sex when alone with them—are barking up the wrong tree and futilely attempting to protect Sleeping Beauty from pricking her finger by burning spinning wheels.

Outward methods of "protection" offer no true safety from compromise. When our hearts need new understanding and vision needs an overhaul, you will never sustainably uphold some so-called moral "high ground" by walling people off and removing them from "tempting" you. You need to ask yourself why you are so afraid of being tempted, get curious about what wound is crying out for attention or what need is going unmet there, and tend to that root as you remember that you have the Spirit of the Living God animating your very own spirit, propelling you toward love and good deeds, providing "everything you need for life and godliness."

When a male pastor at a local Baptist church I used to attend is having to include his wife on all text threads to any female congregation members so that he is "held accountable" and "leaves no room for compromise," I have deep concerns about how quickly he's willing to compromise the moment he's off his "leash." That type of forced "accountability" already assumes failure and gets us in the mindset of being a prisoner on parole. This is *not* the posture God calls us to walk through life with. This is not an accurate representation of Him. And it reeks of fear and control.

Jesus, operating in the total freedom we now have available to us thanks to Him, intentionally went out of His way on His own to meet the woman at the well. Now that I understand more of her backstory and context of her situation at that time and in that culture, I believe He did so to protect her dignity, or to infuse in her what she'd lost. I think He knew that it would have been embarrassing to her and she wouldn't have opened up the way she did to Him had his "band of brothers" been with them in that transformative moment. I believe when we're led by the Holy Spirit, we'll know when to do which, when us + God are all that's needed, and when in wisdom, "there's safety in numbers."

In contrast to the above example about the male pastor who abides by the group texting, it meant the world to me when the also male pastor at a local church I previously attended immediately replied to my text about burning questions I had regarding Jesus' stance on women being able to baptize others. At the time, I was still reeling from being met with a door in my face by yet *another* male pastor who told me that though my sister had requested I be the one to baptize her, I wasn't allowed to, and I quote from his mouth, "... because you're a woman." This was on the conference call where I confronted him with Jesus' Great Commission directed at both men and women. Though he agreed with my reply that Jesus commissioned *all* of us to "go and make disciples, baptizing them..." and admitted to it being something they abide by to not upset the older (read: highest tithing), more traditional congregation members. But that's another faulty theology soapbox for another day.

I digress... what I appreciated about the pastor at my previous church texting me back was his willingness to answer my genuine theological questions and not feeling the need to loop me in on a group text with his wife. It was a most refreshing and dignifying experience that felt normal and like what Jesus would do—void of fear and full of best assumptions, which is how it should be.

Not long after that, he reached out to church members individually to meet for coffee one-on-one to hear more about what the

Lord had been doing in our lives, stirring up in our hearts, and see what gifts we might want to exercise in the church, to make sure everyone felt valued and was getting to participate in a role that felt purposeful to them. This went miles for me in bolstering my appreciation for him treating me like a valued person and church member rather than "a woman" and, therefore, a threat to his marriage. Again, his normalcy toward me was unusual for me and felt very much like a conversation Jesus would initiate with me. While I no longer attend his church, to this day, I hold him in the highest regard for shepherding the way he did.

In summary, behavior modification is a futile control measure rooted in fear.

Heart and mind transformation is a fruitful pursuit rooted in love. Beyond a pursuit, it's part of our calling as believers to "put on the mind of Christ" and embrace and grow up into maturity in the "new heart" He's given us.

We have *got* to start seeing each other as the sacred family that we were designed to be. Every step we take is on holy ground, and we should tread on physical and digital ground like it's true. We are of divine origin and carry the Spirit of the God of the Universe inside of us! When we *get this*, we will ache for His love to flow through every inch of an opportunity we have to touch this world in need, joyfully locking arms with brothers and sisters on the same mission. We are not threats but gifts to each other. How in the ever-loving world could we look at each other as anything other than siblings in the same great big family when *this* is our perspective?

My frustrations with this topic burn hot to this day because of how incredibly wrong the "church" back then got it, putting the "cult" in purity culture. I believe it is still a prevalent issue in Christian culture to this day, and I've yet to hear this be boldly addressed through any avenue in Christianity other than the New Testament itself, which is why I'm doing my best to speak up on behalf of us, traumatized and brainwashed, degraded and demoralized by such warped approaches to living.

From operating from the base camp of fear as laid out above to the other end of the toxic spectrum of pastors publicly "thanking God" (read: bragging) for their "sexy" and "smokin' hot wives" from stages, the collective "church" has at times been no better than or even worse than the over-sexed and objectifying culture they call "secular" and contrarily say they aim to avoid the pitfalls of.

Note: I am not saying all churches and pastors, but it has been a recurring message among enough of them to impact many of us with deep relational dysfunction and misunderstanding that is nowhere in the wheelhouse of what God envisioned for us.

When we reduce the opposite sex down to something biological, on a humanistic and natural level, we reduce each other down to nothing but body parts that potentially serve or harm us. I want someone in the church at large to explain to me how this behavior is any better, or really any different than the objectification culture you would call "secular" and claim to stand against. What part of it is "rooted and established in love"? What part of it is honoring? What part of it gives credit to the "Power now animating us," which is "able to keep us from stumbling"? What part of it is not striving in futile human efforts? What part of it is walking by the Spirit, love that assumes the best, or living by faith?

None of it. In many church circles, especially those that embraced and ran with the 90's "purity culture" movement, it seems as though there has been a normalizing of men and women being reduced to extremes—between potential romantic partners to potential moral hazards—in the way that it has missed the mark with relationships as God intended them to be.

If there is to be any true hope for change, we've *got* to understand God's heart on this. We've got to zoom out from a heavenly vantage point with an eternal perspective about people and relationships. Before any of us had these fully formed bodies, minds, emotions, hormones—we had *souls*. At the moment of conception, while we were still a mass of cells in progress of being knit together, we. were. already. souls. And each soul bears individual, unreplicable fingerprints of God. Each one, He's tucked aspects of His Divine nature into.

If we can't look at other human beings and immediately see them as triune—body, soul, and spirit—as God's original handiwork and be struck with awe and wonder of the Divinity they carry as an image bearer of God, then we need to go back to the drawing board and cry out for a mind detox—culturally and religiously.

Wherever we picked up the degrading load of bull from doesn't matter; what matters is that we get it out of our churches, relationships, interactions, and way of thinking altogether. Who the heck would want to be a believer in Jesus if what comes with that is being treated differently as a man or a woman, as though you pose some threat to their "good streak" of morality just by existing?

If we have the power of God living inside of us, if we are supposed to be *more* than conquerors through Him who loved us, then we ought to be so secure in our hearts entwined with His that we're extensions of Him and conduits for His love to reach others. We get to be His hands and feet, serving and loving, encouraging and building one another up. We get to do all of this *better*, with all of our humanity engaged, moving toward others in whole-hearted, minded, and bodied (quality hugs are scientifically proven to release hormones that help with pain relief and immunity boosting—how cool is THAT for a mind-body-soul connection?!) unconditional love.

One Body

A few years into learning the new "language" God was teaching me by speaking to me creatively through numbers, I had an ever-growing list of repeating numbers and the connected meaning, phrase, verse, etc., that He'd been revealing to me.

Early in 2020, one such number that I began frequently encountering and was what I'd call the "focal point" of a few weeks where it seemed to be the highlight of highlights was the number 242. It would pull directly in front of me on license plates. It would be the time when my phone would receive a notification I'd look at. It would be the price on a gas station marquee (ah, a small bright side of the 2020 pandemic). It was so in my face and highlighted to my spirit I couldn't escape it, so I began praying about it, *"Okay God, what are you trying to tell me? What does this one have to do with? Show me. I'm looking. I'm listening!"* I'd smile every time it "found me" again, feeling a distinct sense of God smiling and winking at me, delighting over the fun of watching me on this creative treasure hunt for the meaning.

Not long after that, the search for the meaning behind 242 finally culminated in driving past a church marquee sign that jumped out at my spirit like a billboard. I forget what the rest of the sentence read, "Acts 2:42" was blaring at me like a fog horn, and I knew this must have been what God had been trying to point out to me. I got to my destination and immediately looked up the passage, and came apart in tears, moved by the picture it painted: it was about the original church, and it felt like the most beautiful poetry finally setting the record straight after all of the church burns, confusing messages, and dysfunctional relationships I'd experienced up to that point in my life, of what "church" looked like. Of how His body—us and our brothers and sisters—originally related:

Every believer was faithfully devoted to following the teachings of the apostles.

Their hearts were mutually linked to one another, sharing communion and coming together regularly for prayer. A deep sense of holy awe swept over everyone, and the apostles performed many miraculous signs and wonders. All the believers were in fellowship as one body, and they shared with one another whatever they had. Out of generosity they even sold their assets to distribute the proceeds to those who were in need among them. Daily they met together in the temple courts and in one another's homes to celebrate communion. They shared meals together with joyful hearts and tender humility. They were continually filled with praises to God, enjoying the favor of all the people. And the Lord kept adding to their number daily those who were coming to life."

Acts 2:42-47, TPT

"Hearts mutually linked together."
"A deep sense of holy awe."
"Signs and wonders."
"In fellowship as one body."
"Sharing whatever they had."
"Daily, meeting together to… celebrate?"
"Sharing meals together."
"Joyful hearts."
"Tender humility."
"Continually filled."
"Enjoying favor."
"Coming to life…."

Gasp It was breathtaking. I wanted to be a part of it. I wondered why I'd never experienced anything like *that* in all my years of "churchgoing."

Zooming in even closer from the beautiful vision laid out in the Acts 2 original church body passage, I wanted to explore more of what a healthy, life-giving, God-reflecting relational dynamic is supposed to look and feel like among a single "body" of people who intrinsically make up all of the parts of a whole. The New Testament, especially, is *chock full* of illustrations of what our relationships were meant to look and feel like, but I'll include my favorites below for reference:

> "How truly wonderful and delightful it is to see brothers and sisters living together in sweet unity!"
>
> Psalms 133:1, TPT

> "Now, because of your obedience to the truth, you have purified your very souls, and this empowers you to be full of love for your fellow believers. So express this sincere love toward one another passionately and with a pure heart."
>
> 1 Peter 1:22, TPT

> "Be merciful as you endeavor to understand others, and be compassionate, showing kindness toward all. Be gentle and humble, unoffendable in your patience with others."
>
> Colossians 3:12b, TPT

> "Love others deeply with a pure heart, a clean conscience, and sincere faith."
>
> 1 Timothy 1:5b, TPT

"Be devoted to tenderly loving your fellow believers as members of one family. Try to outdo yourselves in respect and honor of one another."

Romans 12:10, TPT

"Above all, clothe yourselves with love, which binds us all together in perfect harmony. And let the peace that comes from Christ rule in your hearts. For as members of one body you are called to live in peace. And always be thankful."

Colossians 3:14, NLT

"Now this is the goal: to live in harmony with one another and demonstrate affectionate love, sympathy, and kindness toward other believers. Let humility describe who you are as you dearly love one another."

1 Peter 3:8, TPT

Threads of deep love, honor, tenderness, respect, affection, purity, prioritizing, and intentionality are woven throughout these passages. Love is at the root of all of them, and as we know from the last passage above, it is the tie that "binds us *all* together in perfect harmony."

There is no mention of fear—because perfect love casts out fear.

There is no mention of segregation or division by gender, age, or other descriptors—because all are one in Christ.

There is no warning to suppress emotions or withhold displays of affection—rather to express it sincerely and passionately.

How *uncanny*. I am still mystified that all of that wisdom escaped me for nearly three decades of my life. Why wasn't it taught from the pulpits of the churches I was in? Brought up as a small group discussion when I finally made it to a church that had a youth group? Mentioned at the marriage conference I attended? On a podcast or in a book, perhaps?

But nope. The "biblical education" on friendship, familyship—basically any relationship structure outside of the highlighted structure of most churches never seemed to get air time unless it was mentioned as a potential threat or hindrance to the seemingly superior relationship structure that gets *lots* of air time and push toward in churches: marriage. (I had a whole soapbox on that topic that got cut from this book for length. Stay tuned for a riveting Substack post of the idolatry of marriage—when I figure out Substack.)

It's my hope that one day, the church will grasp the vision laid out in Acts 2 as it was in the original church. That one day, our faith communities wouldn't need to section off groups based on gender and relationship status, but rather, embody Galatians 3:28 which says "all are one in Christ." Because good golly, we *need* each other, like our toes need toenails and our legs need joints and our lungs need air and—a body needing *all* of its parts.

If the good Lord puts different aspects of Himself in men and women from creation and in each of us as we were dreamed up and brought to life here, then when we separate and segregate from each other, we grossly miss out on His fullness. We will miss out on vital aspects of God's own nature that were meant to be displayed through each other. Without a well-rounded assortment in our relational portfolio, we are missing out on particular kinds of sharpening and encouragement, missing different angles, strengths, perspectives, and richness of God's character made manifest through each other. It creates holes in our wholeness, lack in our understanding, and gaps in what is supposed to be a complete community.

I've had equally as sweet of friendships with some of my brothers as I have had with my sisters. Granted, coming from my cult-ish background, those relationships have been hard-won and not without consciously and intentionally discarding fear of what others think. But going through the discomfort of untangling the lies and discovering what God truly intended for relationships with my brothers has been 110% worth the fight and yielded a harvest so sweet with a few good bro-relationships that sharpen and encourage me like I'd never have imagined after all of the fear-mongering about boys growing up.

It reminds me of the point Jesus made when disciples interrupted His preaching to a crowded room to let him know His family was outside looking for Him, to which Jesus replied, *"My mother and brothers are those who hear God's word and put it into practice."* Essentially saying that those there in the room with Him, who hear and live by God's heart, were what created "family" beyond the world's definition or understanding of it.

Sisters, your brothers need you. Brothers, we need you, too. We've got to become rooted in love, "rooted and firmly established in truth." Otherwise, we're prone to unwarrantedly treat each other on some subconscious level as a risk or threat, with jealousy, suspicion, distrust, and other erosive concepts. When we look at each other as family, as good gifts from God, we'll show "brotherly love and affection" without fear of that being misinterpreted. As we practice it more and more, we become more comfortable and settle into the sweet unity that we were always designed for with each other. When we see the fruit of it in our lives and in each other's lives, we begin to believe it more and that this is what we were made for—this is what community and unity in Christ is.

If we, as Christ's body, gave each other permission to be free and light and as we are in our own skin among our brothers and sisters, truly living out love, which "always assumes the best" and "never causes harm to another"—if we allowed ourselves and others to live "not partially, but completely and wonderfully free," we'd all be more attuned to the gold in each other and be able to actively and consistently participate in the "building up of one another to love and good deeds," and it would be everyday-common-place to intentionally "encourage one another daily."

May we take this truth to heart: "We are many parts of one body, and we all belong to each other" (Romans 12:5b, NIV).

Chapter 11

Forgiveness & Focus

"... I came to grips with the deep and lingering hurt from these experiences. Although I thought I had left them in the past, I had actually buried them alive."

Josh McDowell[43]

What lies "behind"

I've always been a big believer in not dwelling on the past, not letting that hold you down or back, as is so easy to do and so many often do. It makes sense, as you can't run a race well with your neck turned backward. You'd stumble and fall, you'd go off the road, you'd smack into trees. Plus, focusing on past hardships can be heavy, and I'd rather embrace lightness and joy, aligning with Christ's "easy yoke and light burden." Thus, I struggled with the idea of counseling and therapy, which seemed to often require looking back—a concept seemingly at odds with the biblical focus on forgiveness and moving forward.

Or is it?

One morning about five years ago, I was sitting in my old living room beneath the shiny green leaves of Frederick, my fiddle leaf fig

43 McDowell, J., & Bennett, B. (2021). *Free to thrive: How your hurt, struggles, and deepest longings can lead to a fulfilling life*. Thomas Nelson Publishers.

tree and plant-pride-and-joy, as he cantilevered over the end of the sofa. While meditating on Philippians 3, I grappled with the tension between forgetting the past and the need to address unresolved trauma. Suddenly, the phrase "forgetting what lies behind" struck me differently, almost as a question: *"What* lies behind?" It was revelatory. I burst into tears as it felt like a direct answer to my prayers and wrestling like God saying, *"Here's how* both *co-exist: you're not looking back. You're actually looking to the now. If you don't address what keeps tripping you up presently due to understanding what happened in your past, it will continue to resurface in your future until it's finally given the attention required to be able to lay it to rest."*

At some point, and often many points throughout our lives, we'll each be invited to participate in the transformational, challenging, yet healing journey to engage with our past as it continues to present itself in our present. It became clear that addressing past wounds isn't about dwelling on the past but rather understanding and resolving what still affects us in the present. Sometimes, it's not until down the road that we are in the right place, have the support, knowledge, or maturity to properly process and grieve something we weren't able to for whatever reason at the time.

For example, growing up, I didn't have the experience or understanding to name what I can now identify as spiritual bypassing and toxic positivity as we explored in Chapter 2. I knew that it didn't seem helpful to turn a blind eye to suffering or hardship by slapping a biblical bandage on real pain. The approach handed to me was to focus on God being bigger than all of our problems, and to just "count it all joy," and to focus on how I had more blessings to count than struggles. Telling someone to just lace up their bootstraps and carry on while wounded didn't seem truly effective, but it did alright at containing the pain temporarily. But since that's a form of *denying* truth, and truth is what sets us free, those things never really die, nor can they be left to "lie behind." It's just a matter of time before they rise back up through the soil of our heart like McDowell's reference above to "burying them alive."

Working with my spiritual director at the time, I was able to slow down and examine this conundrum enough to realize that it does not make us more "holy" or "mature" to race through and ignore things that wound us. It does not mean we are tougher, more resilient, or closer to God. It means we're better at denying reality and ignoring injustices, which is neither noble, good, or wise. Learning to sit with hard things and harm done to us, name things we couldn't at the time, grieve losses we didn't know we were allowed to count and process these things in a non-judgemental, safe space with a reliable witness such as a good counselor, is what *is* brave, noble, constructive—even holy—contributing to our growth and healing rather than thwarting it and continually hindering us as we tried to move forward while desperately trying to ignore the fact that we were limping along in the dark.

While the things we're processing are considered a part of our past, we're not really looking back if that's not where we left it. If we've been carrying it with us all this time and have never known we could pause and process because we were belittled into thinking it wasn't a big deal or experienced the classic spiritual bypassing of being told "it's in the past" or to just "let go and let God."

If we've never quite processed or healed from it, if we've never known how to do the inner work or given that a shot, whether it's the help with a therapist or a friend—someone walking through that with us to really journey there, as hard as it may be to unpack some of these things that maybe we thought we put to rest—maybe we thought we let it lie. But I think the indicator of if it's truly been let to lie is if it has been processed in a way that it no longer has that same effect on you—to where it finally stops resurfacing at the same frequency and with less weight or effect in your present. That while you remember it, it is no longer the defining, heavy burden to bear or the rogue rudder of your ship that it once was.

Forgiven but not forgotten

The revelation above also presented another question, though, and that was how to know if you've addressed something to the point that it can truly "lie behind."

You've likely heard the notion "forgive and forget" a few times throughout your life. I'm here to debunk that incorrect, unbiblical, and toxic catchphrase, as it belongs to the family of spiritual bypassing we've been dismantling. While many think it is a verse in Scripture, it isn't; rather, it is a derived sentiment of the verse "Love keeps no record of wrongs." But it is often taken to an extreme and applied in situations where it runs contrary to other calls to "keep (protect) our heart with all diligence" in Proverbs 4:23 (NKJV) or to "let no one deceive you with empty words, for because of such things God's wrath comes on those who are disobedient. Therefore, do not be partners with them... Have nothing to do with the fruitless deeds of darkness, but rather expose them." from Ephesians 5:6 (NIV). How about Jesus' caution as He sent out the disciples in Matthew 10:16-17 (NIV) to "...be wise as serpents and innocent as doves. Be on your guard..." (against men who intended to harm them)? Or the infamous verse in Matthew 7:6 (ESV) about good stewardship of everything entrusted to us by God, including us, to "not cast your pearls before swine."

All of the above passages herald a call to alertness, wisdom, protection, and good stewardship. The issue with "forgive and forget" is that it is not only impractical, as memories are fantastic aspects of our being, and we're not likely to actually *forget* an injustice done to us, but it is *unwise* to not hold others accountable for their harmful actions. While we are absolutely called to forgiveness, which is actually more about embracing our freedom than often believed of "reconciling" with the perpetrator of harm—we are not called to allow, enable, or participate with wrongdoing or those who choose to proceed in a pattern of harmful behavior. While mercy, grace, and forgiveness are all priceless gifts we've been given in abundance by God and are called to extend to others, these can all be gifted to someone who has wounded you, all while enacting boundaries to "guard your heart with all diligence" and retain your pearls, not casting them before the person who trampled them/you.

Another incorrect note about "forgive and forget" is that the original Greek word "forgetting" is translated from *"epilanthanomai,"* a word whose biblical usage spans from "to forget" to "neglecting, no longer caring for" to "given over to oblivion." It is described as *a decrease in focus on.* "No longer" or "given over" involve a form of surrender. To "neglect" or "no longer care" about something isn't to say that you literally have no memory of a hurt to be healed; rather, *it no longer consumes the amount of focus you were once giving it, and it, in effect, no longer requires constant tending to.* Similar to how a flesh wound requires quite a bit of attention when it's actively healing. At first, it requires a major part of your focus, as the pain will keep reminding you of its presence. Tending to it in the beginning requires constant changing of wound dressing, disinfecting or washing it again, reapplying infection-fighting medicine, fresh bandages, taking care to not reinjure it by carelessly hitting it against something or getting it caught on something again. But over time, as the healing takes place, the pain lessens, the wound site doesn't require constant managing, and eventually, the supports can be removed. The new flesh, while still bearing a scar which can be likened to the memory that remains, is healing to a point that we no longer react to what happened with the same intensity as when it occurred. That's what I believe when referencing "forgetting" in this context—not a literal forgetting, but the ability to refocus on the present and reach ahead to where you're going, not being consumed by the past.

Still, to forgive someone who's caused us great harm and much pain, or even smaller offenses, can sound about as appealing as mopping up a mess you didn't make or paying for your own as well as the totaled vehicle of someone who crashed their car into yours—a tall order.

But that's just the thing—I think just as "forgive and forget" has heaped unrealistic and misleading ideals on all of us for too long, we've likewise had the wrong idea about just the forgiveness part! During a beautiful message on forgiveness by Barry Hall at the church home that's been a haven of healing for me these past few years, these impactful notes about what forgiveness is and what it's not, has been so helpful to me:

> "Forgiveness is not letting someone off the hook—it's putting them on God's hook. It's letting Him deal with them."

> "The ones that hurt you are so bankrupt, that they can never repay the debt or heal your heart. Only Jesus can."

> "Forgiveness is accepting the consequence for someone else's sin, and placing it in the hands of a just, moral, and able God—the only one who is able to deal with it."[44]

Forgiveness is *not*: paying for someone else's wrongdoing, reconciling with someone who caused you harm, and does not even need to involve the offending party (though, it can). It can simply take place in your heart.

One of my favorite passages about forgiveness encompasses

---

44 Hall, Barry. "Sermon on Forgiveness." *Encounter Church*, 2024, www.encountergod.co/watch.

the heart of it being more something that moves through us (like feelings!):

> "Tolerate the weaknesses of those in the family of faith, forgiving one another in the same way you have been graciously forgiven by Jesus Christ. If you find fault with someone, release this same gift of forgiveness to them."
>
> Colossians 3:13, TPT

The focus is on *letting* what Christ gave to us *flow through us* to another person. When we think of it as a gift meant to be shared. That is the complete call, to simply release what was extended toward us, to them—it is easier to do. It doesn't involve anything beyond that. It does not say "trust them again" or "let them back into your life." It's simply a heart posture of releasing grace toward them, because you've received the same grace, and it was meant to be shared.

You can forgive and remember for the sole purpose of wisely informing your choices in engaging that person going forward. Not to hold against them, hang over their heads, accuse or harm them back. We're called to "not be overcome by evil, but to overcome evil with good." Even to "bless our enemies and pray for those who persecute us." These are all acts of love that by no means require trust to be extended to our enemies or access be granted to us.

I hope embracing this truth helps set you free from any confusion surrounding forgiveness. I've known some to ironically stay bound to the person who caused them great harm by refusing to extend forgiveness in their hearts because they were afraid that would also require reconciling with or letting this person off the hook, where they might continue causing them harm. I'm here to set you free with the truth that forgiveness is a choice in your heart, between you and God, intended to set *you* free from the heaviness that comes with unforgiveness.

"Forgive as the Lord forgave you" is true. But it does not say trust them blindly, let them back in, and let your guard down. No. We're called to be wise and discerning, and we can fulfill that call while simultaneously extending forgiveness while choosing not to engage with that person again if that is what is the most loving decision, which honors yourself and them with what is true. In the wise words of Prentis Hemphill, "Boundaries are the distance at which I can love both you and me simultaneously."[45]

Inviting Jesus into our healing

Until we participate in the Truth that sets us free, stuffing, avoiding, and denying harm that occurred in the past will continue to cause issues as it resurfaces in our present and future. It will likely continue to do so until we listen to what it's crying out to tell us. Looking to the past isn't what holds us back; ignoring it when it begs to be named and deserves to be grieved, however, does. (*Dwelling* in the past is a different story, and what Isaiah 43:18 cautions against it for the same reason. Dwelling can cause us to miss the new being created in our lives at present.)

With the way we know our bodies and emotions are integrated, we must also consider the physical and mental ramifications of neglecting our emotional well-being. Dr. Claudia M. Elsig reminds us that "Suppressed emotions stay in the body. The effects of suppressed emotions include anxiety, depression, and other stress-related illnesses."[46] (Other thought leaders on this topic who have been greatly helpful in deepening my understanding on this con-

45 Hemphill, Prentis. *What It Takes to Heal*. Random House Publishing Group, 2024.

46 Elsig, Claudia M. "The Dangers of Suppressing Emotions." *Calda Clinic*, 24 Jan. 2022, https://caldaclinic.com/dangers-of-suppressing-emotions/. Accessed 23 Oct. 2024.

nection are Adam Young's *The Place We Find Ourselves* podcast, and researcher Dr. Hillary McBride.)

But we aren't doing this brave healing work alone! God calls us to this work, as we are accountable for tending to that which He has entrusted to us, which is, first and foremost, ourselves. But He does the work with us! Like in Song of Songs 2:15 (TPT), when the king (who represents Jesus) tells his bride (who represents us), "You must catch the troubling foxes, those sly little foxes that hinder our relationship. For they raid our budding vineyard of love to ruin what I've planted within you. Will you catch them and remove them for me? We will do it together." He never leaves or forsakes us, and He partners with us even in the hard things He asks us to do. *Together.*

God lives outside of time and "redeems the time" we live within. He promises to go before us to level the uneven places, and as David so beautifully recounts in Psalm 139:5, "You've gone into my future to prepare the way, and in kindness you follow behind me, to spare me from the harm of my past" (TPT). That verse so perfectly paints the picture of how the past, present, and future are all connected, and what we're really doing here when we're talking about present inner "work" and healing is taking responsibility to tend to present harm caused by something in the past.

When we take His hand as we do this work, when we "in all our ways acknowledge (consider, remember, include) Him," like in Proverbs 3:6, He promises to "make our paths straight." When we remember this, we realize how much of our healing truly comes from the willingness to allow Him to do what only He can do—heal in a deep heart, mind, and spirit way as the "Great Physician" and gentle healer He is.

One of the most profound healing experiences I've had involved confronting a deep emotional wound from my past. It happened during a heartfelt conversation with my dear friend Julia, who not only listened to my struggles but also offered to invite Jesus into the healing process. This was unlike any approach I had previously encountered.

As I shared my pain with Julia, she suggested we pray together and ask Jesus for guidance. With her gentle prompts, she asked Jesus to reveal where the pain began and where He had been during that moment. This brought me back to the first specific childhood memory I could associate with the wound—the root of it. I remembered the feelings of being overwhelmed, alone, and burdened with responsibility beyond my capacity at a young age. I remembered being gripped by fear through it all. Julia then prayed for Jesus to show me His presence in that moment, and suddenly, I could see Him standing nearby me in the memory, quietly watching over me with care, helping me handle all that I did and shouldn't have had to on my own at the time. A wave of warmth and relief washed over me as I realized I *hadn't* actually been alone—Jesus had been there, protecting me all along. Tears of relief rolled hot down my face, releasing emotional weight I had unknowingly carried for years had been lifted. Julia thanked Jesus for His presence and prayed for continued healing. By the time our call ended, I felt distinctly lighter, amazed at how deeply intentionally inviting Jesus into the healing process had touched me.

This experience was a turning point for me. It wasn't just about revisiting an old wound; it was about experiencing Jesus' active presence in my healing journey. I realized that Jesus is not distant or detached from our struggles. Instead, He is intimately involved, ready to bring comfort and restoration when we invite Him into our pain. This breakthrough reinforced my belief that Jesus continues to be a living, healing presence in our lives and that true healing often comes from recognizing and embracing His constant, loving presence in both our past and present.

Pressing on

There's a verse that I love in the Old Testament that details the Israelite army, how they circled a mountain long enough, and God's giving them a new direction. Ironically, "up" or "north" is the direction that they're encouraged ahead: "You have circled this mountain long enough; now, go north" (Deuteronomy 2:3, paraphrase).

Picture reaching this pivotal point of pressing on in your healing journey like this:

Jesus—who has been right beside you all along, patiently and compassionately witnessing your pain and strengthening you along the journey—places one hand on yours, stilling the one that's been swirling around in the dust, tracing and retracing steps, missteps, memories, and emotions that had to be held, felt, and dealt with in honesty. With the other, He gently lifts your chin up to gaze into your tear-worn eyes with His glistening, light-filled ones. When it's time, He softly speaks, *"My dear, you have slayed this giant. Your faith has healed you. Go in peace. Pick up your mat, and walk. You have circled this mountain long enough. Now it's time to go forward and up. Are you ready to see what beauty I have in store for you ahead? Here, take My hand. Let's go together."*

When you have bravely faced your "Goliath" dealing with the weights and wounds you've been walking with—when you have done your best, that "if at all possible, as far as it depends on you, live at peace with everyone" (including within yourself) then maybe it's time to "go north." Sadness, you have every right still to feel. We can make friends with our grief and continue moving forward, hand in hand with it. Healing does not often mean some magical moment where a book closes like a final "the end." To heal often means incremental progress of moving forward. It means we are no longer "benched" by our wounds; rather, we are able to continue moving forward even as we continue learning what it looks like along the way of their continued healing.

The alternative is the extreme you might have witnessed or experienced before, and that is where one cannot seem to let something lie that has already been attended to. Perhaps it's in search of the not-always-attainable closure, perhaps it's the brain on a loop that may require more intense forms of therapy to create a "pattern interrupt" in the brain circuitry, perhaps they've become so familiar with their pain that they have become accustomed to wearing it, and it now feels inseparable from them and destabilizing to think of taking it off or setting it down—like losing part of their identity. Perhaps it's in fear of loss of the known, as these grief-lined hallways have become familiar, like the comfort of home. You likely know if you've encountered this "stuck" place yourself. From what I've witnessed and the times I've encountered this place, it seems to be when the trauma experienced is the constant, primary focus of thoughts and the place conversations always route back to, like a skipping record looping back over the same phrase repeatedly.

Whether you know someone or are the someone currently experiencing this stuck place, I want you to hear that healing is no easy journey, and no two people's paths will look alike or follow the same timeline. But if you find yourself frozen in time like this, not just looking back as you work through the thing, but *living* there— if you're in a trance as you circle the mountain again and again— friend, I ache with you, and I have been on that seemingly endless loop when the past is no longer informing the present healing work, but rather causing us to miss out present, and likely trying to sabotage our futures, too.

If you're at this point in your journey, know that you are worth seeking the help you need and deserve to thrive. It might involve finding a new counselor or therapist or returning to one. It might involve lifestyle changes to nurture your body as it supports your heart and mind hard at work. It might be inviting a trusted friend to walk with you and journey with you to deeper places. Perhaps setting healthy boundaries with yourself and others. Whatever aids you in sustainably moving forward toward greater healing and wholeness—take even the smallest next step. God's heart, and mine, is for your wholeness. I'm cheering for you and continuing to move along with you as you move forward.

Know that being stuck dwelling in or on the past is different than being knocked down again by a swell of pain or grief. It's normal for emotions like anger and sadness to resurface throughout our lives over past harm and losses. For me, the difference I've noticed as I've continued healing is that now I am able to allow the feelings to flow naturally, rather than past defaults of fixating on them, despairing over them, or suppressing them—which created a toxic emotional buildup that only kept me more stuck. Most of the time, I'm now able to let even painful emotions wash over me like a wave that I know will subside and return to calm waters.

I also want to address this sometimes hard to accept but very real fact that, eventually, I learned the hard way to be true: that deep, lasting healing cannot take root if the wounding is still active and ongoing. For example, someone who's been abused before but is no longer in that situation (in effect, the abuse has stopped, and safe boundaries have been put in place to prevent it from recurring) can begin healing those traumatic wounds that occurred previously. But someone who remains in an environment where abuse is ongoing is not going to be able to sustainably heal, as their nervous system will not be able to safely begin regulating itself because its very job is to remain activated and hypervigilant to keep one safe, sensing threatening environments before the mind even identifies it as such. Wounds will continue to be reopened each time more of the same harm is inflicted in the same environment by the same party/parties. While this sounds like an extreme scenario, it is sadly more common than we think, and many live in denial of the dysfunction and harmful situations they've become accustomed to, perhaps even perceiving it as normal. Where spiritual abuse couples with relational abuse to create double damage is when spiritual bypassing is used to excuse abusive behavior and encourage a victim to "forgive and forget," 70x7, turn the other cheek, "suffer as Christ suffered," and other gross and grievous misuses of Scripture.

If you find yourself in a confusing or harmful situation that you need help identifying and navigating, be it of a personal, professional, or religious nature, know that you are not alone. You are not overreacting. It is *good* to be curious, to ask questions, and there are confidential ways to seek help in navigating your situation. There are many online quizzes that help identify various forms of toxic environments and abusive situations, nonprofit support centers, and other resources available to help you. Please don't wait to reach out for a reality check of what is considered "normal."

Just as your body was made with the miraculous ability to heal, so were your mind, emotions, and spirit. You are His precious, priceless, and worthy child, and you deserve to experience the safety in all its forms (physical, emotional, spiritual) you were intended for, where you can begin to heal without continued harm toward the wholeness you were designed for! His heart is for your healing, friend. If a Goliath from our past needs to be slayed from our present path; if time traveling back to a traumatic event to properly name, feel, and grieve the deeply impactful loss; if forgiving while remembering to set wise boundaries is the next step you need to take to "go north" and take hold of greater wholeness God has for you—then onward we go my friends, with great courage and self-compassion.

Focus

If the root of "forgetting" means "a decrease in focus on," it prompts us to ask: where should we direct our newly freed capacity as we begin to heal? How do we intentionally use our minds now that they're healing and increasing inability to focus on more than just damage control and survival mode many of us were subjected to for years of grappling through religious harm and often the relational harm that tends to follow or stem from those environments?

On my own journey of inner healing, I've been astonished at the mental and emotional space it has created, allowing me to re-focus on areas that are actually *life-giving* and fruitful. As I began writing this section and had outlined the ideas of "focus," "fuel," and "fire," respectively, I was studying the origin and meaning of the word "focus" and was delighted to discover it actually came about *because* of its ability to *produce* fire!

> The Latin word focus meant 'hearth, fireplace.' In the scientific Latin of the 17th century, the word is used to refer to the point at which rays of light refracted by a lens converge. Because rays of sunlight when directed by a magnifying glass can produce enough heat to ignite paper, a word meaning 'fireplace' is quite appropriate as a metaphor to describe their convergence point. From this sense of focus have arisen extended senses such as 'center of activity.'[47]

This discovery has so many applications! From the imagery of a magnifying glass being a tool with which we literally focus on something more closely than others to it being a tool of where the sun's energy converges to pass through and ignite a fire—there is so

---

47 "Focus Definition & Meaning." *Merriam-Webster*, Merriam-Webster, tinyurl.com/4htpj6np. Accessed 23 Oct. 2024.

much to draw from regarding how we harness more of and direct accordingly, what will ultimately help produce a life in alignment with what we believe.

What we choose to place our focus on is so incredibly powerful. Like a compass, it shifts the direction we are going, whether it's calibrated correctly or not. We are called to calibrate our focus, allowing ourselves to be transformed with the foundation of total mind renewal. Like a wake-up call now that we are on this side of believing, we learn a new way of seeing, of thinking. Our spiritual "eyes," or as I like to call them, "heart-eyes," are opened when we allow the Holy Spirit to do His transformative, continual work in us.

2 Corinthians 3:16a (TPT) speaks of this spiritual "sight," saying, "But the moment one turns to the Lord with an open heart, the veil is lifted, and they see. Now the 'Lord' I'm referring to is the Holy Spirit, and wherever he is Lord, there is freedom." So, the spiritual eye-opening happens, declaring freedom from our previous and limited, earth-bound way of seeing. I believe the *ability* comes instantly! But the practice of *choosing* to see as the Spirit enables us to is a constant choice that gets easier the more we practice adopting His heavenly perspective. His focus that we want to sync up with is a learned skill as we adjust our focus deeper, beyond the natural, temporal, limited, former focus.

A small illustration of this hit me last summer. I'd walked around to the side of the house to fill up a bucket of water to hopefully entice my smallish, withering garden to come back to life despite this sweltering, early summer heat. As I was standing there waiting for the bucket to fill, I found myself staring at the back of the house in front of me. The nearly 100-year-old reddish bricks show the wear of time, with cracks here and missing mortar there. The thought of paint colors dancing through my head, thinking how much better the bricks would look painted. All of the sudden, though, something else came into focus that had been right in front of me and in front of the brick wall all along. It was the glorious, white hibiscus tree the former gardener who'd lived here some 50 years ago had the lovely thought to plant. Once I'd zeroed in on the hibiscus blossoms, I couldn't unsee them, their white and light petals popping in contrast against the dark old bricks. The sad bricks were still behind the blossoms; they were just blurred out in the background of my vision. Now, my focus is crisply locked on more lovely things.

1 Corinthians 2:6-16 (TPT) teaches that as we grow spiritually, the Holy Spirit reveals God's profound wisdom to us. Verse 10 says, "God now unveils these profound realities to us by the Spirit. Yes, He has revealed to us His inmost heart and deepest mysteries through the Holy Spirit, who constantly explores all things." This means that only the Spirit of God can truly understand His thoughts, and because the Holy Spirit lives within us, we are privileged to know God's thoughts and secrets! It ends in verse 16 by declaring, "For who has ever intimately known the mind of the Lord well enough to become his counselor? *Christ has*, and we possess Christ's perceptions." This means we can actually think like Jesus, perceiving and engaging with God's thoughts in a deeply transformative way!

This truth is foundational to our well-being, and the purpose of this book is to show how essential a close relationship with God is. God desires deep communion with us, and a gift of walking closely with Him is the ability to perceive His thoughts, which enables us to understand and align ourselves with God's will, allowing His wisdom to guide our thoughts and, therefore, our lives.

You know that kind of deep knowing of a dear friend when you are out shopping and see something that just "has their name on it," or you scroll across a hilarious meme on social media and immediately think of them, knowing them so well you can almost hear their laughter and comeback in your mind before you've even sent it? The kind of closeness when dear friends or spouses can finish each other's sentences or, at times, know what the other is thinking with a simple look? *That* is the kind of intimate knowing available to us with God through His Spirit abiding in us, our bodies—His very home.

The above passage also contrasts this divine insight available through close communion with Him with those who live purely on a human level and who cannot grasp spiritual truths because they lack the Spirit's illumination. If someone can live on an "entirely" human level on which they are not able to perceive things only illuminated by the Spirit, it seems there is an alternative to live "partially" on a human level in this regard of focus and spiritual sight.

It brings to mind the verse cautioning against being lukewarm, rather choosing "hot or cold." Or the verse in Galatians 5:9 about a little yeast affecting a whole batch of dough. I believe these can be applied as reminders to live awake to the fact that there will be constant invitations for each of us to take the bait of distraction and decoys when it comes to where we aim our sight. We can end up with our magnifying glasses blocked by the fog and clouds of interference we'll experience in the "world's system" and way of thinking.

Even that can be a decoy as well, as Ephesians 6:12 highlights that our struggle isn't rooted in the physical realm but begins as a spiritual battle that often manifests in the physical realm. This enemy's goal is to distract, discourage, and ultimately destroy us, often by attacking our minds. While thoughts can arise spontaneously—which, as we've learned, is often where we'll hear whispers from the Holy Spirit as we focus in and learn to discern His voice—what we choose to focus on is up to us.

The "helmet of salvation" mentioned in Ephesians 6 serves as protection for our minds, guarding us as we make these choices. As

Psalm 23 (TPT) assures us, "Fear will never conquer me, for You already have," which affirms the truth that, in essence, we cannot be focused on or devoted to two opposing forces at once. Although the enemy cannot dominate our minds, he can still taunt and tempt us, which is why it's crucial to be discerning about which thoughts we entertain. By cultivating awareness and practice, we can quickly identify the origin of our thoughts, discerning whether they align with God's heart and what kind of fruit they would produce if we allowed them to take root.

Fuel

The more we know who God really is, the easier this gets to discern. The verse about "taking every thought captive" means exactly that: you are the "bouncer" at the door of your mind, and you get to meet and greet every thought that comes along. But you decide who gets in and can stay at the party and who is escorted out. When we've effectively "bounced" unwelcome thoughts and bypassed worthless distractions to place our focus on (all the while the Holy Spirit's advocating for us and constantly guiding us), we have effectively defended the battleground of our minds and only allowed our focus to be consumed with that which is life-giving.

Which brings us to the fuel: what kind of thoughts do we want to be consuming? What are life-giving thoughts aligned with God's heart for us made of? And as one of my sweet friends recently mentioned (thanks for pointing this out, Hannah!), why, oh why, is there such an emphasis in Christian culture on reducing our thought-lives down to the heavy yoke of dualistic thinking between right and wrong? My guess on that one is the "doctrines of men and corrupt customs that are worthless to help you spiritually" mentioned in Colossians 2:22 (TPT) or, in short, legalism.

I'd like to invite you to think larger and more lovely than that.

Because God did not give us these incredible, powerful, creative, intelligent, imaginative, and flexible minds designed in the likeness of His own yet as unique as His snowflakes in that no two are just alike—only to reduce engaging with our thoughts along the lines of sorting laundry, the darks from the lights and the wrongs from the rights. It falls short of considering what's good, better, and even best! Like C.S. Lewis's quote about how we settle too easily for less than what's available to us:

> ...like an ignorant child who wants to go on making mud pies in a slum because he cannot imagine what is meant by the offer of a holiday at the sea. We are far too easily pleased."[48]

We don't have to look far in Scripture to aim higher to discover the "holiday at the sea" we were created to run on, thought-wise.

This passage in Philippians 4:8 (TPT) so beautifully enlightens us:

> Keep your thoughts continually fixed on all that is authentic and real, honorable and admirable, beautiful and respectful, pure and holy, merciful and kind. And fasten your thoughts on every glorious work of God, praising him always.

The NIV translation describes the last two qualities as "excellent or praiseworthy," which are great criteria to add to the fuel-list as well.

The other great test of thought quality and origin is the Fruit of the Spirit passage in Galatians 5:22-23 (TPT):

> But the fruit produced (which fruit born of the Spirit can

---

48 Lewis, C. S. *The Weight of Glory: And Other Essays*. Macmillan, 1949.

be experienced in thought, emotion, and also physically such as a sense of peace) by the Holy Spirit within you is divine love in all its varied expressions: joy that overflows, peace that subdues, patience that endures, kindness in action, a life full of virtue, faith that prevails, gentleness of heart, and strength of spirit. Never set the law above these qualities, for they are meant to be limitless.

How about this beauty in Colossians 3:2:

Yes, feast on all the treasures of the heavenly realm and fill your thoughts with heavenly realities, and not with the distractions of the natural realm.

Let's pause and savor all of that deliciousness.

We're encouraged to dwell on that which is *beautiful*. That which is *kind*. That which is *admirable*. We have the Spirit of Truth living inside of us, guiding us into "all truth" and bearing within our thought life peaceful thoughts, joyful thoughts, thoughts of Divine love, and kind thoughts. We're invited to "feast on all the treasures" and "fill our thoughts with heavenly realities..." What a wonderful way to think! The God who dreamed up you and me and all of the magnificent beauty we enjoy on this earth is also the author of life-giving, beautiful thoughts to fuel our days.

It's likely because of it sounding so out-of-this-world-lovely, nearly too good to be true for what we understand in this world, that sometimes those like me deemed as "positive people" or those known for their "positive thinking" can get a bad wrap and thrown under the bus with toxic positivity. There's a misunderstanding that to dwell on such goodness means simultaneously turning a blind eye or blocking out all of the opposite, the sad, ugly, drab, unlovely, harsh, tragic, and so on.

The call of what to fuel our thought life with is about what is a *continual* fixation. Like locking in on a radio signal or programming "favorites" channels, it makes up the foundation of a life-giving thought-life. It does *not* ask us to turn a blind eye to suffering, ignore hardship, and slap silver linings on things, as that would involve denying reality or in the words above, that which is "authentic and real." It *is* one of divine love's "varied expressions" to have strength of spirit when enduring hardships. As is "kindness in action," which can come boldly in the form of standing up to injustice or "patience that endures" when navigating a frustrating and painful situation. As we look closely, we'll still see the likeness of what is beautiful and life-giving, encoded in even the heaviest, hardest of good thoughts that need thinking.

The thoughts we want to "bounce" out of our mind are the ones that don't lead to life but to death. The quickest way to sift through and locate those is almost always to ask, *"Does embracing this thought mean denying one of God's promises?"* If so, kick that soggy, rotten log out of your stack of thought-logs as it will snuff out your fuel and flame.

For example, if I'm thinking that something is impossible, then I'd have to deny that Jesus said, *"With God, all things are possible."* So I choose to think instead that yes, this seems improbable and if possible, incredibly challenging, but it *is* possible, and I've been equipped to do "all things through Him who gives me strength."

Or if I'm thinking that I've made a mistake beyond repair and ruined everything, I'd have to have to deny the promise that God is sovereign and will "work all things together for my good." If I embraced the thought that I'm alone and uncared for, I'd have to ignore His promise to "never leave or forsake me" and forget what He said in Isaiah about being "precious and honored in His sight, because He loves me."

What gets fed and watered grows, and it takes just as much energy to nurture negative, life-draining thoughts. So why wouldn't we want to make it our primary aim to tend to the beautiful, life-giving ones most? We are not aiming toward good thoughts to be "good"— we are *already* good. God said that about His creation when He created it. (*Very* good, I believe were His exact words.) We are aiming toward good thoughts as our baseline because we were *made for life in abundance.* We are eternal beings made in the Divine Image of a good and holy God. It makes total sense that in the same way as our bodies were made to run well on good nutrients and not junk, we were designed to feed our minds the fuel of good thoughts.

When we're harnessing the sun's (or Son's—ha!) bright, warm, illuminating, and fire-starting light through our magnifying glass, focusing it on the fuel of beautiful, life-giving thoughts, we're called to continually fixate on, well, that's how a good fires get started.

Fire

Everything we've been exploring in the chapter so far surrounding our focus and thoughts, is all leading up to something. Setting fire! Thoughts are the kindling for the fire inside of our hearts as we become more awakened to these spiritual realities. I believe the Holy Spirit stokes it, breathes on it, and helps the flames rise higher and higher, making us the beacons of light that He's designed us to be!

Fire can be a life-saving blessing—warmth from the cold, light in the dark, purifying impurities, cauterizing wounds, and so on. It's fierce and, yes, can be dangerous, but I like to think of fire in the spiritual sense as a powerful and constructive source of life, even when destructive. There is a fire that arises in my spirit when I've discovered a lie that needs truth to dispel it or an injustice that needs to be addressed. I have let the fire in my heart incinerate areas of ideology or theology that need burning up to reveal the pure gold of truth that remains!

Fire is also a form of energy, which is another reason I think it serves as such a great illustration to what happens in our hearts spiritually when we're walking close to God and engaging with the Holy Spirit in our daily lives. There is a supernatural energy that comes from being plugged into the Source of Life. Like fire needs oxygen to keep burning, He is the breath of life that keeps our inner fires burning. I love the way Romans 12:11 (NIV) encourages us to, "never be lacking in zeal, but keep your spiritual fervor, serving the Lord." Zeal is described as "a great energy or enthusiasm in pursuit of a cause or an objective."[49] This pairs so well right along with the call in our theme verse for this book, Hebrews 12:1 (TPT), about running the path marked out for us "with passion and determination." The NIRV translation calls zeal "fire," urging us to "never let the fire in your heart go out." Words like passion, determination, zeal, enthusiasm, and fire are less commonly discussed in Christianity compared to faith, hope, and love. Yet, this fire is what propels us, ignites us, and keeps us going. It energizes us to act, helping us remember the purpose behind it all. Zeal drives boldness, risk-taking, and faith-filled leaps with joy and confidence. You've likely heard people say they "got their fire back" after losing it, as if part of them was smothered. But when they regain it? They're unstoppable!

Our fire revitalizes, energizes, purifies—and, like our fiery God Himself, becomes all-consuming (Hebrews 12:29). We often hear about God's love, kindness, grace, and righteousness, but how often is He described as passionate, energetic, and fired up? These qualities, like all others, are gifted to us by our amazing Father and Friend!

---

49 Oxford Languages. "'Zeal' definition". *Google*, https://tinyurl.com/rm35pfss. Accessed 24 Oct. 2024.

It's time to remember the person of God, who is Jesus. It's time to discover where our zeal comes from. From the 33-year-old carpenter who danced at weddings, was moved with compassion to tears over a lost and hurting people, got fiery enough over injustice to flip tables and offend religious leaders with his rhetoric. The one who spoke for hours on end, day in and day out, to heal them and encourage them. The one who woke early and enthusiastically greeted His friends on that fine morning, "*Hey guys! Catch any fish?*" Who made breakfast for them. Who washed their feet. Who braved dying on a cross because of the joy of knowing *you* would be *His* (Hebrews 12:2). That Man is our fiery God. To live an average Christian life, professing to believe in Him but beyond that, living a "vanilla" life of spiritual slumber in the pews or apathy out of them, is tragically not what we were made for. We were made to live, move, and have our being in and through our Passionate God! It all comes from Him—the enthusiasm born out of living with and for the One we were designed to commune with eternally. Don't sell yourself short and miss out on the vibrant life you were made to live, animated by the zeal of the Holy Spirit alive and burning inside of you. It's time to be set ablaze!

Chapter 12

To Freedom, and Beyond!

"His love broke open the way, and he brought me into a beautiful, broad place. He rescued me—because his delight is in me!"

Psalm 18:19, TPT

"... you have broken open my life, and freed me from my chains..."

Psalm 116:16b, TPT

Made for Freedom

Since the initial "rescue mission" following my quarter-life crisis a decade ago, Jesus has continued to set me free in even more exponential ways. Like peeling back more layers, opening new doors I didn't know existed, lifting me higher—in every way from the inside out, my body, soul, and spirit, respectively, and in tandem have all become free in increasing measures. I get teary-eyed thinking about all the ways in which He has led me into greater depths and broader dimensions of freedom.

From relational freedom in the form of true friends and safe people now in my inner circle, to my remarriage to a man of unequivocal character and more grace and patience than I've ever known in a human capacity, to financial freedom from burdensome debt and growth in my business, to time freedom as I'm learning to trade in a frantic and hurried pace for Jesus's "unforced rhythms of grace," to spiritual freedom as He's continued to teach me more and more about the bonds of the religious mindset and the true freedom we were made for in spiritual communion with Him, increasing emotional freedom from past traumas, physical freedom from autoimmune symptoms—I stand in awe. I am living proof of His promises coming to life as I've come to embrace surrendering my life to Him not as a loss but as the greatest gain and promised path to the life I was always meant for. I look back across the path I've journeyed in the last near-decade now and see remnants of chains that once bound me in every area of my life, left in fragments to the left and right, being broken off of me as I've journeyed forward with Jesus every day since. The truth of it is you cannot spend time with Jesus with an open, willing heart to know Him deeper and *not* have Him open your eyes and teach you truth. You absolutely will be influenced by Him for the better.

Freedom is delivered in two kinds of sweeps, it seems: first, it will swoop with an epiphany—an awakening, a pivotal "before and after," from the moment we were under an illusion that we had no other choice, and it just was the way it was, and the next moment when we realize freedom has always been available to us—that He already cut the chains and left the cage door open! Once you've walked out of the initial cage—be it internally, such as a thought system you've decided to call into question or a physical situation you took measures to change—freedom then continues to abide with you, wrapping around you and melting off layers of additional excess you didn't even know was containing the truest, freest, lightest, inner core of you.

Something that's long bothered me deep in my spirit to the point that this book became the way I could herald this very point far and wide is this: if Jesus is who He says He is—God—and the freedom He offers us, is supposed to be the epitome of freedom, then in truth, "believers" in God ought to be the freest people on the face of the earth! Our extraordinary, Divinely created spirits ought to be unhindered by the ordinary, temporal circumstances and systems. So why, then, does it seem that across my life I've known more Christians who seem to be encased in confines of their own constructs (or those imposed on them by others) with cumbersome burdens heavy laden on their weary shoulders, striving so very hard to avoid "sin" and maintain their own "holiness" like a terrifying tightrope walk, ultimately bound to or by something in this world rather than walking in the freedom they claim to believe in?

Believers ought to be the freest people in every way, on earth, just as it is and will continue to be forever in heaven! For that not to be the case is a great grievance against Jesus and all He died and paid for us to experience, and it discredits the gospel—making it seem limited in power to deliver when, in fact, it is the most powerful, freedom-heralding story on earth, alive with might to truly set us free in every way, shape, and form, as testimony to His truth! When we treat grace as "peripheral," as Paul references in Galatians 2:21 (TPT), we by default live as though keeping the law could release God's righteousness in our lives, which then tragically and preposterously would mean that "Christ would have died for nothing."

I think so many believers are sadly asleep. Or don't fully believe. They've turned on the hot and cold water and just let it run and neutralize the hot fire that could be their faith. I think many have yielded to fear. I think many are deceived. And it burns me up and makes the fire inside of my spirit grow even hotter to set the record straight and burn right through chains that have no right to hold them—or you—a moment longer.

I've summarized Romans 13:11-14, which heralds a rallying call to this point:

It is time for us to wake up!

For our full salvation is nearer now than when we first believed.

Night's darkness is dissolving away as a new day of destiny dawns.

So we must once and for all strip away what is done in the shadows of darkness, removing it like filthy clothes.

And once and for all we clothe ourselves with the radiance of light as our weapon.

Fully immerse yourselves into the Lord Jesus, the Anointed One, and don't waste even a moment's thought on your former identity!

Dear sweet people. Precious friends! We have the Spirit of the living God alive inside of us! And "where the Spirit of the Lord is, there is freedom" (2 Corinthians 3:17, HCSB). Or ought to be. I believe this freedom is always there and available to us! The same One that raised people up from death and will continue upending life as we know it here. And did He not say in the context of His power raising the dead, casting out demons, and performing other mighty miracles that we—that is, you and me—would do "even greater things than these"?! When I think about it, it blows my mind!! If we have the ability to do all of that by His spirit alive in us, then we absolutely SHOULD BE COMPLETELY, WONDERFULLY FREE!

The above verse's subtext states, "*Where He is Lord, there is freedom.*" THAT is the key:

Any area of our lives where He is not Lord is where we will remain in unnecessary bondage.

Other things may have slipped in, accidentally taking the place of the Lord if yielded to. Whether He's active or "benched" on the sidelines of our lives, though, has much to do with what we believe about Him and the limitlessness of His liberating power. Given free rein, He will work from the inside out of us in the most unimaginable of ways. We need only have faith, an open mind, and not quench His unexplainable nature—not hinder the ways in which He may move.

When we realize this, believing it in our heart of hearts with childlike faith and wonder and out-of-this-world fearlessness, freedom and power will come flowing through our daily lives like undeniable white water rapids.

It will change the way you *see.*

It will change the way you *live.*

You might just feel like you've come alive from a weighty slumber you didn't know you'd previously "lived" in. You'll have the ability to "walk on water" in ways you might not have imagined nor may be able to explain with mere words. It will likely confound some, even yourself, at times.

Freedom such as this that has been reserved for us to walk in by the King of Kings may appear to look quite like a miracle here in a world that would have you shackled by something at every turn. It will be contrary to popular (un)belief. But I promise you, "This is the way. Walk in it" (Isaiah 30:21, HCSB).

Turn the world on its head by living in a way quite unexpected, even deemed impossible, or sometimes even questionable by the world around you. That's usually a good sign that you're breaking through the glass ceilings and into the freedom you were made for. It is from this awakening into the freedom that's always been ours that we are emboldened to take more leaps and bounds into the "good plans God has for us," one faith step or leap at a time.

Walking by Faith

The thing about walking (or leaping) by faith is that it brings us to a pivotal moment where we "pass the point of no return," in a way. It's why many linger at the fringes, delay, or maybe even never proceed beyond a cognitive belief system. Just as in science, it can be dangerous to test theories, so it is with faith. But if we never take our claims beyond the bounds of our personal, inner belief system and out into the great unknown of applying what we know and believe to situations and relationships all around us, then we miss out on the spark becoming a flame, and we simmer on the edge with our good intentions and hold back from taking bold action.

When we move beyond believing in our hearts and minds to acting on those beliefs in our daily lives, we gain true momentum. This action builds our personal faith journey and establishes our own track record rather than relying solely on the testimonies of others. While it's wonderful to be inspired and encouraged by the faith stories of others—whether in our lives or even biblical faith heroes like Abraham, David, and the disciples—creating our own journey with Jesus allows us to see *our* faith come alive through answered prayers, unexpected provisions, personal healing, and miraculous changes. In essence, faith makes the invisible visible by being so sure of what we don't yet see, that suddenly, we begin to see it! It brings the Divine to life in a felt, sensed, deep inner knowing kind of way and solidifies in our spirits. We no longer just claim to believe in the goodness of God. We have borne witness to His Word unfolding in our lives—just as He says. We no longer have theories—we have proof. More than that, *we*—our very lives—become living proof of the truth of His heart and Word. Experiencing the fruits of our own faith is, in my experience, exhilarating. Having my own experiences to reference now has cemented my faith like taking someone's word for it couldn't have. As Hebrews 10:39 (TPT) puts it—rather than being "held back by fear" and perishing—"we are among those who have faith and experience true life!"

Here's something to be aware of when you hear the "faith without works is dead" verse, admonishing us to put our faith into action. That is not to be confused with working and striving to prove our faith. No. "Faith is a gift from God," and as such, we put it into action and will do "good works" as a byproduct of faith in God, but from a heart posture of rest in Jesus's finished work. Because it was never supposed to be about what we "can accomplish in our own strength" (religious duties, how "good" we can be, etc.), it's *always and forever been about what He's already done on our behalf*, and we live out of response to that wonderful news.

I love this passage that refers to God's pattern of resting on the Sabbath day to celebrate His work of creation, and likens us being able to rest from our "works" as well, but describes it as a whole posture and way of living, calling it a "faith-rest life" we enter into:

> As we enter into God's faith-rest life we cease from our own works, just as God celebrates his finished works and rests in them. So then we must be eager to experience this faith-rest life, so that no one falls short by following the same pattern of doubt and unbelief.
>
> Hebrews 4:10-11, TPT

When we walk by faith and not by sight, from a place of enjoying this sweet faith-rest life in and with God—it is incredible what He is able to do in and through us! Our spirits will feel different, and our days will look different in the most unimaginable of ways when we "walk by faith, not by sight." When you "have faith" in Jesus, not just in word but in action, you will "experience true life," as the verse says. I would be remiss then not to spend a bit of time submerging ourselves into the "greatest" aspect of life and the very essence of God Himself: love.

Allowing Love

"*Let* His love continually pour from you to one another, because God is love."

1 John 4:7-8, TPT

A few years back, God began highlighting 1 John 4:7 to me through one of those creative ways He personally speaks to me, through numbers. Among other series of numbers, He was showing me that correlated to other verses, "147" kept crossing my path in uncanny ways from the time on the clock, to an order number, to the license plate in front of me, to the exit toward my house. It was not long after that my friend Maggie posted this thought on her Facebook, which went right along with the message of the 147 verse:

> "Perhaps the most healing thing that we can do for ourselves is to let ourselves receive God's love. And so often, God's love comes to us through people. So a great work of healing is simply to open ourselves up to another and let ourselves be loved."[50]

We often stand in our own way and hinder love due to deep-seated fears and shame. Perhaps fear, stemming from past experiences where we were unloved or mistreated, led us to trust issues and self-protection. The path to healing involves experiencing genuine, safe, true love, which counters the counterfeits that

---

50 Paulus, Maggie. *Facebook*. Date unknown.

wounded us. It requires courage to apply what we've learned from past wounds, to set wise boundaries to avoid those counterfeits, and to try again. Shame, perhaps rooted in the false belief that we are unworthy or undeserving, might come from others' negative messages or our own mistakes. But as we know by now, the truth is that we have an intrinsic, inherent, immovable, immeasurable value that nothing we could do or say and nothing that was done or said to us could ever alter. You are an image bearer of the Creator of the Universe. Shame is not for you. You are worthy of receiving love just as you are. You're in the process of Christ's mission to completely restore all things to Himself. And we can't wait until we *feel* worthy to receive love because it takes receiving His transformative love to realize our worth that's been untouchable all along!

For the above verse to say "let," it seems God knew we would struggle with this: the *allowing* of a good thing. As Maggie said above, His love often comes through others if we only allow it. It seems counterintuitive, I know. It seems it should be simple. Of course we'd *love* love. Of course we'd give and receive it freely. No problem, right?

But also, as we explored above, it's complicated. And when we're not aware of what's happening on our insides, we often subconsciously bar it from reaching us (often referred to as "self-sabotage" in therapy-speak). This is why self-awareness is *so* important and why therapy can be so helpful in tracing the roots of why we do what we do or don't do. By integrating this knowledge of our mental and emotional patterns, we come to see that what often keeps us stuck is beyond a spiritual issue, but ties into our nervous system, where at some point in time in efforts to keep us safe, self-preserving pathways were carved out in our brains that keep firing when a similar feeling "threat" triggers us. Even if there is no present threat now, until redirected (as new neural pathways can be paved with new experiences—yay brain plasticity!) there can be an element of internal autopilot to this avoidance of love.

Beyond the subconscious ways in which we can interfere with love flowing to and through us, we can often amplify the interference by intentionally choosing what may appear to offer more present surety or comfort, trying to control or policing ourselves and others well. Love requires an openness, a vulnerability, a being seen in our raw state and moved toward anyway, that can be quite foreign and feel risky to some who've yet to give in to its gloriously filling and refreshing current meant to pulse through our whole beings like a rushing river. Damming it, we are thirsty, parched, malnourished, and disoriented about it. We are desperately in need of the very thing we push away and try to limit in understood proportions.

When we experience Love—True Love—the Love that *is* God, showing up through the words, actions, hands, and feet of another, showing up through blessings out of nowhere that don't make sense, in ways that seem near too good to be true—it is disarming in the best of ways. The hope is that we come to realize that love in its purest form is so grand that it will never make complete sense on this side of heaven, so we should stop trying to block, limit, and regulate it until it does. In doing so, we attempt to shrink it down to something our human minds can understand, when love is something that will resonate in our hearts and minister to our souls without making complete sense to our rational minds.

To receive and extend *this* love requires faith. You can feel fearful too, it's okay. Don't be afraid of your own fear. You can take it along with you for part of the journey as you learn to "let" love. Because it will eventually dissolve in the presence of perfect love, which "casts out fear" (1 John 4:18, NKJV). The goal is to get to Love. It will take care of the rest.

It feels like taking a risk and stepping out of your comfort zone.

It feels like being vulnerable to something beyond your control.

When you feel like backing away from it, inch forward.

Keep going until you begin to see the fruit of allowing yourself to be loved and the fruit of freely loving others in this way. Something will shift inside of you. The tide flowing through those wide-open doors of your heart will effortlessly remain open by the sheer force of the rapids of love that flow in and out of you. Once you "let" this love in and out, it's inclined to keep the door open all on its own. And at that point, you wouldn't want it any other way.

Love will transform you, heal you, smite fears on the spot, give you compassion for those who've hurt you, and so much more we can't truly "live" as we were meant to, without. Be encouraged by this moving, accurate telling of God's love in the words of David G. Benner from his book, The Gift of Being Yourself:

> I am convinced that God loves each and every one of us with depth, persistence, and intensity beyond imagination. God doesn't simply like you. Nor does God simply have warm sentimental feelings toward you just because you were created in the Divine image. The truth is that God loves you with what Hannah Hurnard called 'a passionate absorbed interest.' God cannot help seeing you through the eyes of love. Even more remarkable, God's love for you has nothing to do with your behavior. Neither your faithlessness nor your unfaithfulness alters Divine love in the slightest degree. Like the father's love in the parable of the prodigal son, Divine love is absolutely unconditional, unlimited, and unimaginably extravagant.[51]

---

51 Benner, David G. *The Gift of Being Yourself: The Sacred Call to Self-Discovery.* IVP Books, 2004.

Since love is the first fruit of the Spirit detailed in Galatians 5, it would make sense that it's needed in order to fully experience the accompanying good fruits, which I believe is intentional. The second fruit mentioned is that of joy, signifying its importance and necessity in our lives as well.

Strengthening Joy

For a quality that sounds so light, happy, and just straight-up fun, it's wild to me how often joy often gets everything from underrated as an "extra" rather than an essential to even getting a bad "rap" at times. Maybe it's because fundamentalists too easily hear "joy" and think "emotion-expressing happiness," which they equate to some concoction of temporal/lesser/earthly/selfish. (Ask me how I know—former legalist expertly trained in emotional suppression here! *raises hand*) It's as though they're afraid of it—and I believe, in many cases, misunderstand it.

It seems at times when joy is "allowed," it's misunderstood as a potent commodity that requires regulation. I can just hear it, if the churches I'd been to had put words to the atmosphere there, "Yes, ma'am, we do allow joy here—just not too much of it. Nothing overwhelming, embarrassing, or flashy—you know. Just Grape Nut-level, ordinary joy. Gotta curb that enthusiasm in service to the Lord!" As though giving up something too closely resembling "happiness" is some mark of martyrdom.

On the contrary, we ought to be suspicious of places in our lives *void* of joy, as joy is a marker of strength (Nehemiah 8:10), fullness (John 15:11), and "healing to both body and soul" (Proverbs 17:22 ,TPT)! There ought to be an open-door policy for joy as an unregulated, encouraged, and welcomed force. Philippians 3:1 and 3b (TPT) attest to this idea:

My beloved ones, **don't ever limit your joy** or fail to re-
joice in the wonderful experience of knowing our Lord
Jesus!... We worship God in the power and freedom of the
Holy Spirit, *not in laws and religious duties*. We are those
who boast in what Jesus Christ has done, and not in what
we can accomplish in our own strength (emphasis, mine.)

Sometimes, joyful people are treated in a similar fashion to
joy. I'm still unlearning voices that've told me much of my life I'm
"too____," especially when experiencing joy. I.e., I talk too fast, too
much, too wordy, too loud, too enthusiastic. Some of my expressions, I do believe, are rooted in joy, while some may be paralleling
personality traits, but for too long, I let trying to control one or the
other dampen the whole of me that might otherwise be yielding
bonkers crops of joy. So I have to come back to the sweet truth in
the liberating verse above: joy is meant to be *limitless*.

I am reminded again to adopt His heart about joy, in that it
is a good, God-given gift, and fruit of His Spirit alive in ours! His
heart for us is for limitless joy, and we were designed to experience
it. Psalm 16:11 (AMP) gives us a clue to where joy begins—with His
presence: "In Your presence is fullness of joy." Nehemiah 8:10 shares
what true joy yields: *strength*. Genuine, supernatural, Divinely-sup-
plied strength is the byproduct of joy. No wonder the control freaks
try to regulate it.

Not only that, but being near Him—*knowing* Jesus—is meant
to be a "wonderful experience"! If you've experienced anything less
than your relationship with Him being a primary source of this
"limitless joy," anything less than a truly wonderful experience—
then what you've experienced isn't this spirit of Jesus. It's likely the
spirit of religion, which is so very void of life and full of the weight
of rule-following, fear, and often self-loathing. Clearly, that is not
wonderful—therefore, that is not where He is or what He has for

262 • Unhindered

you. There is so much more "wonderful" that awaits simply in a sweet, secure relationship with Him. Let all else you thought you had to do or become, all that self-effort religion has told you it takes to be a "good Christian," fall away. If "His load is easy and his burden is light," then walking with the God of the Universe day by day will feel like it. Light, easy, secure—and *not* dependent on you.

It should be a place where you know deeply how beloved you are. A place where you experience His delight in you, His unconditional love for you in big and small ways daily. We were made for the "wonderful experience" of knowing our Lord!

Not a head knowledge thing.

Not a task list thing.

It's a *wonderful experience*, more like something that happens *to you*, not something you do or fail to do.

Embracing the above naturally evokes a response of rejoicing and worship. And no, I don't mean singing-at-church worship—but true worship, which is simply a heart posture of awe and adoration toward Him. How wonderful, effortless, and powerful does that sound?

Joy is another fruit we were made to enjoy that many of us have had our crops compromised by a spirit of religion that dampened or eroded our joy. "Laws and religious duties" do not produce any of the following the above passage mentions: limitless joy, a wonderful experience, nor worship of God! Those things do not come from Him, and if we want to experience what *does* come from Him, we've got to decline to participate in the exhausting and fruitless hamster wheel of man-made religious ideals. It's an erosive distraction that will keep you from experiencing what you were truly made to experience: freedom, faith, love, joy, and all of the fruit of true, abundant life!

Abundant Life

I love how Hebrews 10:39 contrasts us as those surely "not held back by fear" but those who by having faith, experience true life! If Jesus is "the way, the truth, and the life," then one could surmise the above verse means that when we live from faith (a simple definition might be "belief in the good we hope for, that is not fully yet seen") and not fear, we'll experience Jesus Himself. Which invites us to dive deeper: what could it look like to experience "Life" or Jesus Himself daily in a practical way, resulting in truly living a fully alive *life*? As John 10:10 attests to the very reason He came to earth was so that we may have life—life in abundance, at that.

When we're familiar with the heart of Jesus, we know His heart is one of pure, unconditional, perfect love. Let's consider the beautiful description of Love in 1 Corinthians 13 as The Passion Translation so beautifully paints it, paraphrased here as a portrait of Love as a person:

Love also is large and incredibly patient.
Love is gentle and consistently kind to all.
Love refuses jealousy over others' blessings.
Love doesn't brag about itself or have an inflated sense of importance.
Love doesn't traffic in shame nor disrespect.
Love is not easily irritated or quick to take offense.
Love celebrates honesty.
Love grieves injustice.
Love is a safe place of shelter.
Love never stops believing the best for others.
Love doesn't take failure as defeat, so it knows how to get back up and keep moving forward.
Love is endless—it never stops loving.

In Galatians 5:22-23 (also TPT), "Divine love in all its varied expressions" include these fruits of the His—Love's—Spirit:

Joy that overflows.
Peace that subdues.
Kindness in action.
A life full of virtue (goodness).
Faith that prevails.
Gentleness of heart.
Strength of spirit.
These expressions of Divine Love are meant to be limitless.

Just imagine combining those descriptors above and running every thought, decision, and action through a lens framed by the heart of perfect Divine Love. Imagine that not even taking much thought or effort, because like learning to drive a car, something that you practice and do repetitively has a way of becoming second nature, of taking root, and becoming a "way" by which you simply do without even having to think it through. This is the *way* I believe living abundantly can become for us, and through us, here and now, as we sink our roots deeper into the Source—into Living Water Himself.

The gospel is not just about our then, after, later. That matters too, but, people spend their whole lives "living" with a one-time kind of "fire insurance" faith and tragically *miss* the true life offered to us each and every day, here, now, as we walk this earth by faith as ambassadors for Life Himself, in sweet, constant communion with Him.

Did you ever read the book *Are You My Mother?*[52] The point of the book is about reuniting the displaced from his nest baby bird

---

52 Eastman, P. D. *Are You My Mother?* Random House, 1960.

with his mother so that he is back home safe and sound with his true family rather than all of the impostors he questioned along the way as to whether they might in fact, be the parent or place he was searching for. The point of the gospel is about connecting displaced kids back to their original and forever family. It's about restoring things back to their original intent. It's about reuniting with our Dad. The bird did not need arm twisting, fear-mongering, and convincing that "if he didn't find his mother and obediently get back in the nest, he would die." No. Inherently, he was always searching for her. I believe on some level or at some point in our lives—perhaps after we've found her/him, we'll realize we were searching all along to come back home, too.

If evangelicals would pause long enough to re-think *why* they're doing what they're doing, sharing how they're sharing, they might realize that their motivation in "winning others to Christ" (news flash: Christ has already defeated death and the grave, in essence—He has already won for all of time) has become more of a frantic and alarming foghorn trying to help them avoid a believed dreadful fate. This model of "witness" completely misses the model Jesus shared this good news by, which by contrast was a compelling invitation to the life *here*, and *now*, and *beyond*, that they were always created for.

I don't think this is just about an "afterlife" kind of true life we'll experience in heaven, but a right now, everyday life. What evangelical fundamentalists often fail to consider is this: even if there was no afterlife, no eternity—would this life here on earth still be worth living "as it is in heaven?" I believe the answer is indubitably yes. I believe all of God's creation here on earth in this temporary life, is still holy and meant to be lived wholly because *He* created it. It may have been broken, but then Jesus came, and the restoration mission began. He valued us, and all that was broken, enough to come start restoring *"all things"* to Himself. He sees us and our right here, right now life, as valuable all on its own and interconnected with forever. He wants to be in close community with us here, *now*. Eternity is already in motion.

The "good news" is that Love and His kingdom are not some far-off-someday, unreachable destination. It is *here*—the kingdom is *already* at hand. And we get to live *now* "on earth, as it *is* in heaven." We are invited to live an out-of-this-world kind of life that does not operate from fear and all its compadres but is rather drenched in fruits of faith such as overflowing joy, unquenchable hope, incomprehensible peace, fierce love, and so much more. Don't draw back and perish even as you "live." Have faith, and experience *true* life! *Now.* His way cannot help but produce life, cultivating and bearing *good fruit.* Our days here on earth are meant to be like abundant gardens of such fruit that we partner with Him in tending. You're His creation! His child! Do you not think He's more personally invested in your well-being than even you are, just as a parent is for their child? It's never been about what *we* can do; it's *always* been about what He has done and continues to do, and His primary "doing" is loving us irrevocably.

Take a deep breath. Take the burdens off your shoulders. Let Him love you and show you a more alive life than most churches have ever known how to tell or show us it could be. Perhaps we're meant to be the ones who come alive first, and through living the "wonderful experience" of knowing Him, others still confused by the emptiness and confusion of a religion that over-promises and under-delivers might, too, be set free.

I believe with all my heart that as we embrace the truth of who God really is, who we really are as His, and what that means for who we all are, belonging to each other through Him—we'll experience a falling away of what doesn't align and an empowerment that enables us to begin walking in the abundant life He dreamed and desires for us to awaken to and discover with Him! When you do, I just believe—everything will begin to change.

You'll face the wind and rain with grace, resolve, and endurance that surprises you.

Your capacity to hold pain and joy at the same time will increase.

You'll let fear fall away like skin that can't contain you any longer.

You'll step with a firm footing towards a more courageous love than you've ever known, with an urgency that knows there's no more time to lose believing lies and living in shadows, "safe" against the wall, beneath the overhang.

Dare to step out, throwing off what hinders and holds you back.

Open your arms and heart wide in confident expectation of good.

Leap freely in the direction faith beckons, and run into the abundantly *full* and *whole* life you were created for.

Conclusion

"For now we see but a faint reflection of riddles and mysteries as though reflected in a mirror, but one day we will see face-to-face. My understanding is incomplete now, but one day I will understand everything, just as everything about me has been fully understood."

1 Corinthians 13:12, TPT

How I wish we could perfectly see it and fully understand it—just how out-of-this-world His love is. Across all of our "faint reflections" in our mirrors, no matter at what point of the process of filling in the cracks with the beautiful mosaics from those who exemplify His heart toward us, the common frame around each one is His irrevocable, warm, and kind love.

My own broken mirrors and hard-to-believe, beautiful frame that holds its stories have been much of my healing and perspective-shifting journey. Being brought up in the fundamentalist, legalistic religious culture I was that had me carrying the shame of being "bad" and sick with a "wicked heart" for much of my life and seeing it as "normal" to view myself in such a self-deprecating way it often seemed that my daily outlook was just being grateful that Jesus would stoop to the depths loving of the likes of me.

That message was corroborated throughout my life in arenas where I was constantly on the receiving end of much critique, complaint, and scrutiny in unhealthy relationships from familial to romantic to spiritual leaders to leaders in places of employment. Like many of you, too, I'm a recoveree from walking on eggshells, watching my back, and beating myself up when I inevitably could not measure up in the eyes of esteemed others in various high places in my life across time.

In the last half-decade, though, with a compounding and expediting effect towards these last few especially redemptive years, He's sweetly dismantled each lie that once marked me, instead revealing to me more and more of the truth of His actual posture toward me—His kind, adoring heart that delights in my very own human one.

He's convinced me now—through leading me out of broken sanctuaries, patching up my broken mirrors, and filling in cracks with those who beam of His light and exude His love that is so grand—that He didn't begrudgingly and with a sigh, roll His eyes and give up His life for mine. Not even close.

He passionately, persistently, and irrevocably *adored* me to the point of joyfully covering me.

What's attached to His name is now attached to mine, too. That's it. That's all. Anything else that ever was diminishing to or of me has fallen away. "I am my Beloved's, and He is mine. His banner over me is *love*." End of story. Or, more like the beginning of the *true* story.

The true story is that He was never disgusted by or disappointed in me. Wounded, misled beloveds of His too, likely quietly disgusted with themselves, gave me that impression.

But Jesus has positioned Himself ever-so-near to me, as though to whisper sweet-everythings in my ear, and impressed on me these kinds of truths instead:

"I have loved you with an everlasting love."

Jeremiah 31:3, MSB

"Because you are precious and honored in My sight, and because I love you."

Isaiah 43:4A, MSB

*"I will never leave you, never! And I will not loosen my grip
on your life!"*

Hebrew 13:5b, TPT

It resonates with me in another way now, too, familiar from my
unstoppable mother's heart for my Liam love. He is precious and of
immeasurable value to me just as he is now, in all his inexperience
and naivety, with all his wide-eyed wondrous, childlike hope and
faith. I hold only overwhelming adoration for him. I cannot imagine clinging to him any tighter, my love for him is so secure simply
because of who he is—mine.

Let His love wrap tightly around your lovely heart which He
adores. Exhale a sigh of relief, that you are His, you are held, you are
priceless, precious, wanted and welcomed, pursued and delighted
over by the Divine.

Then let's love each other like that. Imagine more mirrors and
portals referencing what it's like to be loved by Him in the way we
delight over and adore one another. No more eggshell-walking,
back-watching, making up for, and proving—grappling for accep-
tance and approval from Him or anyone else. It is not a slave and
taskmaster, nor judge and show-pony dynamic.

Love is not pain or proving. Love is not even suffering, as we've
been told, in that it does not willingly inflict pain or require it. Love
is only associated with pain in the way Jesus willingly gave it all up
for us and the way I willingly labored 42 weeks, 32 hrs, and an emergency C-section for my Liam love to be born safely into this world.
The joy of knowing he would be mine far surpassed any pain I could
face in the process of bringing him out of the darkness where he began and freeing him into the light and warmth of my embrace that
was always intended to be his home. Just like my arms were eagerly
waiting to hold him all those months leading up to his birth—know

that the heart of God aches for you to know that His strong arms are *already* holding you close to His heart. He's eager to stir you awake from what's perhaps felt like a nightmare and discover what's real. He's been here, holding on to and loving you wholly all along.

Afterword

A very special thank you to my publisher, hope*books, for being the bridge between the book in my heart and the book you now hold in your hands. I waited for years until it made sense—and from the first news of hope*books launching, there was a "light bulb" moment in my spirit, and I knew—you all were the who and the how I'd been waiting for, the team God envisioned all along to help this book take form. To h*b's visionary leader, Brian Dixon—thank you for your passion, heart, and mission. To the entire h*b team, thank you for your patience and persistence in holding me to the course. To my "A team"—Angela Abbot, my incredible developmental editor, and Amanda McMullins, my awesome copy editor—thank you! I remain astounded by God's divine orchestration to have had this book go through both of your wise, encouraging, and compassionate eyes first. I will never forget the first two souls to have read these more vulnerable words from my own heart. Bless you both. To my dear friend Timothy Fisher, thank you for translating my wild batch of words, photos, inspiration, and vision into cover art that still moves me to tears. You were always the one meant to make the art for this book, and I love how it all came together. You also deserve copy edit creds as the beta reader who caught the most typos before it was too late—whew! You are a God-send to my life and to this project. To my partner and best friend, and biggest believer in this book years before it came to be—Forrest, my co-captain, partner, and best friend. You've steadied me through the overwhelm and helped me see the light and the end. Sometimes, it feels like I made it here to the end simply because you believed without a doubt that I always would. Thank you for your faith in me and in our good, big God.

And to you, dear reader and friend—thank you, immeasurably and endlessly, for taking this journey with me toward living increasingly unhindered.

My parting words to you, my beloved sisters and brothers, I'm borrowing from 3 John 1:2 and 1 Thessalonians 5:23:

> *"Dear friend, I pray that you may prosper in every way and be in good health physically just as you are spiritually. Now, may the God of peace and harmony set you apart, making you completely holy. And may your entire being—spirit, soul, and body—be kept completely flawless (whole, sound, intact) in the appearing of our Lord Jesus, the Anointed One."*